ETHIOPIAN DEVOTIONS

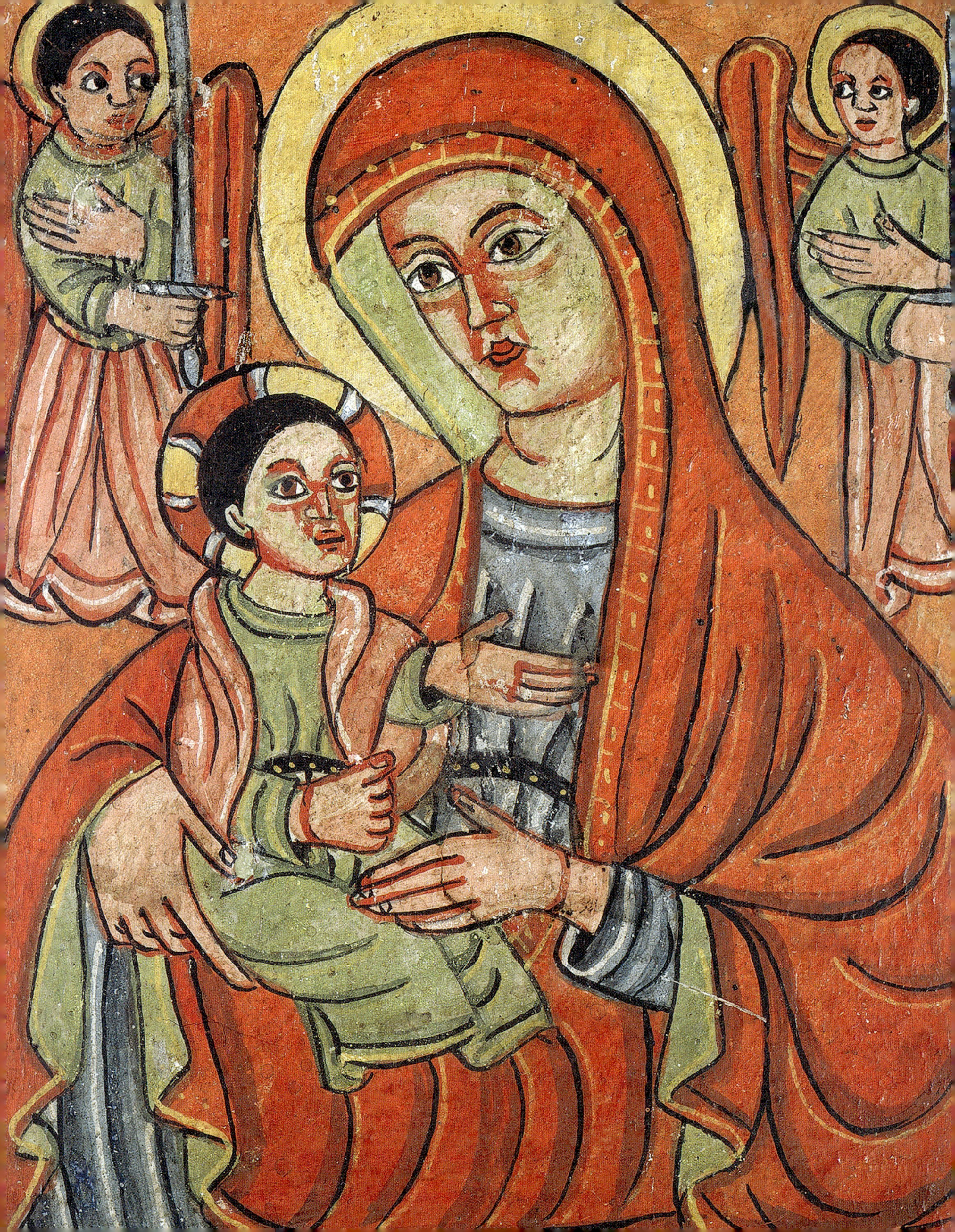

ETHIOPIAN DEVOTIONS

Paintings, Illuminated Manuscripts, and Processional Crosses from the Fourteenth to the Twentieth Centuries

Edited by
Marilyn E. Heldman

National Museum of African Art
Washington, DC

Distributed by Smithsonian Books
PO Box 37012, MRC 513
Washington, DC 20013
smithsonianbooks.com

Smithsonian Books
Director: Carolyn Gleason
Senior Editor: Jaime Schwender
Editorial Assistant: Paige Elliott
Digital Imaging Technician: Bill Whitcher
Edited by Jane Friedman
Designed by Studio A

This book may be purchased for educational,
business, or sales promotional use. For information
please write the Special Markets Department at the
address or website listed here.

The publication by the National Museum of
African Art is generously supported by Lilly
Endowment Inc.

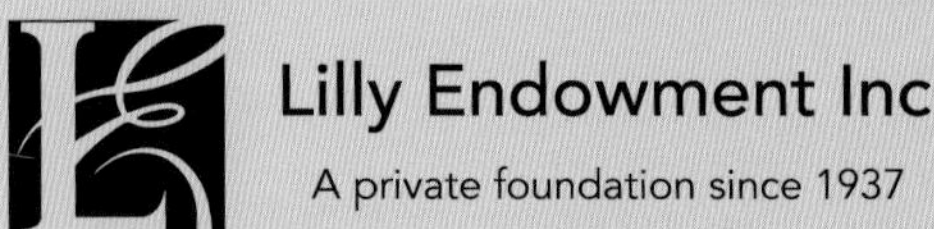

Frontispiece: Ethiopian Orthodox artist,
Saint Mary and Her Beloved Son flanked by Saint
Michael and Saint Gabriel, early 16th century.
Distemper and gesso on wood,
6⁹⁄₁₆ × 10½ × ⁹⁄₁₆ inches (16.7 × 26.7 × 1.5 cm).
Photograph by Franko Khoury, National Museum
of African Art, Smithsonian Institution,
Gift of Mary Garland in memory of Robert Lewis
Garland, 98-2-1

National Museum of African Art
Director: John Lapiana
Deputy Director: Heran Sereke-Brhan
Production Manager: Lisa Vann

For more information about National Museum
of African Art publications, write to:
Office of Publications
National Museum of African Art
Smithsonian Institution
MRC 708, PO Box 37012
Washington, DC 20013-7012

Library of Congress Cataloging-in-Publication Data
available upon request.

Hardcover ISBN: 978-1-58834-807-4

Printed in China
Not at government expense
29 28 27 26 25   1 2 3 4 5

For permission to reproduce illustrations appearing
in this book, please correspond directly with
the owners of the works, as seen at the end of
each caption. Smithsonian Books does not retain
reproduction rights for these images individually, or
maintain a file of addresses for sources.

Contents

Preface

KAY KAUFMAN SHELEMAY

G. Gordon Watts Professor of Music and Professor of African and African American Studies, Harvard University

The essays in this volume were brought together by art historian and Ethiopianist par excellence Marilyn E. Heldman, who conceived this publication and the exhibition it was intended to accompany. Due to a lengthy illness and her subsequent death in 2019, Dr. Heldman was unable to write the planned introduction, and, in its place, I offer on behalf of all the contributors an informal biographical sketch of Marilyn Heldman, combined with a brief overview of her distinguished career.[1]

It is customary to refer to Ethiopians by their first names, and this tradition informs the references to Marilyn here. Born Marilyn Jean Eiseman on June 12, 1935, in St. Louis, Missouri, she retained the surname Heldman after her divorce from her first husband to ensure continuity with her prior publications. Raised in the St. Louis suburb of Kirkwood, Marilyn attended the University of Missouri at Columbia (known as Mizzou), where she received both her undergraduate degree as well as an MA in art history (1964). In the words of her stepdaughter Nina Gilden Seavey, Marilyn "was a real Missouri girl."

Initially an art teacher for middle school students in St. Louis, Marilyn moved into new intellectual and artistic terrain during 1966–67, when she accompanied her former husband, an archaeologist, to Ethiopia, and volunteered to serve as curatorial associate at the Museum of the Institute of Ethiopian Studies in Addis Ababa. Marilyn organized the icons and canon tables in the Institute collection and was intrigued by their antiquity; she committed herself to learning more about their history and significance, moving enthusiastically into Ethiopian Studies.

On her return to St. Louis in 1967, Marilyn entered a doctoral program at Washington University in St. Louis, where she completed her PhD in art history in 1972 with a dissertation titled "The Gospels of Princess Zir Ganela, an Ethiopic Manuscript dated 1400/01 A.D." When she decided to write her dissertation on early Ethiopian Christian art, Marilyn encountered resistance from her professors, who advised her that her Ethiopian topic was both "irrelevant" and "dangerous" for a foreign woman needing to travel to "potentially unhealthy Africa alone." Marilyn stood her ground as a woman and an Africanist, pursuing her intended topic. She went on to travel extensively throughout Ethiopia and other parts of Africa (frequently alone), contributing to a more vibrant, feminist, art-historical discipline.

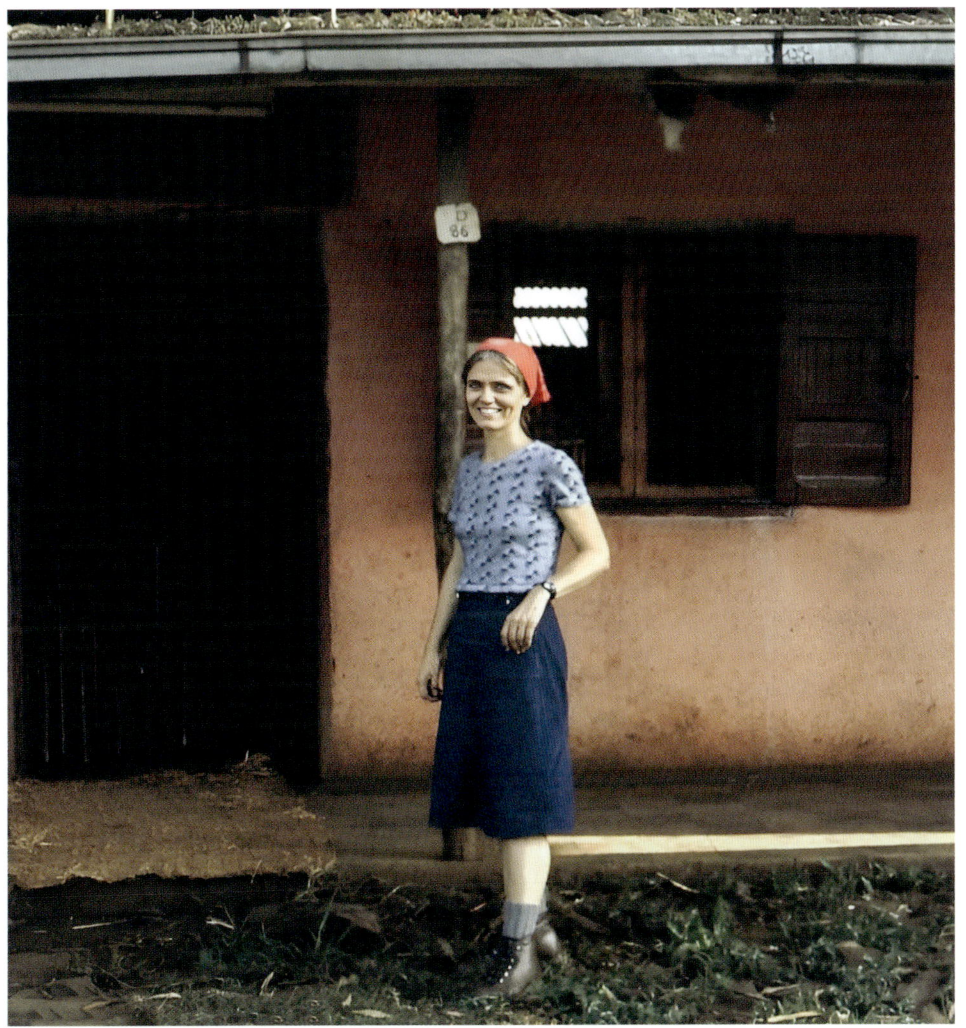

FIG PR1
Marilyn E. Heldman in Finote
Selam, Gondär, Ethiopia.
Photograph by Kay Kaufman
Shelemay, ca. 1975

Marilyn's first return to Ethiopia took place shortly after she completed her PhD, when she received a fellowship from the National Endowment for the Humanities for 1973–74 to support her travels to Ethiopian monasteries and churches. This was the first of many trips she would make to Ethiopia in the years to come. Marilyn and I met and began our friendship and professional collaboration at the First United States Conference on Ethiopian Studies, held at Michigan State University in May 1973, several months before we both departed the US to carry out research in Ethiopia. We shared many research experiences during fall 1973, just prior to the Ethiopian Revolution, when we were still able to travel freely for research across the northern portion of the country, as well as in the decades that followed.

While in Ethiopia during 1973–74, Marilyn met many Ethiopians, including a then-young student named Almaz Baraki, whom Marilyn mentored and who remained a close friend. Marilyn also met and established supportive relationships with many Ethiopian artists, whose work she actively promoted. At the Fifth International Conference on Ethiopian Studies, held in Chicago in April 1978, Marilyn met distinguished Ethiopian scholars by then living in the rapidly growing Ethiopian American diaspora, most notably Getatchew Haile, who became a deeply respected colleague and confidant.

In 1975, Marilyn accepted a tenure-track position as assistant professor of art history at Trinity University in San Antonio, Texas. But life intervened to bring Marilyn back to St. Louis: In December 1975, she married civil rights attorney Louis Gilden, whom she had met shortly after her return home from Ethiopia in 1974 and to whom she remained dedicated until his death in late 2000. From 1976 until 2005, Marilyn served as a visiting assistant professor of art history at Washington University in St. Louis and, subsequently, as an adjunct associate or full professor at the University of Missouri, St. Louis.

Marilyn's professional status over time became that of an independent scholar who devoted herself to her research and writing without the support of university resources. Her independent status renders her accomplishments all the more impressive. She garnered various major fellowships, research grants, and residencies, including funding from the American Philosophical Society (1996); the Sylvan C. Coleman and Pamela Coleman Memorial Fund Fellow at the Metropolitan Museum of Art (2003); the Community Associates Research Fellow at the Art Institute of Chicago (2004); Fellow in Byzantine Studies at Dumbarton Oaks (2005); Distinguished Visiting Scholar for Medieval and Renaissance Studies, University of California, Los Angeles (2006); and, from 2009 until her death, Visiting Scholar-in-Residence at the Smithsonian National Museum of African Art. Marilyn also curated important exhibitions, including the international presentation of Ethiopian sacred art entitled *African Zion* (1993), initially presented at the Walters Art Gallery, Baltimore, and *Aläqa Gabra Selasse, an Ethiopian Icon Painter* (2000), which opened at the University of Missouri, St. Louis.

But it was to the world of scholarship that Marilyn devoted most of her energy over these decades. Her interests were extraordinarily broad, spanning both broad swaths of time and multiple locales in Ethiopia and beyond, enhanced by Marilyn's skill at linking historical data and cultural significance to visual imagery. She was the primary author of *African Zion: The Sacred Art of Ethiopia*, an exhibition catalogue published by Yale University Press in 1993. Her monograph, *The Marian Icons of the Painter Frē Ṣəyon: A Study in Fifteenth-Century Ethiopian Art, Patronage, and Spirituality*, was published by Otto Harrassowitz in 1994. In addition to more than twenty-five important juried and invited articles, and numerous entries for the *Oxford Encyclopedia of Archaeology in the Near East* as well as *Encyclopaedia Aethiopica*, Marilyn presented innumerable papers and lectures at international colloquia and at campuses worldwide.

Largely because her work is so nuanced, contextualized, and often provocative in its conclusions, Marilyn's research and writing has inspired scholars from a variety of disciplines. Her range of media and subjects—encompassing architecture, painting, and iconography—has enabled her to offer a truly synthetic appraisal of whatever subject she tackled. Marilyn's broad knowledge of church architecture throughout Ethiopia permitted her, for example, to provide important insights into the construction of Ethiopian Christian churches in the Ethiopian American diaspora.

During her fellowship at Dumbarton Oaks during 2005–6, Marilyn used the results of recent radiocarbon tests that dated the parchment of richly illuminated Byzantine canon tables from the monastery at Äbba Gärima in northern Ethiopia to 300–600 CE, to confirm her stylistic analysis dating these Byzantine miniatures to this period. It is best to let Marilyn's discussion of these miniatures, published in a Dumbarton Oaks newsletter during her fall 2005 residency, speak for itself, for one finds here that the early exposure to canon tables that launched her initial interest in Ethiopian art and architecture illuminates a broader field of findings:

Few decorated canon tables datable to before AD 600 are extant, either as fragmentary or complete sets. Hence the importance of the Äbba Gärima miniatures with richly illuminated Early Byzantine canon tables, the architectural frames of which, embellished with grasses, fruits, flowers, and birds, suggest doorways to the path of salvation. One set of canon tables concludes with a full-page miniature of a circular temple whose roof is upheld by four columns, an architectural device symbolizing the unbroken unit or harmony of the Four Gospels, the purpose of the canon tables themselves. The "finispiece" of the second set of canon tables takes the form of a rectangular structure with [a] steep stairway and is unique to our present knowledge of late antique canon table decoration, although architectural motifs play an important role in the iconography of extant floor mosaics of early Byzantine churches in the eastern Mediterranean. I argue that within the context of Gospel book decoration, this unique composition suggests the symbolic temple of Christ's body. My fellowship research will result in a publication that establishes the strategic importance of these miniatures for the history of Bible illumination.[2]

In honor of her decades of brilliant research on Ethiopian art and architecture, we offer a heartfelt dedication of our essays in this volume to Dr. Marilyn E. Heldman.

Foreword

HERAN SEREKE-BRHAN
Deputy Director, National Museum of African Art

I first encountered Marilyn E. Heldman's work through the exhibition *African Zion: The Sacred Art of Ethiopia*, on view at the Schomburg Center for Research in Black Culture in 1994. I remember my unbridled excitement as a young visitor, soaking in the possibility that Ethiopian and, by extension, African, art could be studied and presented to a mainstream audience in such a way and at such a scale—and that it was, as I had always believed, a critical pillar of and contributor to civilization throughout the ages. Marilyn contributed five essays to its accompanying catalogue, providing a foundational introduction to Ethiopian art with this seminal exhibition. The exhibition also properly situated Ethiopian Christian art in the broader context of African and Black art, demonstrating its diversity of cultural expression and meaning as well as its overall relevance, even with acknowledged gaps in our understanding, since antiquity.

Marilyn and I met during my graduate studies at Michigan State University, and we later had the opportunity to reconnect when I was working on Richard and Rita Pankhurst's Festschrift publication.[1] We kept in closer contact once we were both living in the Washington, DC, metropolitan area. We attended one another's talks, and many an evening we would curl up on her living-room sofa over delicious Turkish barley soup, surrounded by open books and references, traversing time and space as she spoke with mercurial fluency about Ethiopia's visual culture and history. Marilyn invited me to consider contributing to this very publication on the topic of women saints in the Ethiopian Orthodox Church, a subject I knew little about, but which sparked my curiosity about the sixteenth-century saint Wälätä Petros in tangential relation to my research interest in nobility familial networks and Ethiopian social and political history.

So, it is by dint of serendipitous happenstance that I find myself writing this foreword to honor a friend and distinguished scholar who kept her curiosity fresh and her knowledge of centuries-old materials exciting and accessible, inviting all to journey along in discovery. This publication also offers an opportunity to honor Marilyn's colleague, our mutual friend and early mentor, leading Gəʿəz language scholar and philologist Getachew Haile, who contributed to this publication and who died in 2021, a few years after Marilyn's passing.

This publication has been years in the making, and its completion marks a collaborative effort between Marilyn's family, the distinguished contributors, and the

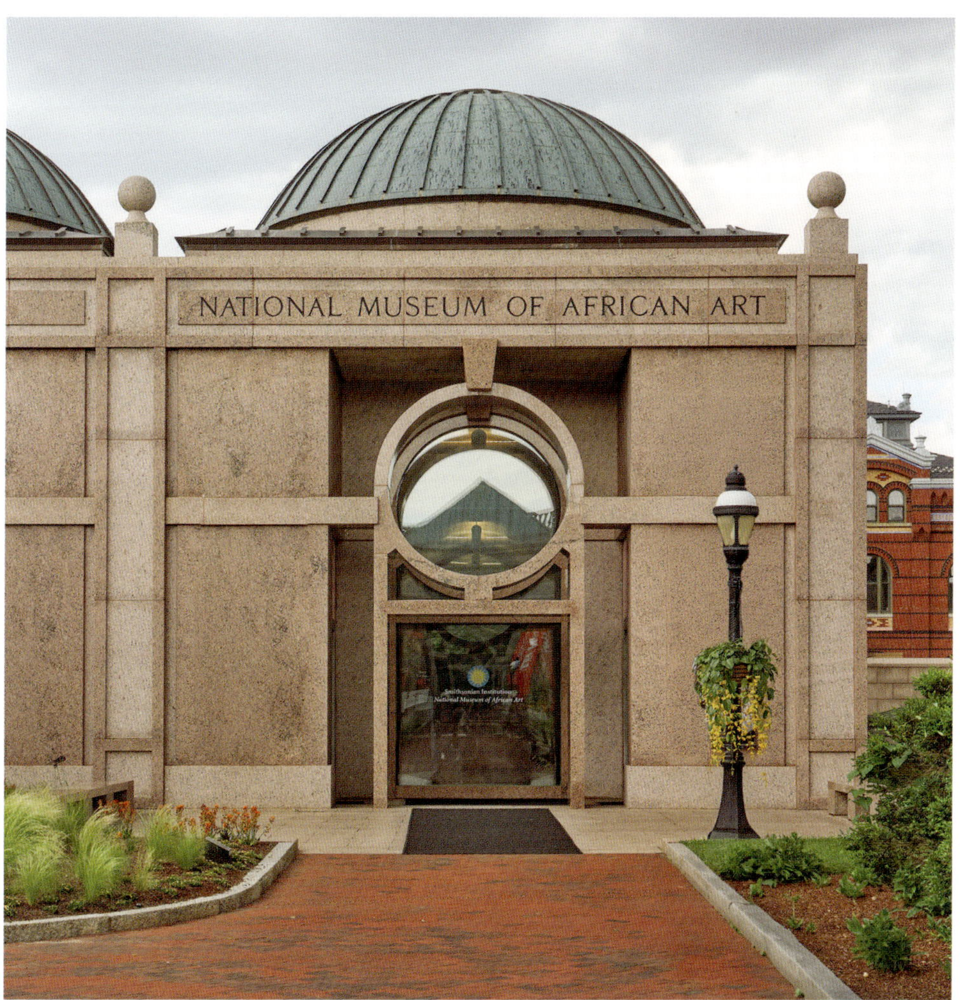

FIG FO1

National Museum of African Art, Washington, DC. Photograph by Brad Simpson, 2024, Smithsonian Institution staff at the National Museum of African Art. The impetus to finalize the now-posthumous project was energized by a renewed commitment to honoring Marilyn's life and final work. In so doing, we hope to reflect upon Marilyn's decades-long interest in Ethiopian Christian art, spirituality, and material culture. Her abiding love for the country and its rich history of producing sacred books, illuminated manuscripts, church murals, and devotional icons is apparent in the meticulous care, rigor, and breadth of her scholarship, of which only a fraction is presented here.

From the time of her early research to her preparation of this publication, Marilyn's encyclopedic knowledge of Ethiopian Christian art spanned the Early Solomonic period of the thirteenth century to the twentieth century. Her early research interest in Solomonic Ethiopic Gospel books and manuscripts examined Ethiopia's connection to the broader Byzantium world at a time when few understood its significance. She worked to reconstruct the evolving cultural landscape while exploring essential questions regarding artistic production and patronage. Marilyn's research interests were likely shaped through her involvement as a volunteer curatorial associate organizing the collection of the Museum of the Institute of Ethiopian Studies in Addis Ababa, Ethiopia.[2] Founded by another notable scholar of Ethiopian Christian art, Stanislaw Chojnacki, who himself spent over a quarter of a century living and working in Ethiopia, this early collection and catalogue are now among the most comprehensive and geographically diverse available, due in no small part to its methodical acquisitions over the years.

A chance turn of events around 1966, which had Marilyn accompanying her then-husband, archaeologist Donald P. Heldman, to Ethiopia, would prove to be her intellectual mainstay and the field of study that she would shape and influence from its very inception. It is not surprising, then, that beginning in 2009 and up until her untimely passing in 2019, Marilyn was still working diligently on her research pursuits when named scholar-in-residence at the National Museum of African Art, Smithsonian Institution. This publication is an outcome of that research.

The book has seven main chapters, three of which were written by Marilyn, as were the six short essays interspersed throughout the book to augment the chapters or serve as bridges. Marilyn's framing essay situates the broader historical and cultural significance of the three Abrahamic faiths—Betä Ǝsrael, Christianity, and Islam—in the geographic setting of the Horn of Africa and presents their shared practices in Ethiopia. Marilyn then focuses our attention on the visual art making of the Ethiopian Church. Her two additional essays and the works of other contributors examine expressions of material culture, political and social history, and the evolution of related spiritual and devotional practices. Taken as a whole, the essays encompass a wide chronological swath, from the fourth century CE to the mid-nineteenth century.

Specifically, the essays explore: the inspirational role and special reverence of the Blessed Virgin Mary as institutionalized by imperial decree during the reign of Emperor Zär'a Ya'əqob (r. 1434–68), the beliefs surrounding Mary's miracles, and her worship through iconic portraits (Heldman and Haile); a historical consideration of the literary traditions of Ethiopic hagiography (primarily Lives and Acts of local saints) produced in monasteries across north, east, central, and southern Ethiopia, as well as an overview of its form and important traits (Denis Nosnitsin); the relationship between the Christian state and its religious centers, particularly between monarchs and monks, as reflected in manuscript production and the impact of royal patronage from the late thirteenth until the early sixteenth century (Marie-Laure Derat); the flowering of high-quality artistic production (painting and illuminated manuscripts), craftsmanship, and architecture as well as the innovative construction of imperially commissioned castles and churches, most notably in the Gondär Period from the mid-sixteenth to the late eighteenth century (LaVerle Berry); and the centrality of music in Ethiopian religion through an analysis of a mid-eighteenth century miniature painting of the Life of Saint Yared, who lived in the fourth century CE and is considered the originator of the core elements of Ethiopian Orthodox musical liturgy, its annotation, and performance (Kay Kaufman Shelemay).

Our hope is that this publication and the arc of Marilyn E. Heldman's life and work continue to elevate our understanding and inspire ongoing inquiry into and discussion of the contribution of African civilizations past and present to the cultural achievements of all humanity.

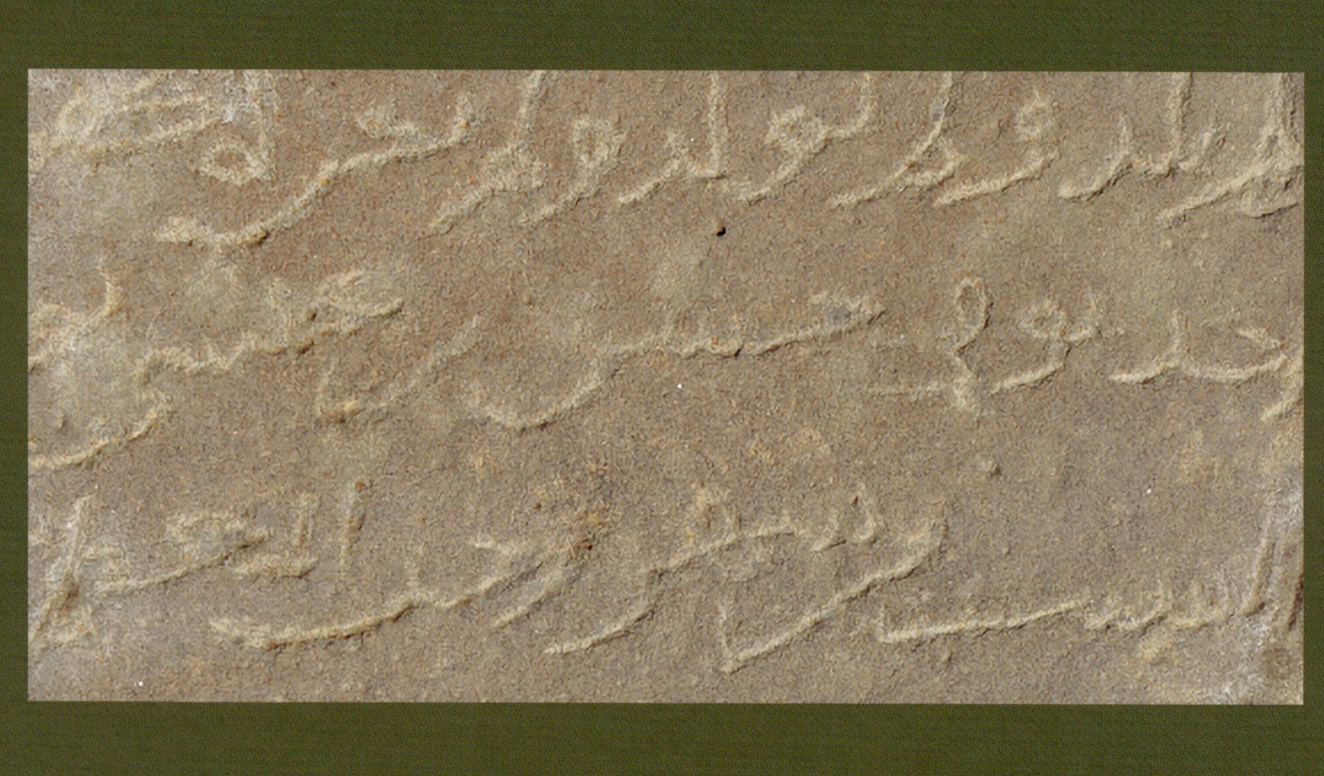

Introduction

The Abrahamic Tradition in the Horn of Africa

MARILYN E. HELDMAN

For many centuries the Horn of Africa has been home to three sibling beliefs: Betä Ǝsra'el, Christianity, and Islam. These are known as the faiths of the "People of the Book," or the faiths of the Abrahamic tradition. This essay briefly explores the historical and cultural contexts of these three faiths.

Abrahamic faiths look to Abraham as a founding figure in their belief systems, and each reveres the Sacred Word. The Betä Ǝsra'el, like other branches of Judaism, consider sacred the scriptures of the Old Testament. In Eastern Orthodox congregations, the sacred text is the Christian Bible, comprising the Old Testament and the New Testament (the four Gospels and records of the Early Church). The Qur'an, the sacred book of Islam, incorporates figures of the Hebrew scriptures and the Christian New Testament within its suras, or chapters. The Prophet Muhammad is the last of the sacred prophets to receive divine revelation from God. The four preceding sacred prophets are Abraham (subject of sura 14), Moses, Jesus Christ, and King David. Although no sura is dedicated to Jesus, Moses, or David, their names appear in many passages of the Qur'an. Sura 19 is devoted to Mary, the mother of Jesus.

FAITHS IN ETHIOPIA

Around 350 CE, several decades after Constantine the Great declared Christianity a legal religion of the Roman Empire, the Aksumite King 'Ezana (r. 303–ca. 350 CE) adopted the Christian faith as the religion of Aksum, a commercial trading state in the Horn of Africa. Although international trade with the Mediterranean world via the Red Sea was drastically curtailed after 600 CE amid the Arab encroachment into their lands, Aksum became the historical religious center of what for many centuries was known as the Highland Christian kingdom of Ethiopia, ruled by Christian emperors who supported the Orthodox Church. The church and state were joined in a close, symbiotic relationship. As armies led by Ethiopian emperors restored or expanded the boundaries of the Christian state, Ethiopian monks followed and introduced the Christian faith.

Although written documentation is scant from the seventh century, when the Aksumite state collapsed, until the fourteenth century, some of the military exploits of Emperor Amda Ṣəyon (r. 1334–44 CE) were passed down in the so-called *Short Chronicle* of 1855 (presently in London), which documents the history of the Ethiopian state

Detail of a grave marker that documents the presence of Islam in Ethiopia as early as the 12th century, Təgray region, Ethiopia and Church.[1] This important text includes the earliest extant references to Islam and Betä Ǝsra'el and reveals that the Highland Christian kingdom was a fairly heterogeneous realm.

The arrival of a group of Muhammad's followers at the Ethiopian court in 615 CE constitutes one of Islam's first contacts beyond its Arabian Peninsula homeland. According to tradition, the group was warmly received. The Islamic faith was recognized in Ethiopia and elsewhere in 622 CE, when the Prophet Muhammad emigrated from Mecca to Medina. The earliest physical documentation of Islam in Ethiopia is literally etched in stone: grave markers recovered by archaeologists in the northern Ethiopian Highlands (fig. 1) indicate that Muslim trading posts along local trade routes existed by the twelfth century. By the fourteenth century, Muslim mercantile trading centers were established along trade routes leading to ports at the Red Sea near the Dahlak islands.

The *Short Chronicle* of 1855 records Amda Ṣǝyon's victorious military campaigns over the loose confederacy of Muslim commercial trading settlements in present-day south and southeastern Ethiopia. And in what appears to be the earliest surviving reference to the Betä Ǝsra'el who lived north of Lake Ṭana alongside Muslims, the text states that Ṣǝyon sent troops to areas in the northwest to wage war against the "renegades who are like Jews." Although the emperor's military campaigns were successful, Muslim settlements did not disappear, and the communities gradually recovered. The High-

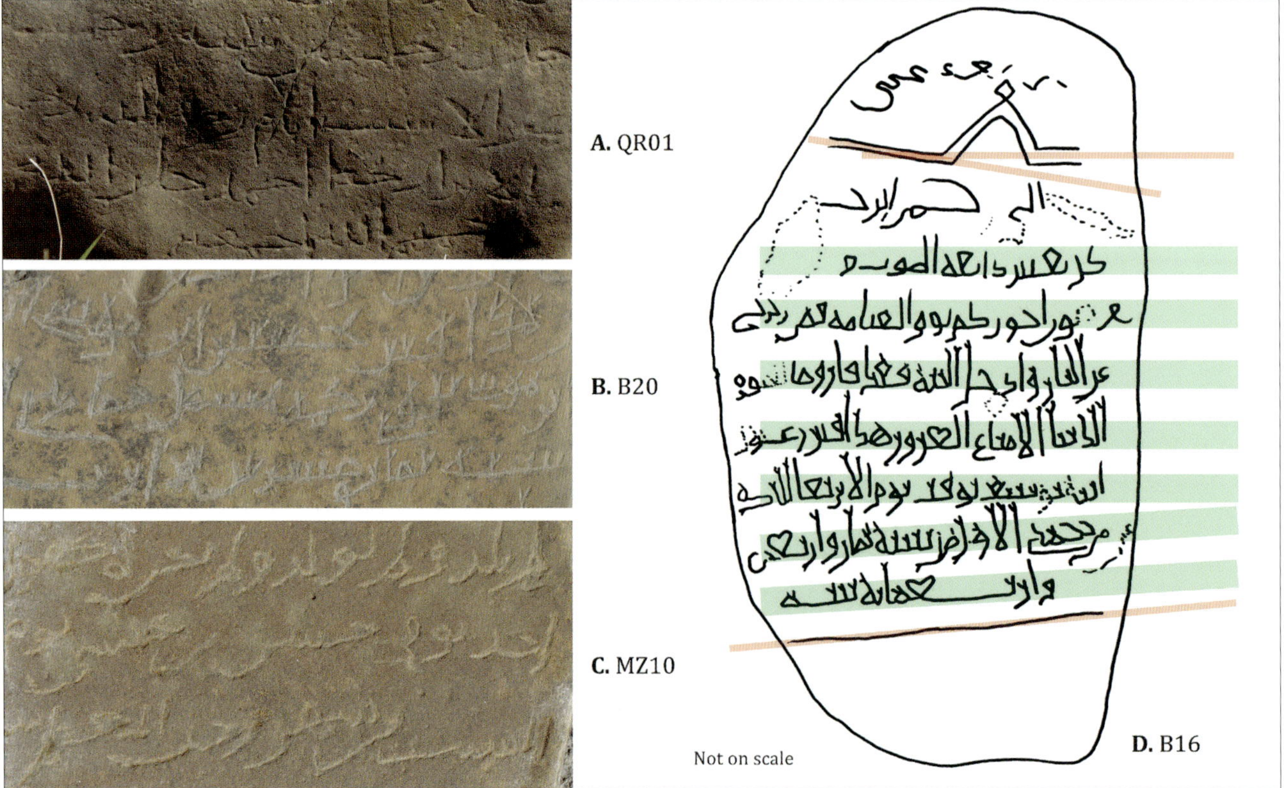

land Christian kingdom would be ruled by a succession of Christian emperors until the Ethiopian Revolution of 1974, after which the monarchy was dissolved, along with the long-standing symbiotic relationship of church and state.

Emperor Yeshaq (r. 1414–30 CE), one of Ṣəyon's successors, adopted his predecessor's expansionist policy. He focused his military campaigns not only on the southeastern regions but also on the northwestern area of the kingdom; the latter included a sizable population of Betä Ǝsra'el, who rebelled against his rule. In retaliation, Yeshaq decreed that persons who had not received Christian baptism could not inherit family lands, thus effectively stripping the Betä Ǝsra'el of all family landholdings. To survive, they were forced to practice low-prestige craft occupations—women became weavers and potters, men became blacksmiths.

Life for the Betä Ǝsra'el improved somewhat in the early seventeenth century, when Emperor Fasilädäs (r. 1632–67 CE) established a permanent royal capital at the site of the small trading center of Gondär. The new capital provided Betä Ǝsra'el craftsmen with an array of building opportunities. They developed outstanding skills in carpentry and stone masonry as they constructed castles and churches at Gondär for a succession of emperors. For example, Queen Mäntəwwab, regent for her son Emperor Iyasu II (r. 1730–55), commissioned a castle at Gondär (fig. 2) and a magnificent church and castle on the outskirts of the capital (see chapter 6). Such grand building projects ceased by the late eighteenth century, however, when the Gondärine dynasty was no longer in power. The Betä Ǝsra'el thereby fell back on their low-status occupations of weaver, potter, and metalworker, the last of which, according to one Betä Ǝsra'el source, included the production of metal processional crosses for Ethiopian Orthodox churches.

SHARED PILGRIMAGE SITES

In addition to sharing a founding figure and a reverence for the divine word, Ethiopia's Abrahamic faiths also participate in shared rituals and pilgrimage sites.

The three faiths recognize the Holy City of Jerusalem as the center of the universe, making it a primary destination for religious pilgrimage. Since the twelfth century, the Ethiopian Church has had a chapel at the Church of the Holy Sepulcher, and beginning in the fourteenth century, the presence of Ethiopian pilgrims in Jerusalem was noted in Western travel accounts. Although documentation of the pilgrimage journey itself is rare, Ethiopian monks likely walked the difficult path to the Holy City, while Christians and Muslims often joined caravans of Muslim commercial traders en route to Jerusalem.

In addition to pilgrimages to Jerusalem, the Abrahamic faiths also share major pilgrimage sites in Ethiopia. These include Mount Zəqʷala, an extinct volcano with a crater lake located about thirty miles south of Addis Ababa, the modern-day capital of Ethiopia. Evidentially, the site was visited in the fifteenth century by Ethiopian Christians, who identified the mountain slopes as the location where the venerated hermit saint Gäbrä Mänfäs Qəddus manifested his holiness. According to the pious account of his life, Archangel Gabriel transported the saint from an Egyptian desert to

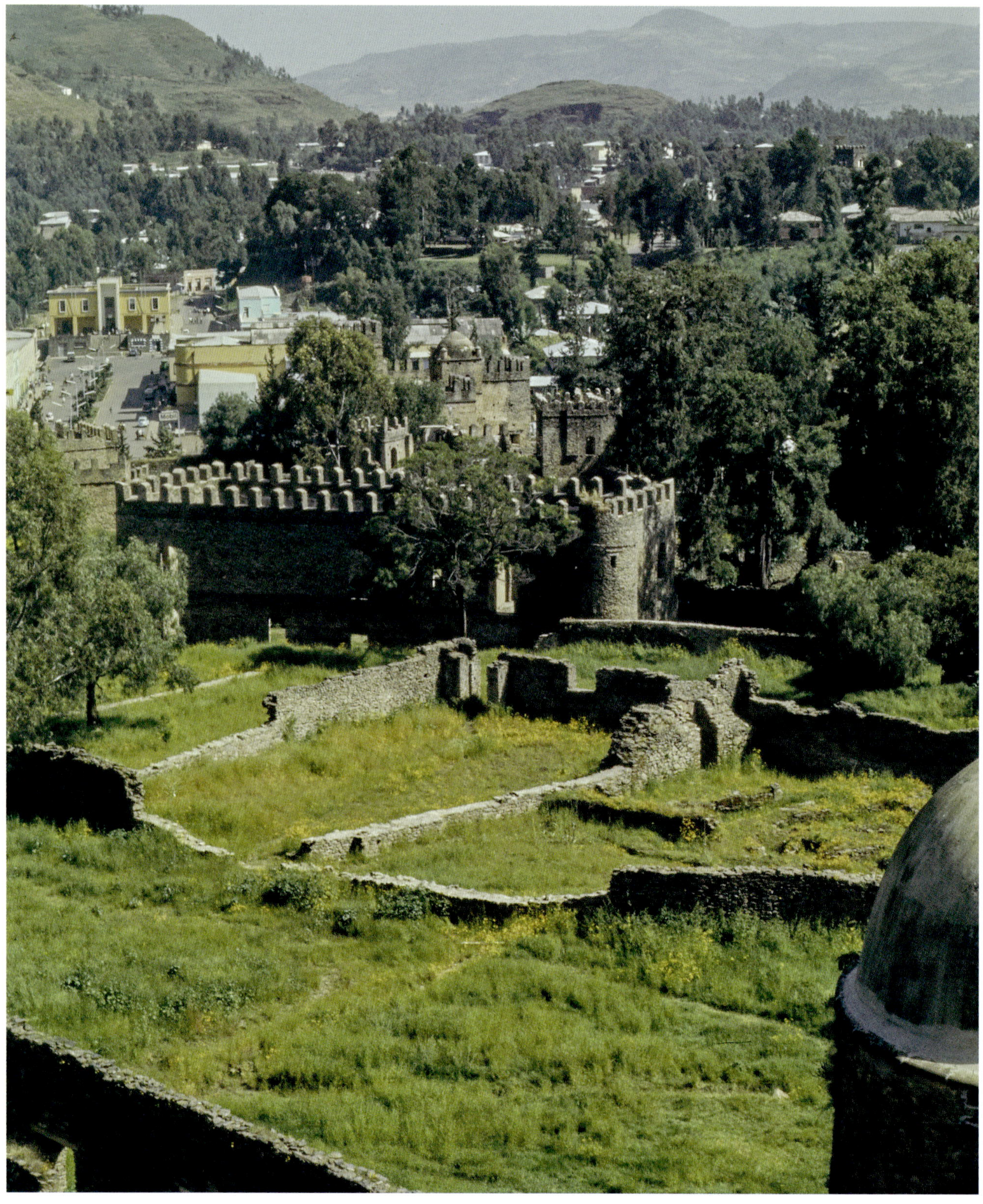

ETHIOPIAN DEVOTIONS

Mount Zəqʷala, where he stood praying, refusing food, water, and sleep for long periods of time. According to a seventeenth-century version of his Life, the saint's body was miraculously covered with holy hair, sent by God to clothe his naked body. Wild lions and tigers came to visit him and were tamed by his holiness (see page 56).

Mount Zəqʷala is presently a pilgrimage site of the Ethiopian Orthodox Church and the Oromo people, whose sixteenth-century ancestors emigrated northward from adjacent regions now known as northern Kenya and southern Ethiopia. By the seventeenth or the early eighteenth century, the Oromo had largely assimilated, and today many are either Christian or Muslim. Nevertheless, certain pre-conversion religious beliefs or sensibilities persist. Oromo religious tradition recognizes a male deity of the heavens whose divine spirit permeates mountains and other physical elements of our natural world. Oromo pilgrimage focuses on the mountain, the crater lake, and the groves of trees at the site, while Orthodox Christians visit the local monastery and attend services at the churches.

Qullebi, a small village located in southeast Ethiopia in the Chercher massif not far from the two predominantly Muslim cities of Harar and Dire Dawa, is another shared pilgrimage site. It is home to the pilgrimage church of the Archangel Gabriel. Founded in the late nineteenth century to fulfill a vow, the church, commonly known as Qullebi Gabriel, has been rebuilt several times. Christians and Muslims make pilgrimages to the church. According to the Qur'an, the Archangel Gabriel sent the Qur'anic revelation to the Prophet (sura 2 Al-Baqara). According to the Hebrew Bible, Gabriel saved three Hebrew youths from death in a fiery furnace (Daniel 3:12–30). A popular chromolithographic print (fig. 3), once available at Qullebi and other Ethiopian churches, appears to be both a devotional and a promotional image for the pilgrimage. It shows the Archangel Gabriel hovering above the three Hebrew youths amid flames that cannot harm them. Below them, mid-register, Christian and Muslim pilgrims advance toward the present church building.

Pilgrims recite a variety of prayers to Gabriel for his divine intervention; for instance, women may come to pray for a child, the logic being that the Gabriel came to the Virgin Mary, announcing that she would give birth to Jesus Christ (Luke 1:27–35). Undoubtedly, pilgrims come to pray for salvation.

DEVOTIONAL IMAGES

The three religions have varying stances toward the creation or reproduction of holy images. The Second Commandment reads: "You shall not make a carved image for yourself or the likeness of anything in the heavens above or on the earth below; or in the waters under the earth" (Exodus 20:4). The Betä Ǝsra'el interpret the commandment broadly. For them, the sacred book itself is a profound symbol of one's faith; further embellishment is neither needed nor allowed. Thus, their sacred scripture has no decorative elements.

As for Islam, manuscripts of the Qur'an receive decorative illumination in the form of a single- or double-page frontispiece of abstract design preceding the holy text.

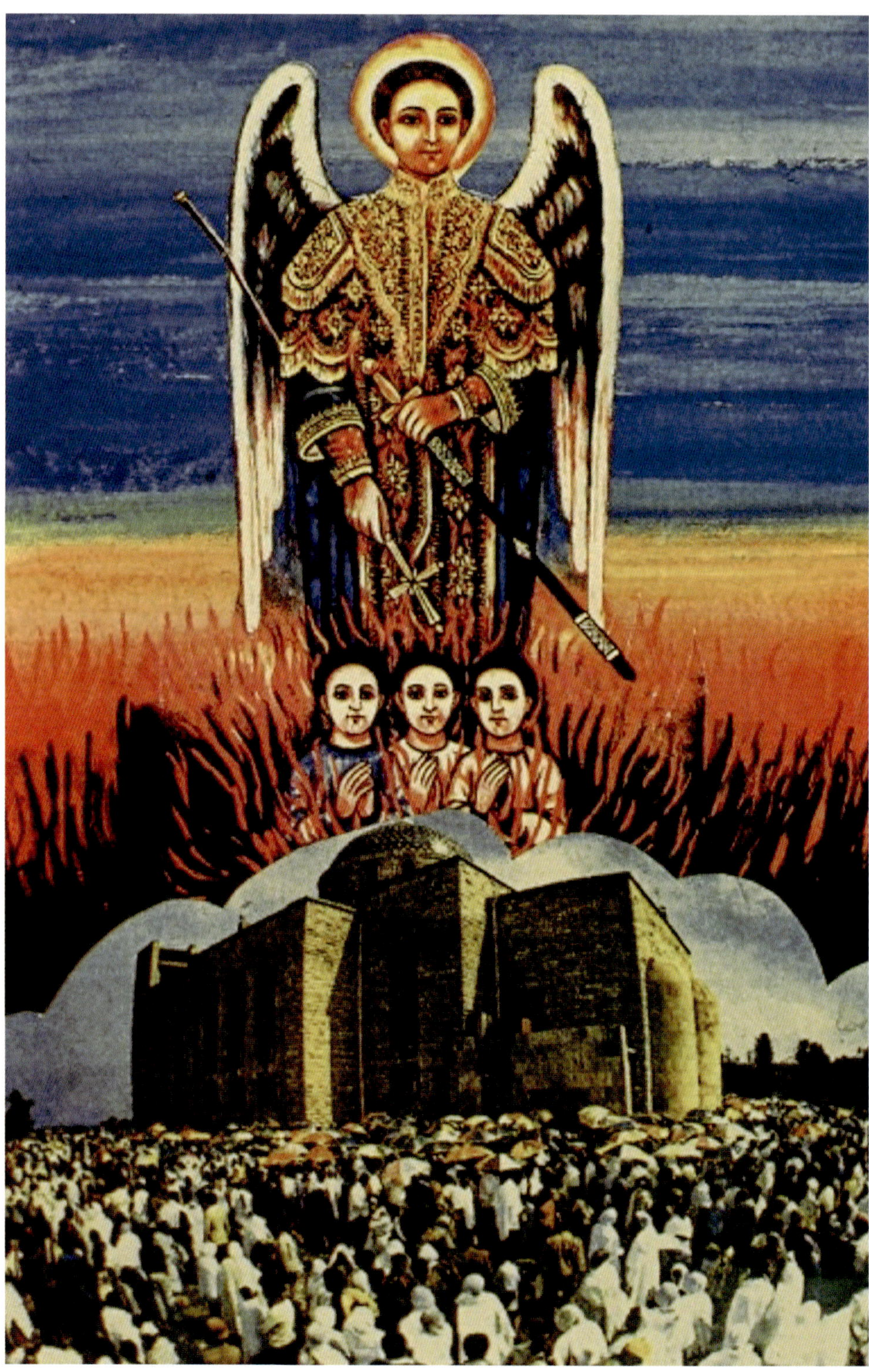

FIG 3

Archangel Gabriel and the Three Hebrew Youths; pilgrims advancing toward Qullebi. Chromolithograph promoting the Qullebi pilgrimage.

This decorative frontispiece, a traditional practice, was first introduced to Qur'ans in the eleventh century. Although theologians initially objected to it, the decorative frontispiece has become a standard element of Qur'anic manuscripts (fig. 4).

The Ethiopian Orthodox Church interprets the Second Commandment narrowly. Carved imagery—for example, three-dimensional sculpture—is forbidden, but two-dimensional images of the human figure are permitted. Artists are free to paint icons of saints as well as narratives and other religious subjects in church murals, illuminated manuscripts, and Gospel manuscripts (fig. 2.5). The wide range of artistry in the Ethiopian Orthodox Church stems from the tradition of royal patronage, which included training programs for painters and supporting monastic centers and their scriptoria. Other members of the ruling class also patronized religious art by commissioning illuminated manuscripts for private use and icons for their private chapels; they also commissioned icons and mural programs for churches. Such visual treasures of the Ethiopian Orthodox Church are the focus of this book.

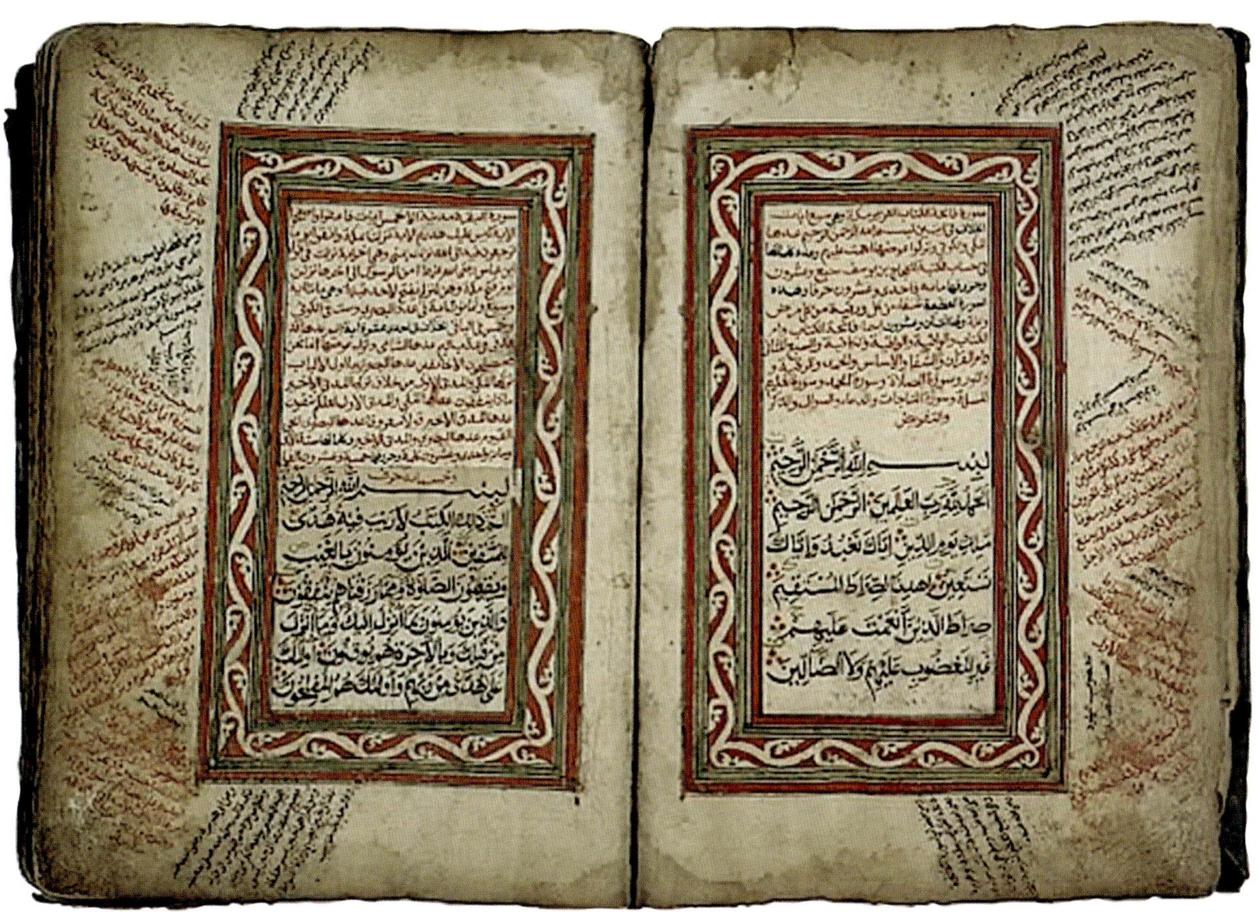

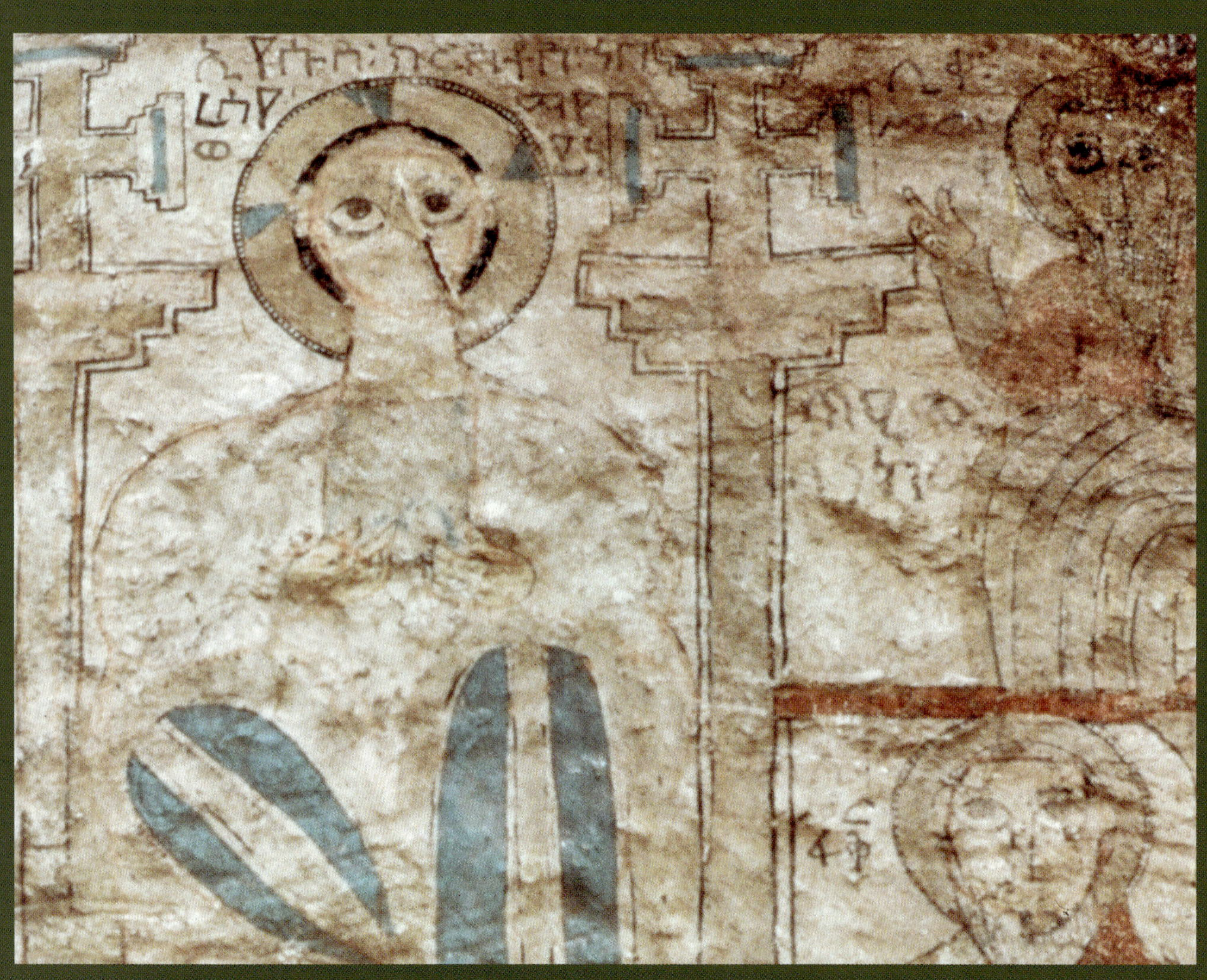

Chapter 1

The Church of Gännätä Maryam

MARILYN E. HELDMAN

DETAIL OF FIG 1.6
Detail from Wedding at Cana

Carved from living rock, the freestanding basilica of Gännätä Maryam rests on the broad ledge of Mount Makina, overlooking the vast gorge of the Takkazi River in the modern-day province of Wällo. The church sits a relatively short distance from the village of Gännätä Maryam; it is visible from an all-weather road that runs through the village and connects the town of Woldiya with the pilgrimage site of Lalibäla.[1]

Gännätä Maryam was built by Emperor Yəkunno Amlak (r. 1270–85), who in 1270 CE overthrew the reigning Zag^we kings of Lasta.[2] Yəkunno Amlak deliberately chose to locate his dynastic church, Gännätä Maryam (fig. 1.1), at Bugna in Lasta, about ten miles east of Lalibäla, the ceremonial center of the defeated Zag^we dynasty and home to its ten rock-hewn churches.[3] The church was excavated and decorated with murals dedicated to Yəkunno Amlak, founder of what has come to be known as the Solomonic dynasty.[4]

We know that the church and its murals date to the period of Yəkunno Amlak's reign. We also know that Abbot Nəhyo Bäkrəstos oversaw both the excavation and the decoration of the church, and that the church was originally dedicated to Äbba Mätta', the venerated monk who came to Ethiopia from the Greco-Roman world in late antiquity.[5] Äbba Mätta' was also the reputed founder of the monastery of Däbrä Libanos near the village of Ham, in present-day Eritrea, once an important center of Ethiopian monasticism.[6] An inscribed portrait (fig. 1.2) in the church reads: "In giving thanks to God. It is I who has this church built, I, Yəkunno Amlak, whom God made king by his good will. My father Nəhyo Bäkrəstos was an agent for me to have this church built in the name of Mätta'. May God have mercy upon me in the Kingdom of Heaven with my fathers Mähari Amlak and Nəhyo Bäkrəstos. Amen."[7]

One of Lalibäla's ten rock-hewn churches was dedicated to Äbba Mätta', or Äbba Libanos, as he is also known.[8] Because this is the only church at Lalibäla devoted to a saint who flourished in Ethiopia, the dedication of Yəkunno Amlak's church to the same individual is significant. It may attest to a reciprocal relationship between Yəkunno Amlak and the monastery of Äbba Mätta' whereby the emperor supported the monks of Däbrä Libanos just as the rulers of the Zag^we dynasty had generously supported their monastery.[9]

With its freestanding piers, Gännätä Maryam's exterior elevation represents an architectural quotation of the church of Mädhane 'Aläm (the Redeemer), the most

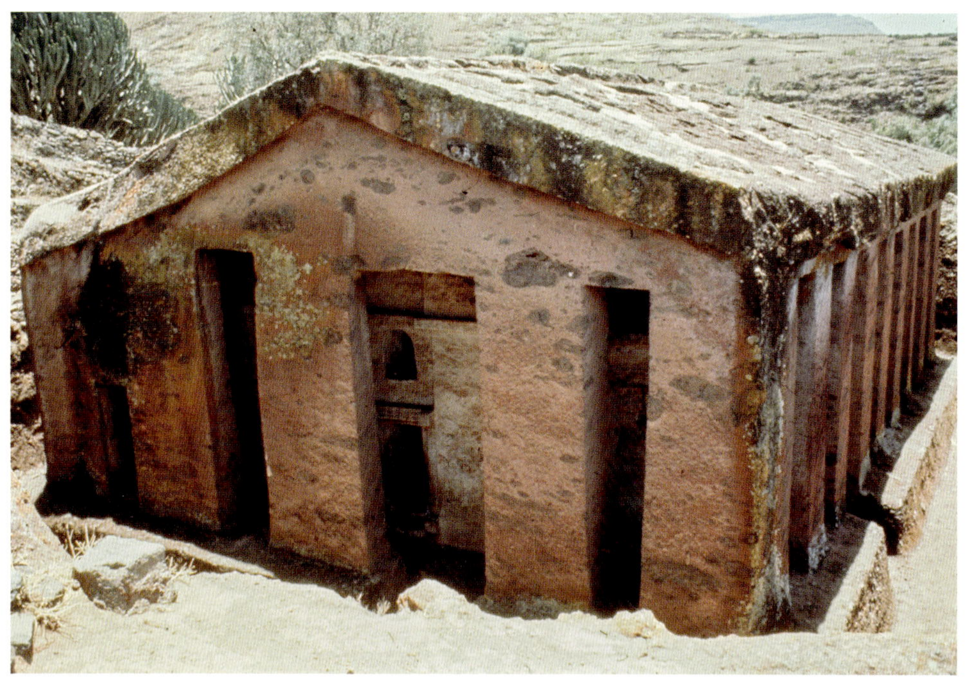

   ETHIOPIAN DEVOTIONS

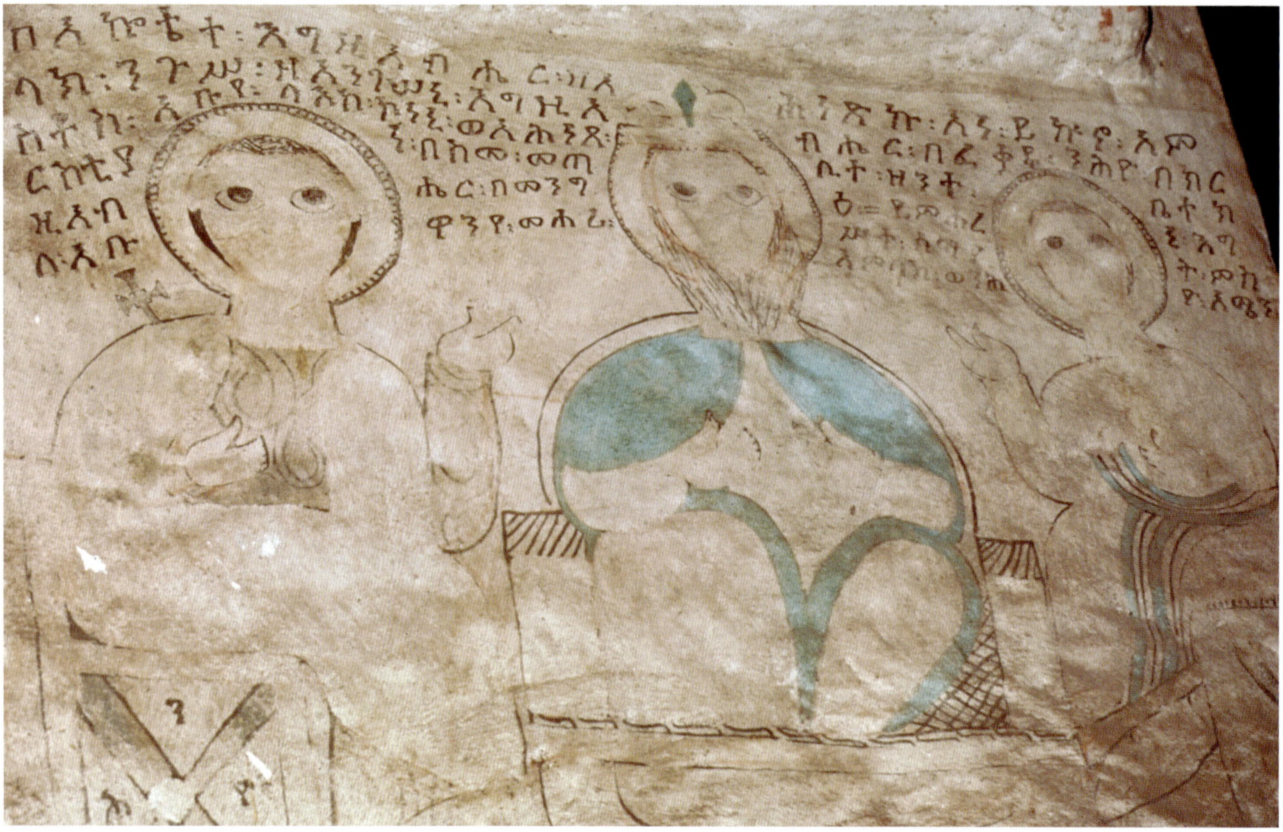

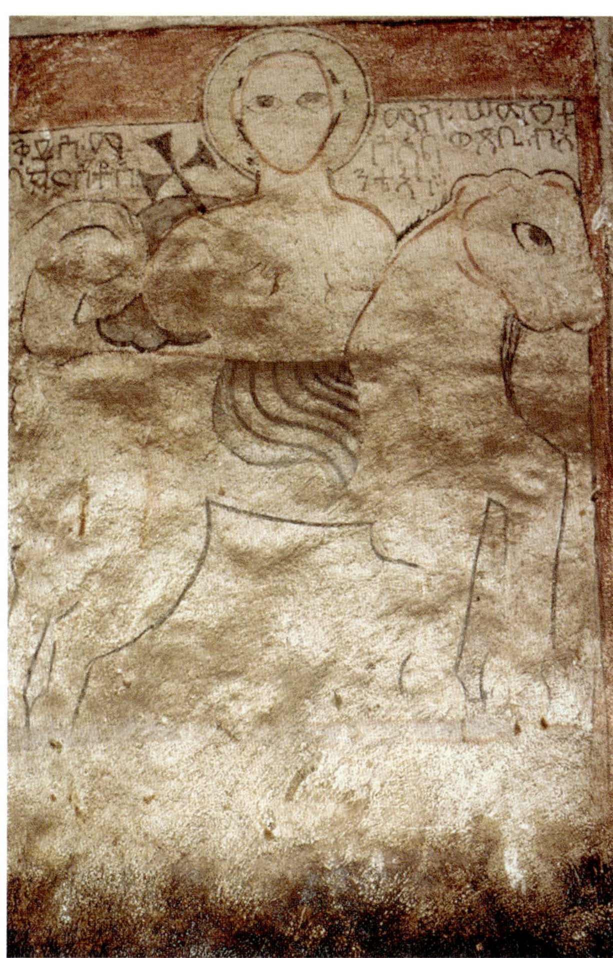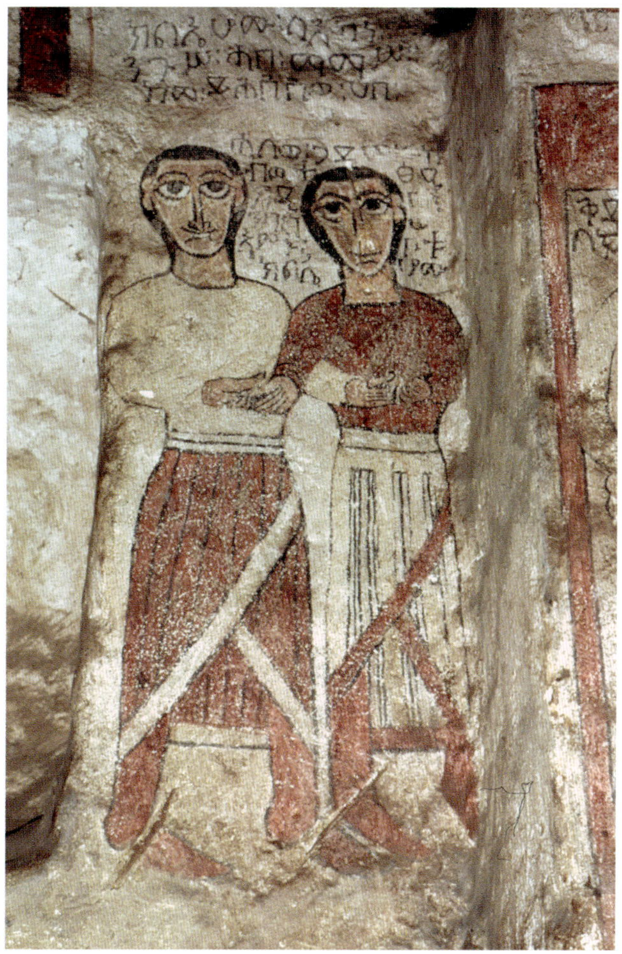

grandiose religious structure in Lalibäla, which is itself perhaps a copy of Ethiopia's cathedral at Aksum.

Numerous chambers cut into rock faces in the immediate vicinity of Gännätä Maryam were used as monastic cells. A series of portraits of abbots, hermits, and holy men and women throughout the church constitutes a monastic scheme. A monastic community of monks and nuns was either present or anticipated when the original mural scheme was formulated.

The north and south walls of the church feature portraits of male and female monastic saints. The south aisle is decorated with a series of portraits and several episodes from the Life of Saint Mamas Martyr. Two episodes from Mamas's life adorn the central bay of the aisle, and an icon of the saint that shows him riding a lion is on the adjoining engaged pier (figs. 1.3 a and b). The inscription reads: "Saint Mamas, martyr of Christ, pray and supplicate for us."

The east bay of the south wall is divided into two registers. The upper register shows Saint Mercurius slaying Julian the Apostate (fig. 1.4) and is inscribed with

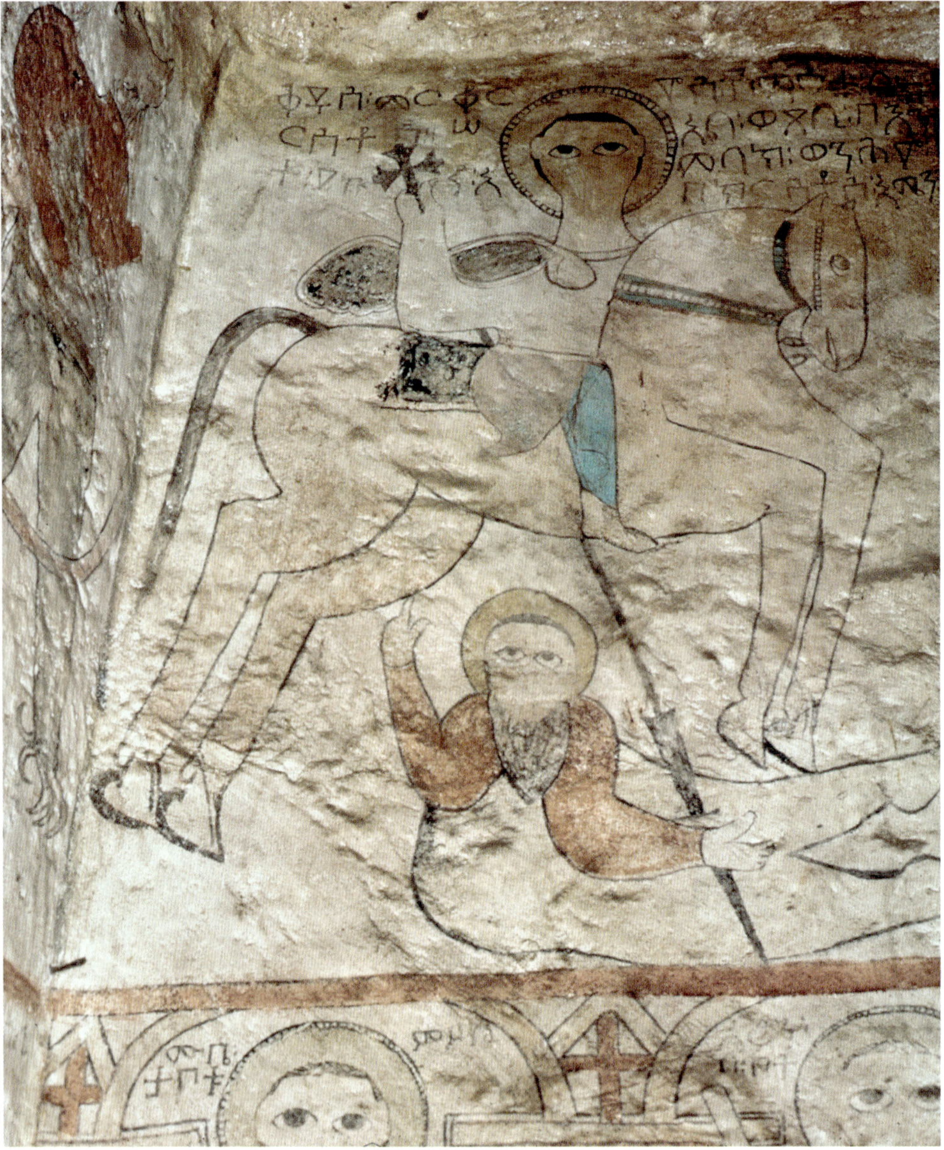

a more specific prayer: "Saint Mercurius, martyr of Christ, pray and supplicate for Yəkunno Amlak and Nəḥyo Bäkrəstos. Amen."[10] This apotropaic portrait of a mounted soldier-saint is mirrored at the opposite end of the south aisle by an equestrian portrait of Saint Qirqos, also known as Cyriacus, whose inscription reads: "Saint Cyriacus, martyr of Christ, pray and supplicate for us." The depiction of Qirqos as a horseman is unusual, for he is usually portrayed as a youth standing beside his mother Julitta, with whom he was martyred.[11]

The north aisles are devoted to scenes of Saint Mary of Egypt. As the story of Saint Mary's life is not found in the Ethiopian Book of Saints (Synaxary), the painters likely followed the Synaxary of the Egyptian Church, thus suggesting that the

   ETHIOPIAN DEVOTIONS

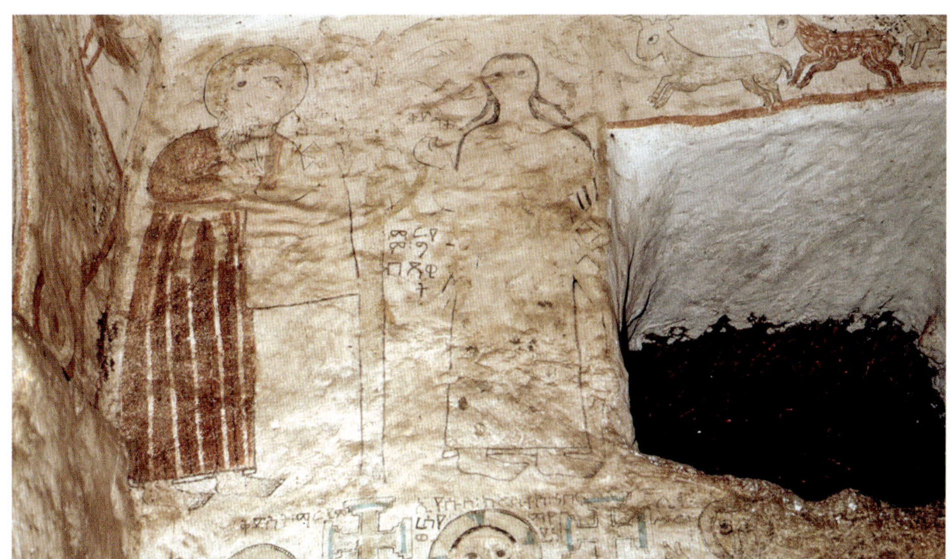

FIG 1.5 A AND B

Ethiopian Orthodox, Scenes from the Life of Saint Mary the Egyptian, Gännätä Maryam, Lalibäla, Ethiopia, 13th century. Photographs by Marilyn E. Heldman, ca. 1993. National Museum of African Art, Smithsonian Institution, Marilyn E. Heldman Collection, Eliot Elisofon Photographic Archives, EEPA 2013-013-0227, 0220

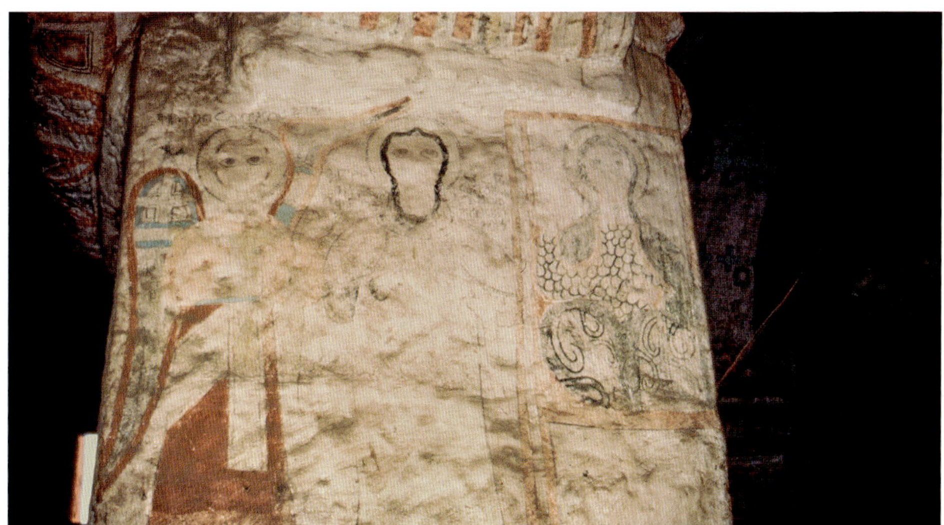

Ethiopian Book of Saints was created at a later date. Saint Mary of Egypt's encounter with the priest Zosimas in the Jordanian desert is pictured above the Wedding at Cana (figs. 1.5 a and b, 1.6). An earlier episode in the saint's life appears on the north face of the adjoining northwest pier.[12]

The individual portraits included in the north aisle depict an almost equal number of holy men and women, most of whom are Egyptians, attesting that the painters were using the Egyptian Book of Saints, or Synaxary, although the cult of Saint Mary the Egyptian was popular in the Universal Church. In addition to Mary, we can note the inclusion of the Egyptian monastic saints Äbba Hor, Äbba Menas, Äbba Samuel, and Äbba Daniel, and the Egyptian martyr saints Barbara and Juliana (fig. 1.7).[13]

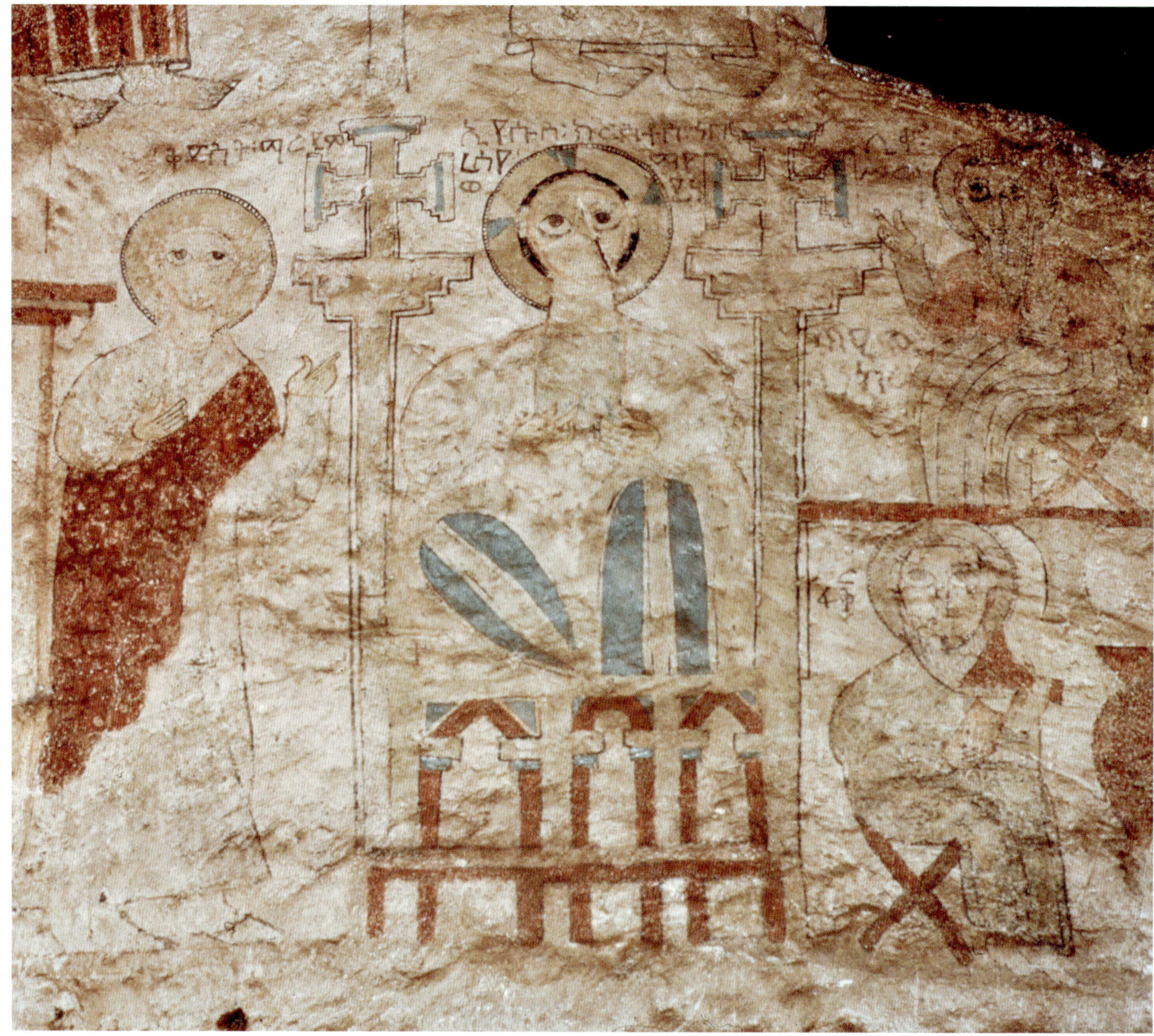

FIG 1.6

Ethiopian Orthodox, Wedding at Cana, Gännätä Maryam, Lalibäla, Ethiopia, 13th century. Photograph by Marilyn E. Heldman, ca. 1993. National Museum of African Art, Smithsonian Institution, Marilyn E. Heldman Collection, Eliot Elisofon Photographic Archives, EEPA 2013-013-0228

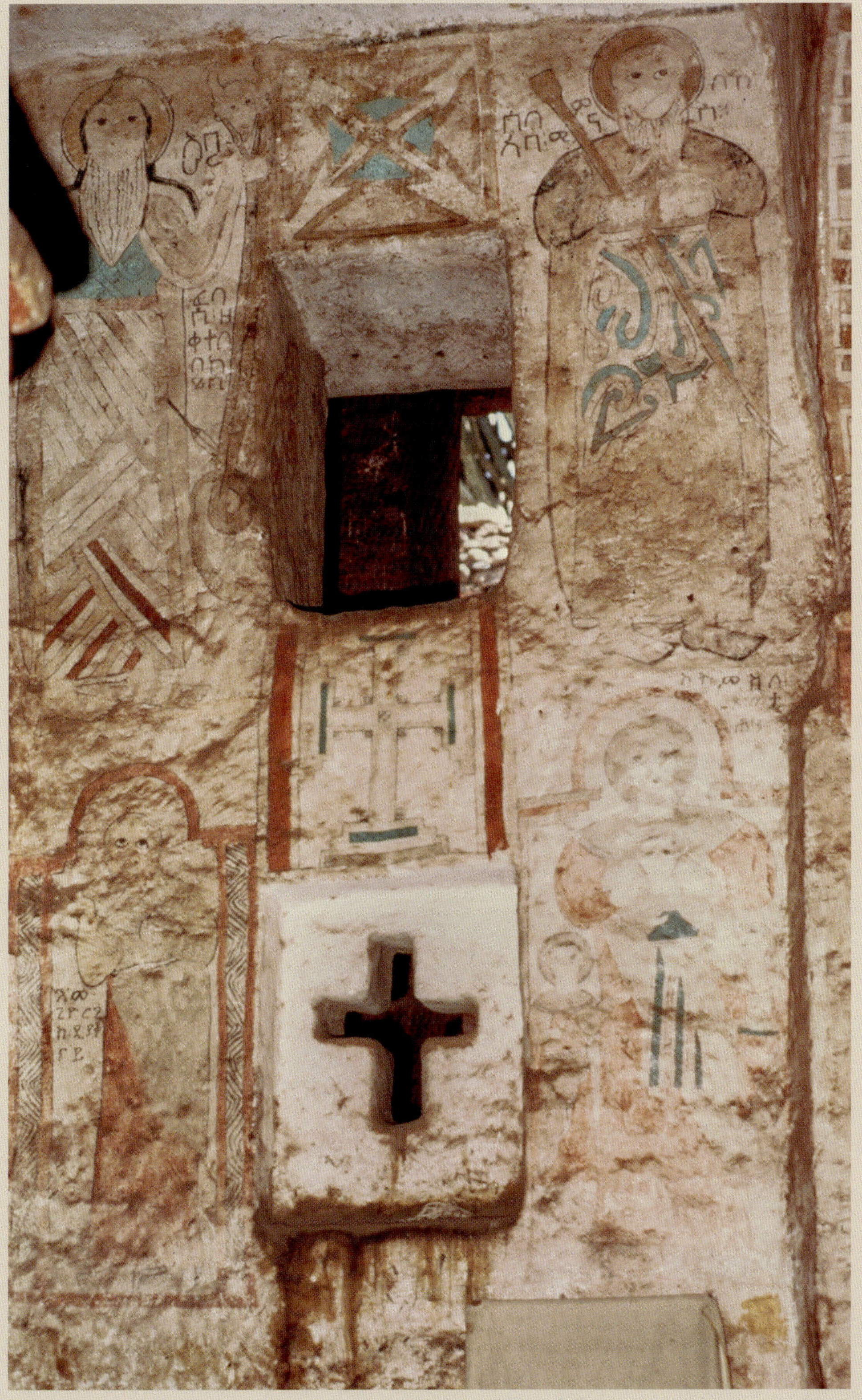

FIG 1.7
Ethiopian Orthodox, Äbba
Hor and Äbba Menas, Gännätä
Maryam, Lalibäla, Ethiopia,
13th century. Photograph by
Marilyn E. Heldman, ca. 1993.
National Museum of African Art,
Smithsonian Institution, Marilyn
E. Heldman Collection, Eliot
Elisofon Photographic Archives,
EEPA 2013-013-232

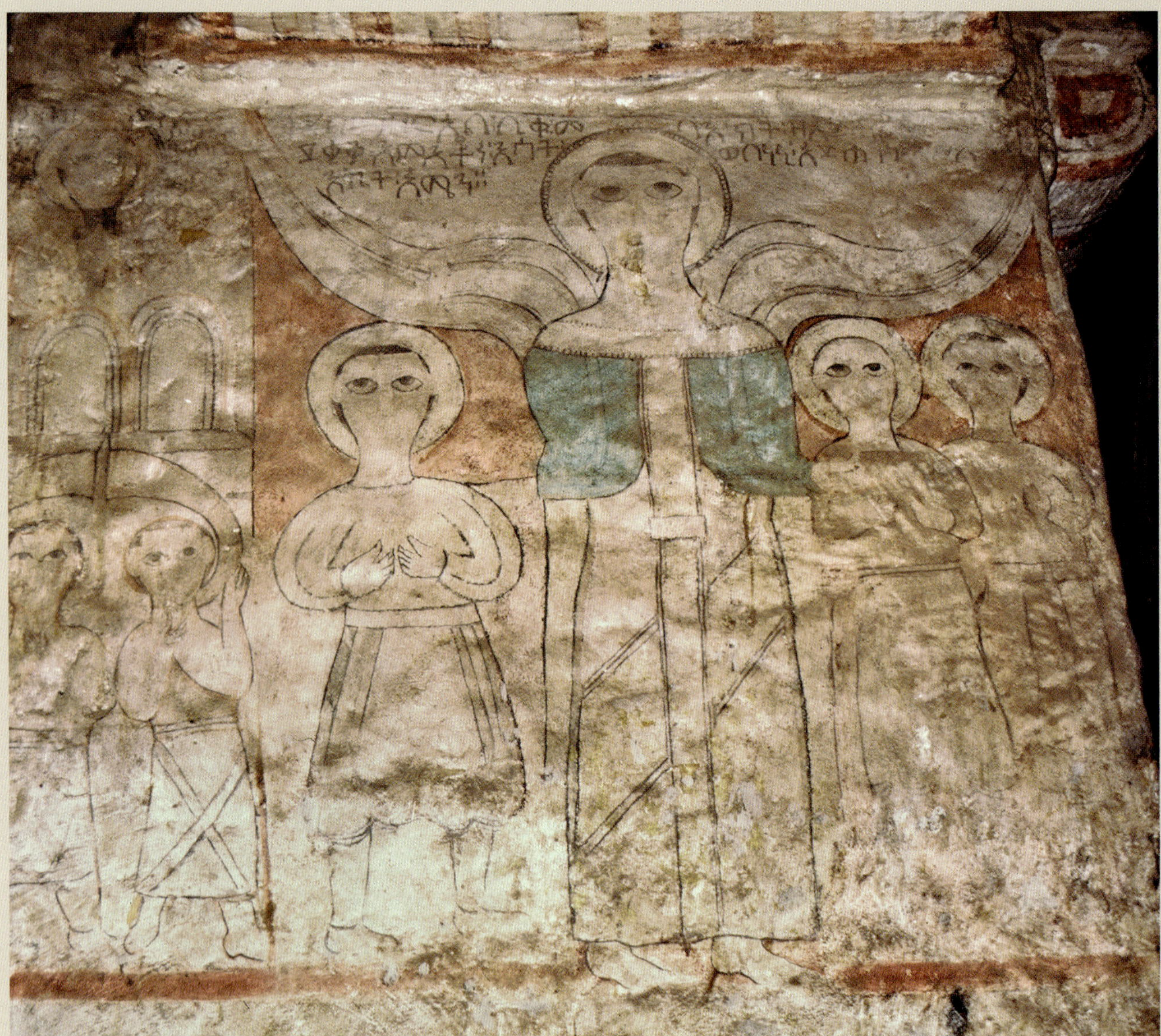

FIG 1.8
Saint Sophia with Her Three
Virgin Daughters, Faith,
Hope, and Charity, Gännätä
Maryam, Lalibäla, Ethiopia,
13th century. Photograph by
Marilyn E. Heldman, ca. 1993.
National Museum of African
Art, Smithsonian Institution,
Marilyn E. Heldman Collection,
Eliot Elisofon Photographic
Archives, EEPA 2013-13-0226

Portraits of Saint Anba Marina accompanied by a small boy appear at the west end.[14] Just east of these two is an equestrian portrait of Saint George riding with the young boy George the Deacon, painted upon an engaged pilaster (the opposing engaged pilaster features the earlier-described depiction of Saint Mamas riding a lion). Flanking the cross-inscribed window to the east, in the lower register, are two portraits—the mother of George the Deacon and Saint Sophia with her three virgin daughters, Faith, Hope, and Charity (fig. 1.8). Saint Sophia is described in the Ethiopic Synaxary as a blessed mother who taught her daughters goodness, piety, the fear of God, and Church doctrine. When her daughters were brought before Hadrian, the pagan emperor of Rome, she encouraged them to endure their beatings so that they might join Christ the Bridegroom and enter with him into the heavenly wedding feast.[15]

Moving east to the next engaged pilaster, opposite the portraits of Saints Barbara and Juliana on the north face of the northeast pier, is a portrait of Saint Äbba Samuel. Adjoining the latter portrait in the lower register of the wall of the north aisle's eastern bay is a portrait of Äbba Daniel. The remaining figures pictured on the wall relate to the narrative scenes of this bay's east wall, although the figure of the great Old Testament matriarch Sarah, in the register above Äbba Daniel, relates to the mothers at the center of the north wall—Saint Sophia with her three virgin daughters and the mother of George the Deacon.

Some of these icons are inscribed with supplications, indicating that they functioned as devotional images:

Saint George, pray for us; may your prayer be upon us.
Saint Sophia with her children, may her prayer be upon us.
Saint Äbba Samuel, salutation to you; pray and supplicate for us.
Saint Barbara with her sister Juliana, pray and supplicate for us.
Saint Äbba Daniel, salutation to you; pray and supplicate for us.

Other leaders of Egyptian and Ethiopian monasticism pictured in portraits in Gännätä Maryam include: Äbba Anthony, founder of the institution of monasticism; Äbba Shenuti, the great fifth-century reformer of Egyptian monasticism; Arsenius, the famed Egyptian ascetic; Äbba Nafer, the great hermit whose Egyptian name morphed into Onnophrius; and the Nine Saints of Ethiopia and the abovementioned Äbba Mättaʿ, said to have introduced monasticism into Ethiopia in the fourth century.

The inscriptions demonstrate without a doubt that the church murals were devotional images intended to receive the prayers recited before them. Gännätä Maryam is the earliest Ethiopian church with murals to include devotional images. Only later, during the reign of Emperor Zärʾa Yaʿəqob (r. 1434–68), were portable devotional icons painted on wooden panels introduced.

Holy Sanctuary

MARILYN E. HELDMAN

The layout of a typical Ethiopian church has changed throughout the centuries. The rectangular plan of the modern-day Ethiopian church is similar to the basilica plan of the earliest churches, with the sanctuary located at the east end of the structure (figs. E1.1 and E1.2). A revolutionary modification introduced around 1500—the sanctuary (*maqdäs*), where the holy Eucharist was celebrated on the altar table—greatly altered the shape of the church's most sacred space.[1] Although there was not space for many worshippers, the plan afforded absolute privacy for the celebration of the Eucharist.

The most popular version of the *maqdäs* calls for a circular plan with a small, free-standing, square sanctuary at its center (fig. E1.2). Doors on the west, north, and south sides of the sanctuary allow priests and deacons to enter and exit. Its exterior walls are painted with rows of devotional images as well as narratives, such as the story of the Holy Family's Flight into Egypt or the Passion of Jesus Christ.

Icons of Our Lady Mary and the Crucifixion, and perhaps of the Archangels Michael and Gabriel as guardians of the holy place, adorn the entrance to the sanctuary. The liturgical Gospel book, which signifies the presence of Jesus Christ within the church, is removed from the sanctuary and carried among the congregation beneath a decorative umbrella that functions as an honorific dome (fig. E1.3). During the celebration of the Eucharist, curtains are used to shield the *maqdäs* from view.

The most recent church plan, developed in Addis Ababa in the mid-twentieth century, resembles the early basilica plan, with the sanctuary at the east wall.[2] Murals or framed images of saints and major events in the life of Christ decorate the walls. The liturgical furnishings have remained constant: chalices and patens for the celebration of the Eucharist, processional crosses (figs. E1.4 a and b) censers (fig. E1.5), and prayer staffs (fig. 7.3 a) are used during the musical performance of the service to enhance the religious experience through the sensorial pleasures of sight, smell, and sound. The incense also serves to raise up the prayers of the priests to God, as did the incense from the censers of the twenty-four Priests of Heaven (Revelation 4:1–8), who carried the of saints' prayers to the throne of God.[3]

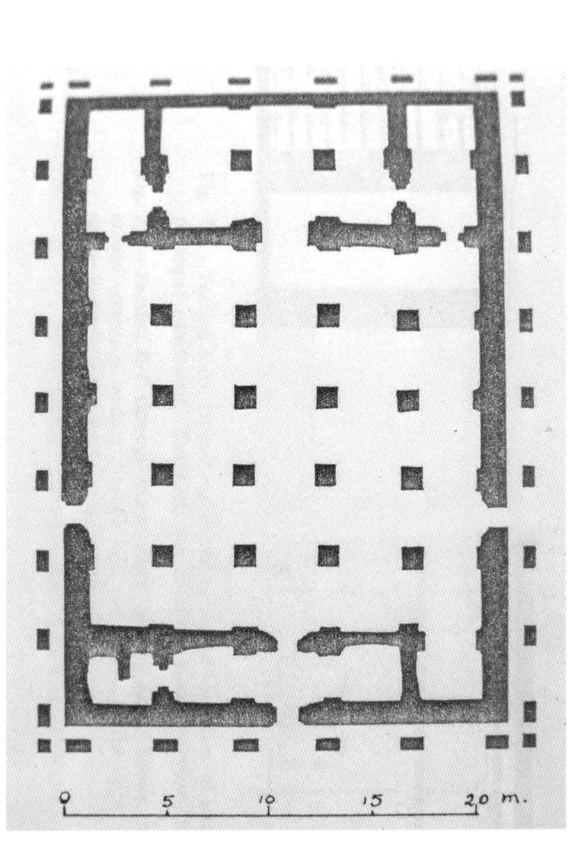

FIG E1.1

Floor plan of Ǝmäkina Mädḫane, ʿAläm, Lalibäla, Ethiopia. Photograph by Marilyn E. Heldman. National Museum of African Art, Smithsonian Institution, Marilyn E. Heldman Collection, Eliot Elisofon Photographic Archives, EEPA 2013-013-0144

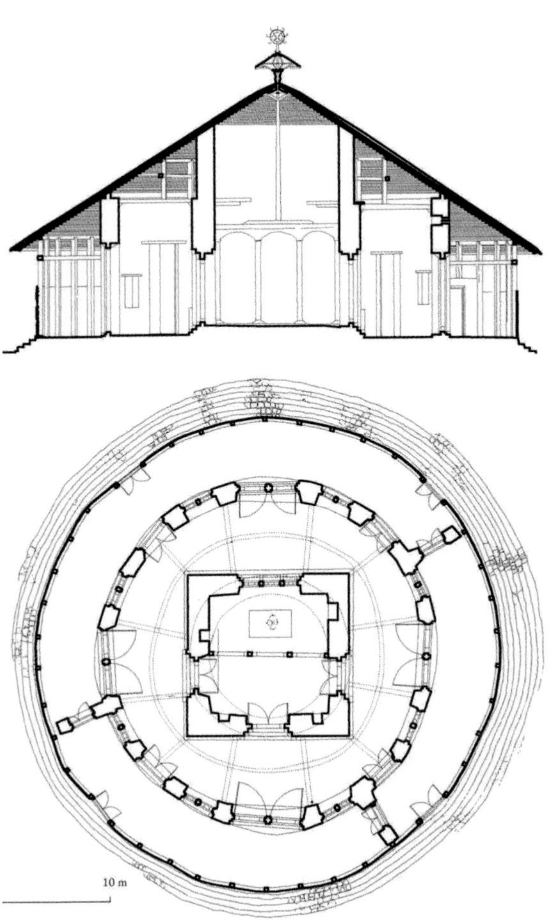

FIG E1.2

Section and plan of Ura Kidäne Meḥrat, on the peninsula of Şegē (from reliefs by Mezmir Abiye). In Mario Di Salvo, *Churches of Ethiopia: The Monastery of Nārgā Śellāsē*, with texts by Stanislaw Chojnacki and Osvaldo Raineri (Milan: Skira Editore), page 91

FIG E1.3
Liturgical Gospel prayer book
carried among the congregation,
Debra Selam Kidist Maryam
Ethiopian Orthodox Church,
Washington, DC. Photograph
by Marilyn E. Heldman and
Kay Kaufman Shelemay, 2007

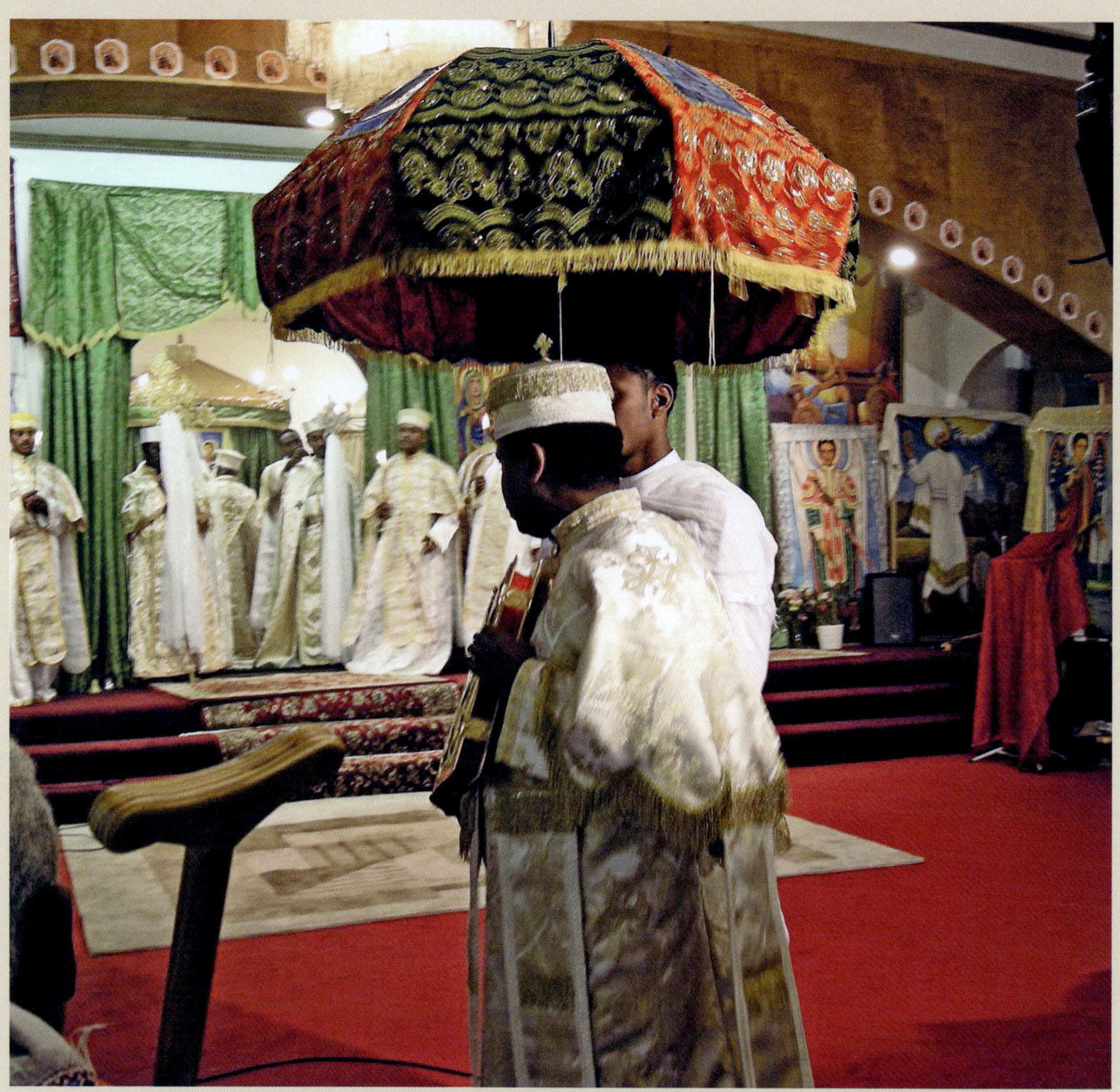

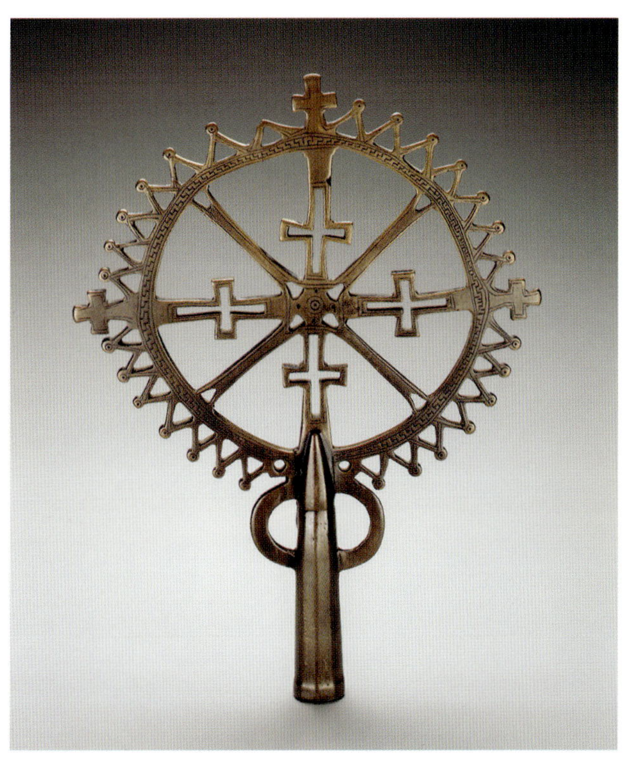

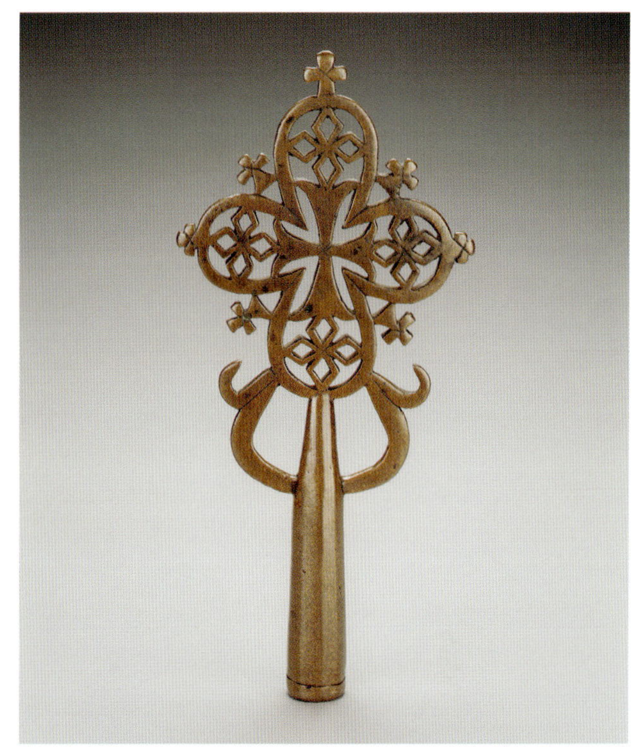

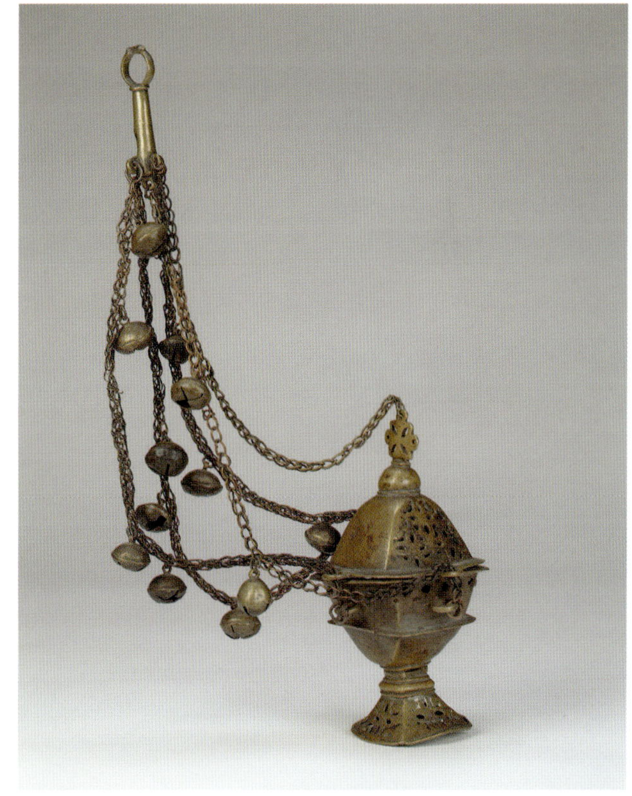

FIG E1.4 A AND B

Ethiopian Orthodox, processional crosses, 14th to 15th century. Copper alloy, (a) 12 ³⁄₁₆ × 9 ⅛ × 1 inches (30.9 × 23.2 × 2.5 cm), (b) 9 ¾ × 4 ⁷⁄₁₆ × ⅞ inches (24.7 × 11.3 × 2.3 cm). (a) National Museum of African Art, Smithsonian Institution, museum purchase, 97-19-1, (b) National Museum of African Art, Smithsonian Institution, 97-19-3

FIG E1.5

Ethiopian Orthodox, censer, 18th to 19th century. Copper alloy, 10 ¼ × 6 ⁵⁄₁₆ × 6 ⁵⁄₁₆ inches (26 × 16 × 16 cm). National Museum of African Art, Smithsonian Institution, Gift in memory of Nancy E. MacDonald, 2015-7-10

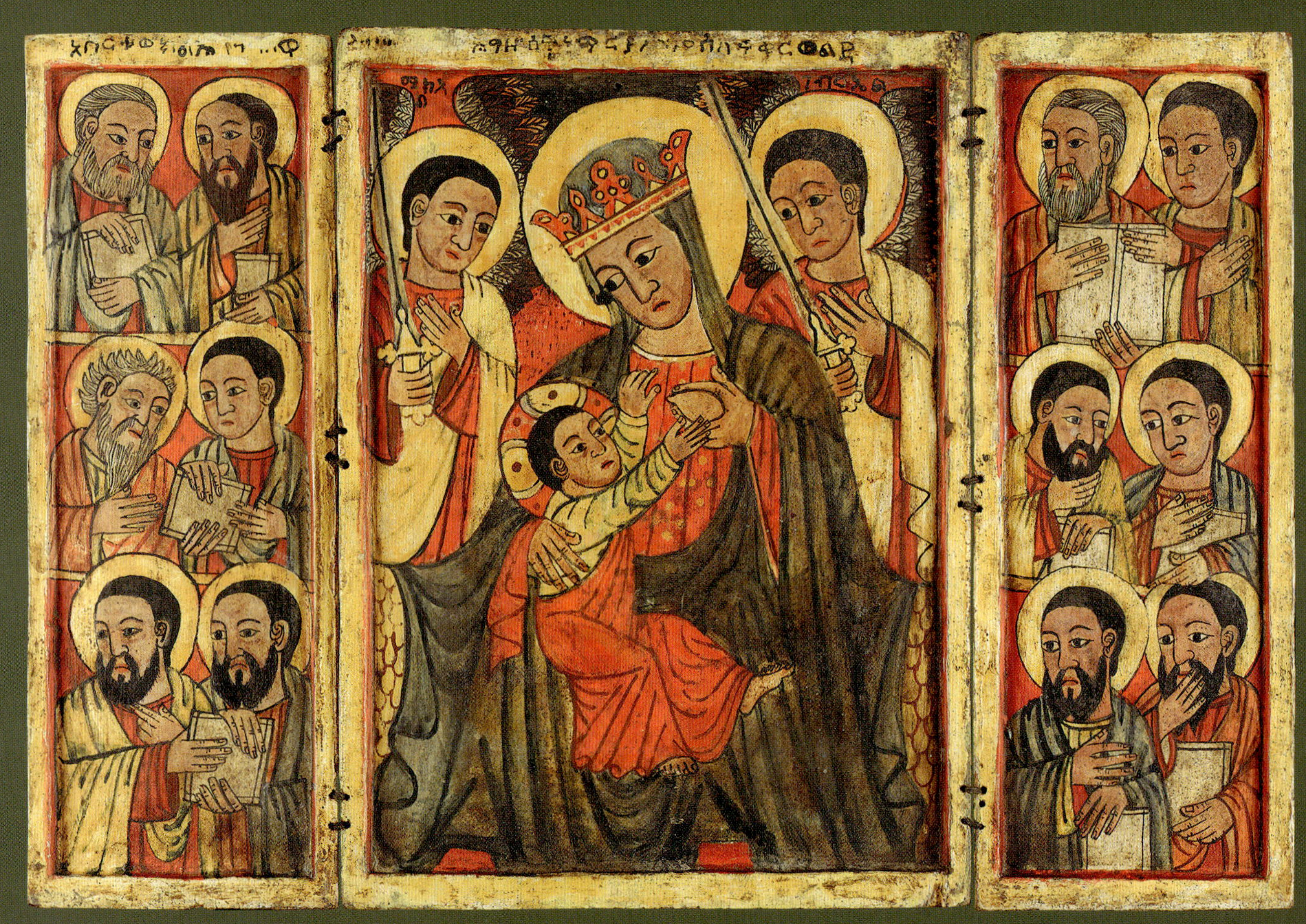

Chapter 2

Emperor Zär'a Ya'əqob and the Cult of Our Lady Mary

MARILYN E. HELDMAN

In the Christian tradition, the sign of the cross is a symbol of Christ's victory over Death. On the day of Zär'a Ya'əqob's birth in 1399, his mother made the sign of the cross on his right hand in the name of "Our Lady Mary, Mother of God."[1] His mother's remarkable dedication so inspired him that as emperor, Zär'a Ya'əqob (r. 1434–68 CE) mandated that the sign of the cross be placed upon the forehead of every Christian. He also authorized the cult of Our Lady Mary.[2]

Zär'a Ya'əqob's father, Emperor Dawit (1380–1412), personally committed himself to the devotion of Our Lady Mary and had her image installed in his palace. Emperor Zär'a Ya'əqob went even further, committing his people and the Church to the ritual devotions of Our Lady Mary and the commemoration of her feasts. He established a court church in her name where collections of the Miracles of Mary were edited, decreed that every church have an altar dedicated to Mary, and demanded that all Ethiopian Christians prostrate themselves in Mary's honor whenever her name was mentioned. The mandatory rite of prostration was prescribed in the Introductory Rite of the Miracles of Mary.

Within the context of Zär'a Ya'əqob's theology, the theme of Mary and the Christ Child with the Twelve Apostles glorifies Mary and symbolizes the Orthodox Church, free of improper teaching and practice (fig. 2.1). The emperor's collection of homilies, entitled *Epistle of Humanity*, was written to promote orthodoxy and condemn heresy, popular superstition, and magical practices, and draws extensively on the Sinodos, the Ethiopian Church Orders.

Those who rejected Zär'a Ya'əqob's cult of Our Lady Mary faced excommunication. This was no idle threat. A monk named Ǝsṭifanos and his followers, who came to be known as Ǝsṭifanosites, rejected the mandatory rite of prostration in Mary's honor, explaining that prostration was an act of worship reserved for the Triune God. Seeing their resistance as a threat to his authority, Zär'a Ya'əqob persecuted the Ǝsṭifanosites; their excommunication was not lifted until the early sixteenth century.

Along with mandating prostration, the Introductory Rite prescribes the reading of three tales from the Miracles of Mary on the thirty-two (or thirty-three) Marian feast days and during the Sunday service. The reading was to be accompanied by hymns of praise and by censing an icon of Our Lady Mary or burning incense in front of her icon.

FIG 2.1

Ethiopian Orthodox, Mary and the Christ Child with the Twelve Apostles, mid- to late 15th century. Paint on wood, triptych, 11 ¼ × 16 ⁵⁄₁₆ × ¹³⁄₁₆ inches (28.5 × 41.5 × 2 cm). National Museum of African Art, Smithsonian Institution, Gift of Joseph and Patricia Brumit, 2004-7-6

FIG 2.2

Ethiopian Orthodox, Covenant
of Mercy, 17th century. Icon.
Tempera on wood, triptych,
13 ¾ × ¹³⁄₁₆ inches (34.9 × 2.1 cm).
Peabody Essex Museum, Harvard
University, Gift of Mr. and Mrs.
Charles Longmuir, E67887

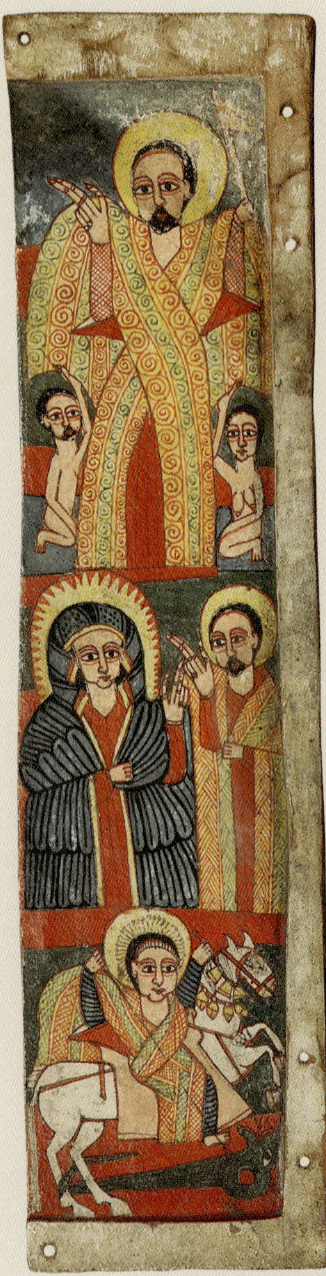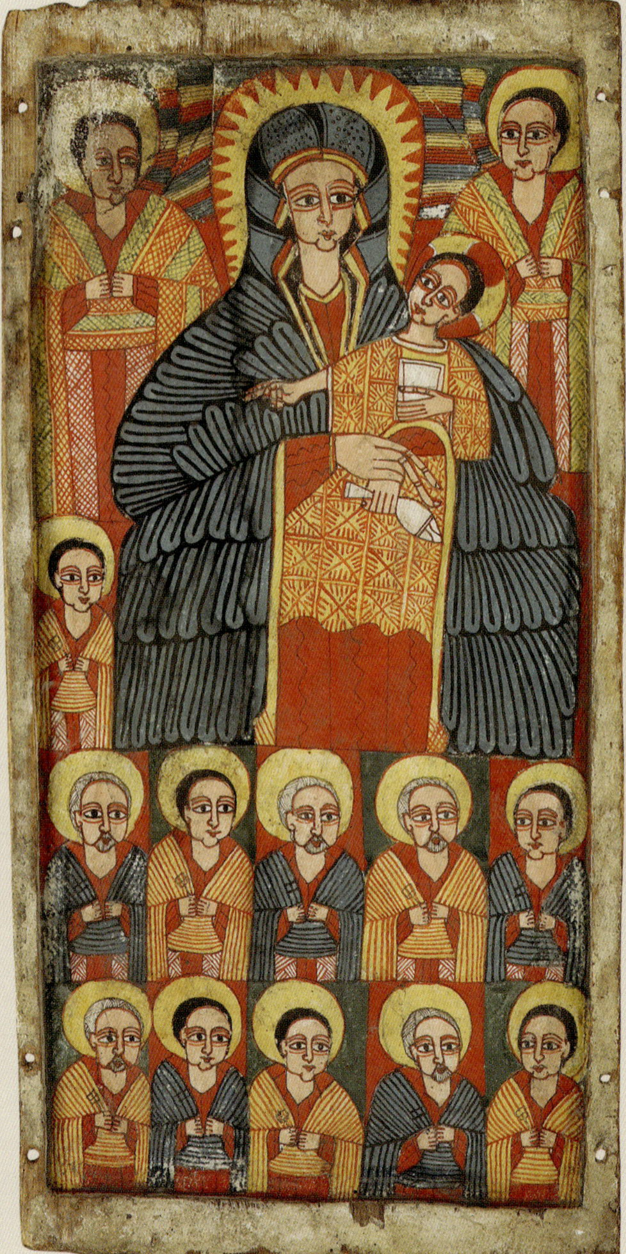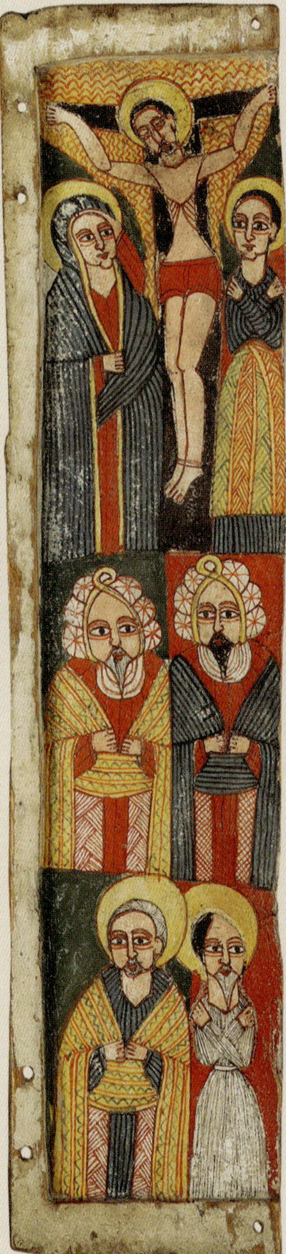

An early sixteenth-century European witness to this ritual wrote that the ceremony of veneration included a procession before the icon.

The Marian feasts commemorate major events in her life and celebrate aspects of her cult. These include her Conception; Dedication at the Temple; Assumption (*Felsata*) on 16 Nehase; Dormition (*'Erafta*) on 21 Tərr, including the twenty-first day of every other month as a secondary feast of her Dormition; the Annunciation to Mary by Gabriel; the Nativity of Christ; and the Flight of the Holy Family into Egypt. The Marian feast of 22 Tahsas recognizes aspects of her cult by celebrating the miracle of Bishop Daqseyos or Ildefonsus of Toledo, the subtext of which promises divine reward for those who write homilies in her honor.

Three Marian feasts—Maryam Sedeneya, Sane Maryam, and the Covenant of Mercy—function to renew popular support for the cult of Mary. The feast of Maryam Sedeneya—the miraculous icon of Mary at Sedeneya (near Damascus)—encourages the faithful to regard the icon of Mary as a vehicle for working miracles. The tale of the miracle-working icon is not routinely included in the Miracles of Mary, although this feast, celebrated on 10 Maskaram, was also compulsory. The feast of 21 Sane, which celebrates the building of churches dedicated to Mary, encourages the founding of churches in her honor. The feast of the Covenant of Mercy, celebrated on 16 Yekatit, promises that the faithful who commemorate her feasts or give even a drop of water in her name will be forgiven for their sins.

The mandatory ritual that precedes the reading of the three tales on feast days requires a small, portable wooden panel, known as an icon, of Our Lady Mary (fig. 2.2). An early sixteenth-century account of the rite describes the "bringing out of a figure of Our Lady," which the priest held before his chest, while two others stood beside him holding lighted candles. In his *Book of Light*, Zär'a Ya'əqob gives instructions for the midday prayer service of the Sunday Sabbath, advising how to display Mary's icon upon a high throne (*manbar*) with a baldachin (*debab*) above it and a cross placed at its right. He adds that, if a church does not have an icon of Mary as required, then a manual cross should be placed upon the throne instead. Icons are still displayed in this manner, resting upon a symbolic throne draped with precious fabric.

The emperor's explicit instructions for displaying Mary's icon suggest that the Ethiopian faithful were not familiar with the ritual use of an icon in worship services. His advice to use a manual cross in the absence of an icon also suggests that Marian devotional images were in short supply; otherwise, each Ethiopian church would have had at least one such image. The zeal with which Zär'a Ya'əqob promoted the ritual veneration of Mary indicates that he sponsored the production of Marian icons, just as his scriptorium at the court church of Saint Mary produced copies of the Miracles of Mary along with copies of his theological tracts for dissemination throughout the empire. Therefore, it seems likely that the monks and scholars at the capital worked with painters to create icons for this new Marian cult.

The most important painter at Zär'a Ya'əqob's court was Frē Ṣəyon, a monk. We know his name because he signed a large wooden panel painting at the top of which

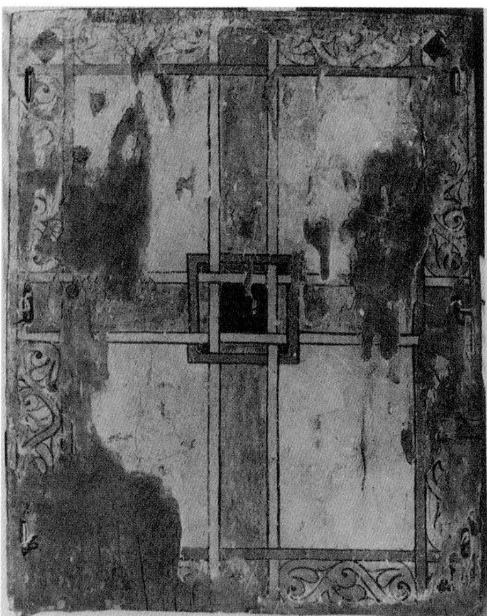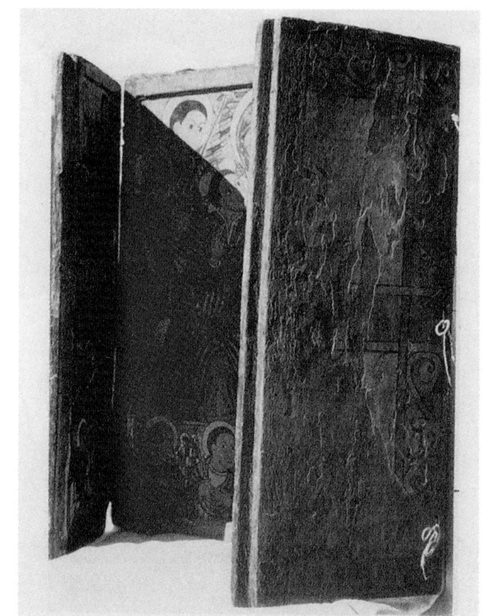

Frē Ṣəyon, Ethiopian, Our Lady Mary Holding the Christ Child. Icon, triptych, partially opened. Institute of Ethiopian Studies, no. 4186. In Marilyn E. Heldman, *The Marian Icons of the Painter Frē Ṣəyon: A Study in Fifteenth-Century Ethiopian Art, Patronage, and Spirituality* (Wiesbaden: Harrassowitz, 1994), pages 36 and 37

appears a portrait of Our Lady Mary and her Beloved Son and the Archangels Gabriel and Michael carrying swords. Below is an inscription, flanked by portraits of Saints Peter and Paul, which reads: "This picture was made in the days of our king Zär'a Ya'əqob and our Abbot Yeshaq of Daga. The painter [is I], the meek Frē Ṣəyon the sinner from Däbrä Gwegweben. Remember me in your prayers, O children [monks] of this place, forever and ever. Amen." This panel painting is unique in Ethiopian art for both its style and its scale. It remained at the Daga Ǝsṭifanos Monastery at Lake Ṭana until the twentieth century if not later.

The panel's similarities to Western painting in terms of its style and scale suggest that Frē Ṣəyon came into contact with European art. There was a good likelihood of this, given that Emperor Zär'a Ya'əqob reportedly received visitors and paintings from Western Europe. The size of the painting, standing nearly five feet tall, resembles that of decorated church altars in Roman Catholic Europe from this period (figs. 2.3 a and b). In addition, Frē Ṣəyon signed his name to the painting—a distinctively Western practice; Ethiopian painters did not usually sign their works because devotional images are created for God, not for the artist's reputation.

Although direct evidence of Frē Ṣəyon's career is limited to his signed panel, the distinctiveness of his style enables us identify the icons he created at the court. The works attributed to the artist include a diptych with portraits of Church Fathers Peter and Paul in the left panel (figs. 2.4 a and b), and Abraham, Isaac, and Jacob in the right panel. As Peter and Paul also figure in the large panel at Daga Ǝsṭifanos commissioned by Zär'a Ya'əqob, this diptych was presumably created for the emperor as well.

The diptych's connection to Zär'a Ya'əqob is even more likely given the figures depicted in the right panel. Zär'a Ya'əqob's name translates to "seed of Jacob."[3] In Genesis

Frē Ṣəyon, Ethiopian, Old and New Testament Patriarchs: Saints Peter and Paul; Abraham with Isaac and Jacob, 1445–80. Icon. Tempera on gesso-covered wood panels, diptych, (a) left panel: 22 1/16 × 12 1/8 inches (58 × 30.8 cm); (b) right panel: 22 1/16 × 11 7/16 inches (58 × 29 cm). Photographs by Marilyn E. Heldman. National Museum of African Art, Smithsonian Institution, Marilyn E. Heldman Collection, Eliot Elisofon Photographic Archives, EEPA 2013-013-0233, 0235, Institute of Ethiopian Studies, no. 4324

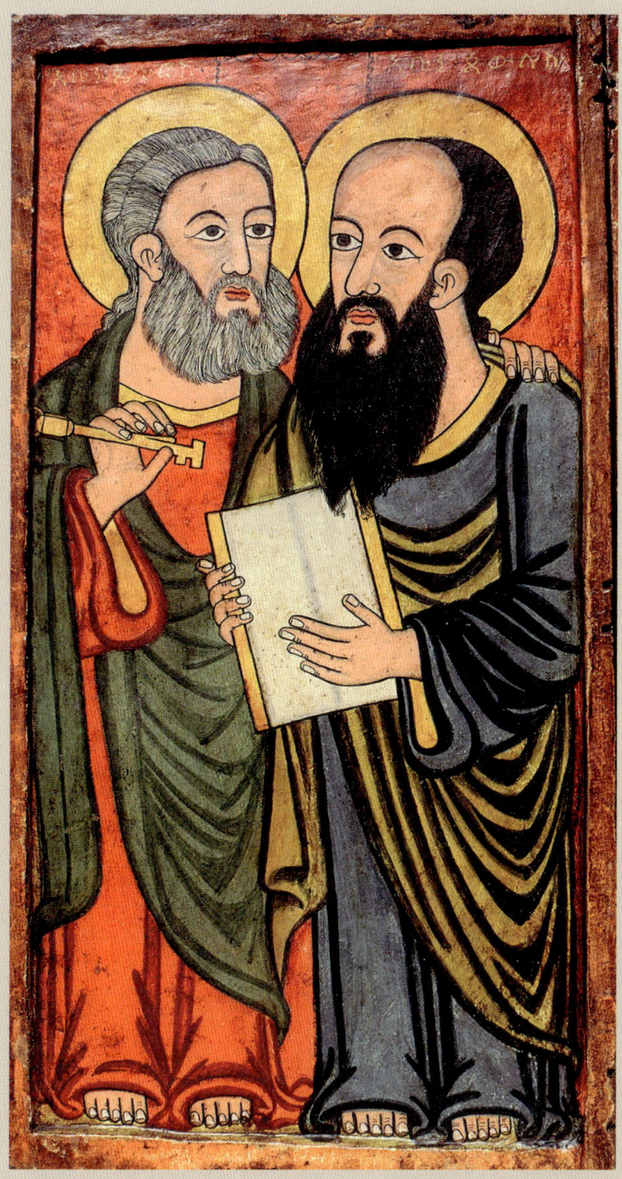
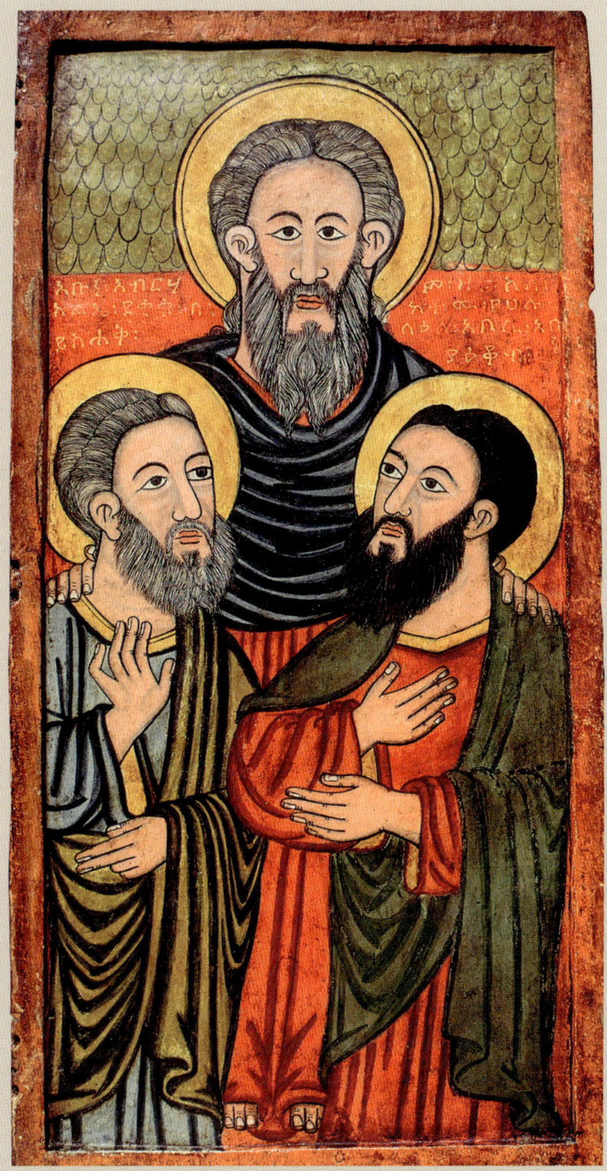

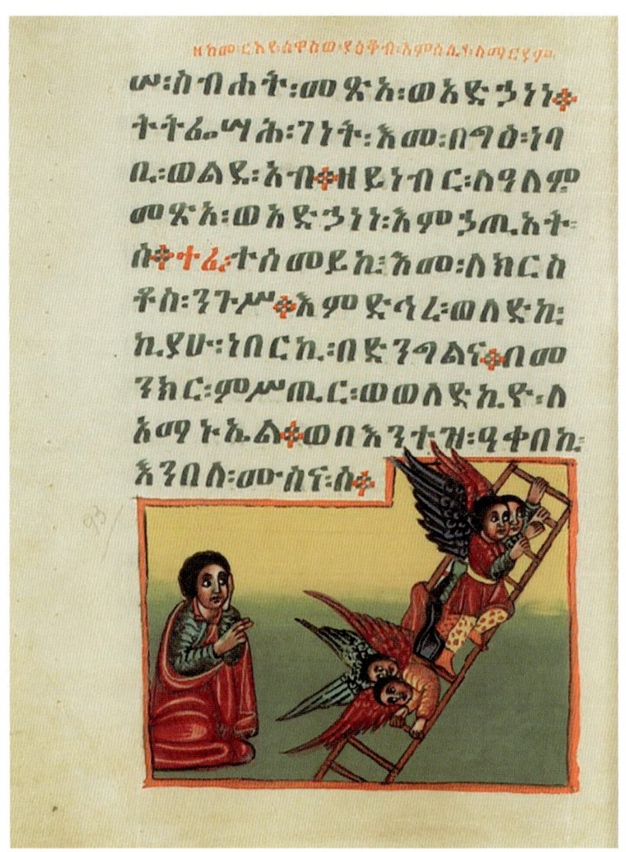

22–28, Jacob is described as the grandson of Abraham and the son of Isaac. All three were beloved by God. Genesis 28 tells of Jacob's journey to Harran: along the way the sun set, and Jacob lay himself down using a stone for a pillow. He dreamt that he saw a ladder reaching from the earth up to the heavens, and as he watched angels going up and down its steps, he noticed the Lord was standing beside him (fig. 2.5).

God said to him
I am the Lord, the God of your father Abraham and God of Isaac. Your descendants shall be countless as the dust upon the earth, and you shall spread far and wide, to north and south, to east and west, and your descendants will be blessed. (Genesis 28:13–14)

Emperor Zär'a Ya'əqob's parents must have known of this biblical passage. They may also have been familiar with the passage in the hymn praises of Mary (*Wǝddase Maryam*), a portion of which related to Jacob's ladder was recited every day at Daga Ǝsṭifanos. The Thursday passage from *Wǝddase Maryam* reads:

Thou art the Ladder on which Jacob saw the Son of God, for thou hast carried
in thy sealed womb Him Who could not be touched. Thou hast become for us an

     ETHIOPIAN DEVOTIONS

intercessor with our Lord Jesus Christ, Who became incarnate of thee for our salvation. Rejoice thou.

OUR LADY MARY WITH THE APOSTLES

The Introductory Rite includes the following hymn:

Blessings be upon this our Lady, the holy Mary, who gave birth to our Salvation.
    Hallelujah, Hallelujah upon all thy people.
Unto Thy Cross, O Lord, we will ascribe glory; Hallelujah, Hallelujah.
Salutation unto thee, O John, Son of Thunder … O John
    Apocalypt … O John Theologos … O John, the beloved of the Lord … O John,
Salutation unto you, O Peter and Paul, and James, and John,
And Andrew, and Matthew, and Philip, and Bartholomew, and Thomas, and James the son
of Alphaeus, and Thaddeus, and Nathaniel, and Matthias, and Luke, and Mark, and James
the Bishop. Bless ye us, your children by the command of the Spirit.

This liturgical catena of praise, as well as the daily prayers addressed to Our Lady Mary, resonates with Frē Ṣəyon's painted panels described above.

The iconography of the artist's Rēmā panel (fig. 2.6) reveals a particularly close affinity with the Introductory Rite hymn. It shows Mary with her Beloved Son, accompanied by the apostles in auxiliary roles. John the Evangelist, whom the hymn names before all others and showers with salutations, is placed at Mary's feet in a position of honor. This scheme is a visual transcription of the catena of salutations in the Marian hymn of her ritual veneration.

The Marian triptych in Addis Ababa (fig. 2.7) is the most visually complex of Frē Ṣəyon's devotional images, with the wing panels (the apostles on one and the Old Testament prophets on the other) establishing a visual dichotomy with Mary and the Christ Child in the central panel. Other fifteenth-century devotional images may adhere to the basic scheme of Mary with the Christ Child, prophets, and apostles, but this is exceptional in its presentation of the theme in such a complex yet legible manner. The triptych visualizes aspects of Zär'a Ya'əqob's *Revelation of the Miracle*, especially the idea of seeing in spirit and seeing in reality with bodily eyes.

The composition is dominated by a large, central figure of Mary with her Beloved Son enthroned, with the Archangels Gabriel and Michael to either side; the Apostles Peter and Paul are also pictured. The left panel (Mary's right) is filled with apostles, evangelists, and saints, persons who lived during the time of the Incarnation. The apostles are joined by Ethiopian monastic leaders and the Evangelists Mark and Luke, while Saints George and Gäbrä Krəstos are in the lowest register. In the lowest register of the right panel (Mary's left), the equestrian Saints Victor and Theodore are visually and iconographically an extension of the bottom register of the left panel. In the registers above the horsemen, prophets converse beneath a vision of the Ancient of Days. We see Isaiah, Daniel, Ezekiel, and Moses in the upper register and Habakkuk,

FIG 2.6

Frē Ṣəyon, Ethiopian, *Our Lady Mary with Her Beloved Son, Saint John the Evangelist,* Rēmā Mädḫane 'Aläm, Daga Ǝsṭifanos Monastery, 15th century. Photograph by Marilyn Heldman, 1993. In Marilyn E. Heldman, *The Marian Icons of the Painter Frē Ṣeyon: A Study in Fifteenth-Century Ethiopian Art, Patronage, and Spirituality* (Wiesbaden: Harrassowitz, 1994), page 73

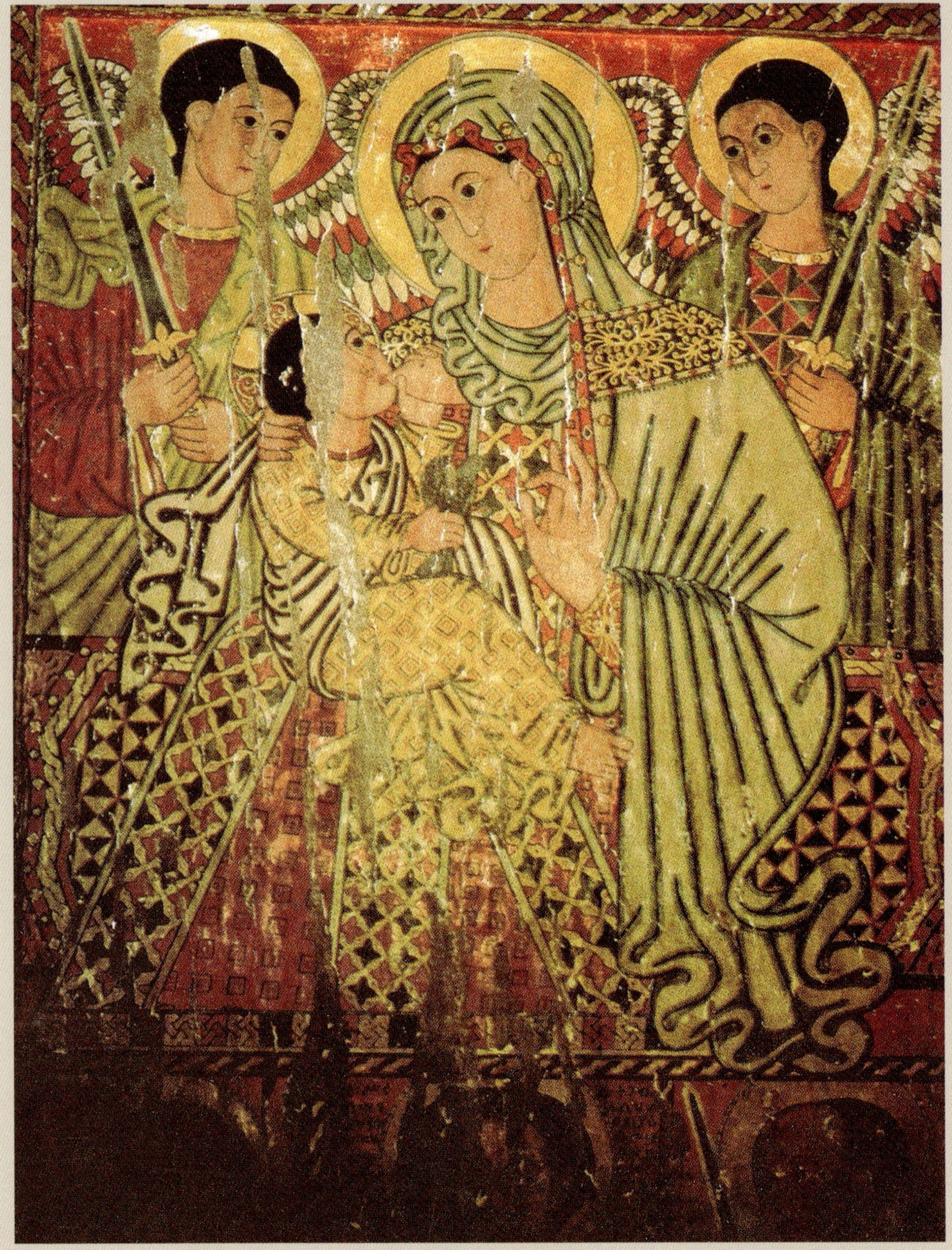

ETHIOPIAN DEVOTIONS

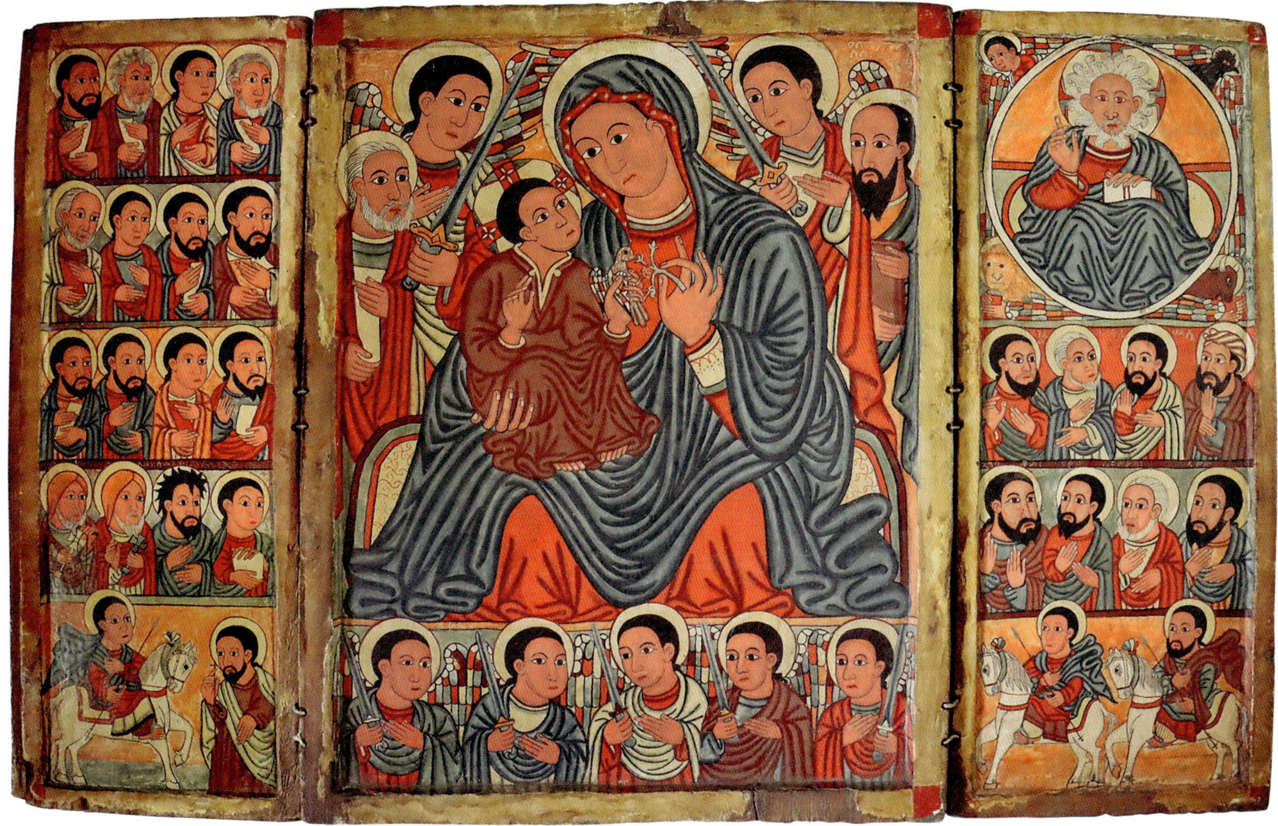

Nahum, Jeremiah, and Amos below. The Addis Ababa triptych thus presents Our Lady Mary joining the prophets and apostles, as per Zär'a Ya'əqob's statement: "it is Mary who brought together the two Laws—the Old and the New Testaments—into one holy Church, catholic (and apostolic)."

THE CIRCLE OF FRĒ ṢƏYON

A single work, the left panel of a small diptych (approximately 24 by 13 centimeters), seems to represent the circle of Frē Ṣəyon's fellow artists. Signed by a painter named Täklä Maryam, the icon features Saint George and small, half-length figures of Our Lord Jesus Christ with Peter and Paul above (fig. 2.8). The inscriptions read:

St. George and Martyr. May his prayer keep Elsabet and me the sinner, its painter Täklä Maryam. And forget not the one who commissioned the painting, Zena Hawareyat. Salutation to George, head of the martyrs. May your intercession be shield [and] grace for us. Amen.

Neither Elsabet nor Zena Hawareyat can be identified. However, by characterizing himself as "the sinner," the painter identifies himself as a monk. Täklä Maryam may

FIG 2.7

Frē Ṣeyon, Ethiopian, Our Lady Mary, The Ancient of Days, Apostles, Prophets, and Saints, Central Ethiopia, 1445–80. Icon. Tempera on gesso-covered wood panels, triptych, open: 24 13/16 × 40 3/16 inches (63 × 203 cm). Institute of Ethiopian Studies, no. 4186

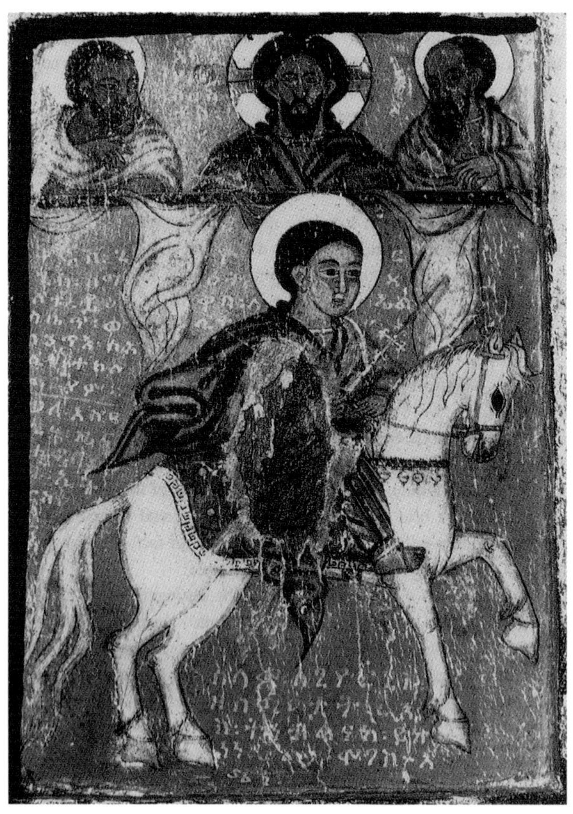

have occupied a fairly important position in this monastery, for the individual who commissioned the icon is named in a secondary position, after both Elsabet and Täklä Maryam. If, however, Zena Hawareyat were also a monk, his auxiliary role may have been dictated by monastic standards of humility. Elsabet may have been a nun or abbess of Täklä Maryam's monastery. Many Ethiopian monasteries were composed of dual communities, an abbess leading the women and an abbot leading the men.

Significantly, Täklä Maryam is the monastic name of a renowed holy man, Abuna Maba'a Ṣəyon, abbot of Endagabtan during Zär'a Ya'əqob's reign. His Life states that he trained as a painter before taking his monastic vows. The painter of the Saint George icon is presumably the same Täklä Maryam, since the likelihood of two renowned mid-fifteenth-century painters having the name Täklä Maryam is very small.

Although Täklä Maryam's icon is stylistically close to the works attributed to Frē Ṣəyon, distinctions include exaggerated pseudo-modeling, best seen in the faces and in the outline of the white horse, and the illogical fall of the draped curtains and cape, features not characteristic of Frē Ṣəyon's work. Still, Täklä Maryam and Ṣəyon share the unique distinction of each having signed a painted panel. This, combined with the stylistic similarity of their works, indicates that the two painters had collaborated.

    ETHIOPIAN DEVOTIONS

The Introductory Rite of the Miracles of Mary and Zär'a Ya'əqob's *Book of Light* provide clear instructions concerning the ritual display of Marian icons. The Introductory Rite requires that Mary's icon be carried in procession before the congregation and thence displayed upon a throne. For a panel to be carried easily by a single person, it should be no wider than 50 to 60 centimeters. Because the ratio of an icon's height to its width is commonly 4:3 or 7:5, the icon's height should not exceed 70 or 80 centimeters. Numerous extant fifteenth-century painted panels (once part of diptychs or triptychs) are only slightly smaller than this suggested measurement. A typical icon would measure roughly 40 by 54 centimeters when open: small enough to be carried easily by a single priest and large enough to be visible to a congregation.

Not all of Frē Ṣəyon's painted panels are appropriate for the ritual as described in these sources. The monumental panels in Ethiopia's Rēmā (see figs. 2.3 a and b) and Daga monasteries are life-size and quite heavy. Displaying such large panels upon a high throne or altar chest would have been nearly impossible. Despite the unlikelihood of their use as altarpieces, the two panels' close resemblance to Italian altarpieces, along with an unequivocal reference to the placement of a Marian icon upon the altar, suggests that the Daga and Rēmā panels were indeed created as altarpieces in the Italian fashion.

The Marian triptych of Our Lady Mary, the Ancient of Days, Apostles, Prophets, and Saints (fig. 2.7) may have been made for private devotion. The figures on the side panels are too small and the program too complex for the icon to have been seen and apprehended from a distance, although the central portrait of Mary is larger in scale. The exterior of the central panel is painted with a cross, a design repeated on the exterior of the closed wings. To open the wings and reveal the vision of Mary with her Beloved Son, the cross on the wings must be parted.

An ebony icon is the cross a priest or ordained monk holds and transforms into a private devotional image. One such cross in Addis Ababa, attributed to Frē Ṣəyon (figs. 2.9 a and b), is documented by the Life of Saint Krəstos Sämra, a female monastic who established a monastery at Lake Ṭana during the fifteenth century. The hagiography describes how she prayed holding a cross "upon which was represented the Ancient of Days and Our Lady Mary with Immanuel her Son and with Michael and Gabriel." Once, as she prayed with the icon in her hand, Our Lord spoke to her saying, "Do not hold my head!" This account describes the vivid religious experience of a holy person for whom an icon was the focus of prayer. It does not suggest, however, that her devotional image was a holy image with miracle-working powers.

Miniature diptychs (fig. 2.10) and triptychs were carried on the person and worn as amulets. A single panel of a diptych, measuring 11.2 by 9.1 centimeters, and a triptych, measuring 9.7 by 9.1 centimeters when closed, are only slightly larger than double-sided diptychs of later periods.

Although Zär'a Ya'əqob denounced the pagan use of charms and amulets, he wore an image of Mary upon his chest. Äbba Täklä Hawareyat, a monastic leader who came

Frē Ṣəyon, Ethiopian, *Mary with Her Beloved Son*, *Saint George* (verso); *The Ancient of Days*, *Twenty-four Priests of Heaven and Saints* (recto). Icon-cross. Incised ebony. Institute of Ethiopian Studies, no. 4329

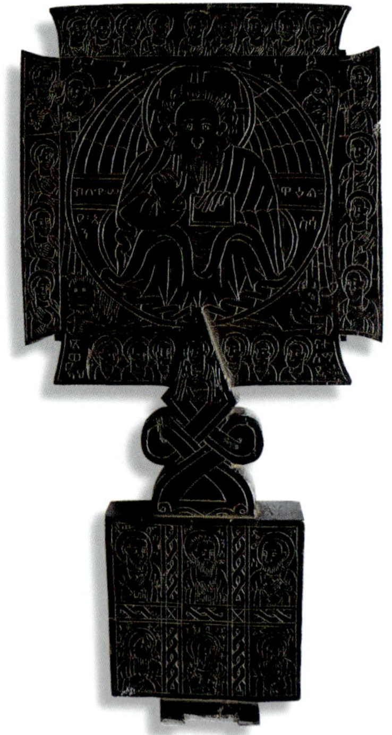
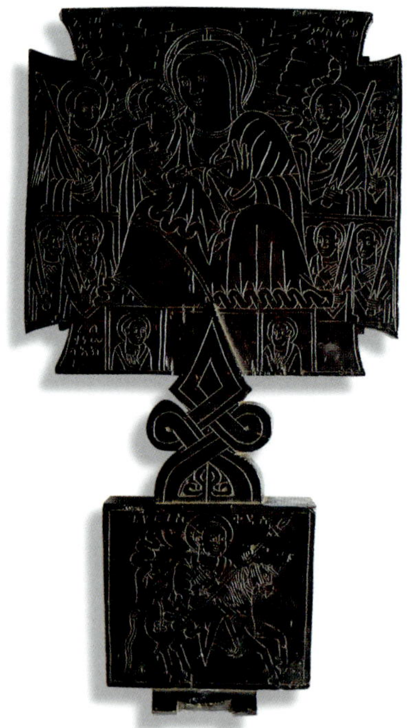

Ethiopian Orthodox, *Saint George*; *Mary and Her Beloved Son*, 18th century. Wood, paint, and ink, 3 ⅞ × 8 ³⁄₁₆ × ⅝ inches (9.9 × 20.8 × 1.6 cm). National Museum of African Art, Smithsonian Institution, Gift in memory of Nancy E. MacDonald, 2015-7-9

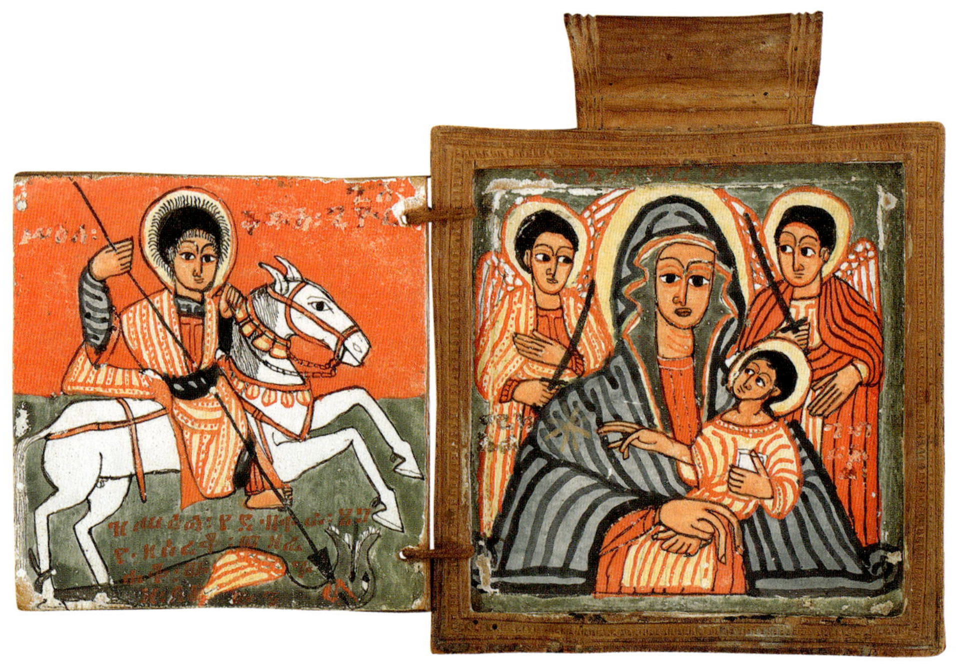

into conflict with Zär'a Ya'əqob, wore an "image of Mary with her Beloved Son" in the same manner. Once, while Saint Krəstos Sämra was at prayer, Our Lord Jesus Christ, carrying a painted panel with the Ancient of Days, appeared and hung the panel around her neck. Surely the author of her hagiography wished to demonstrate that Our Lord himself sanctioned the wearing of an icon in this manner.

An episode from the childhood of the fifteenth-century abbot and painter Mäba' Ṣəyon attests to a special amuletic form known as a *sensul,* or "chain" of paintings (fig. 2.11). A wandering pilgrim, invited to spend the night in the home of Mäba' Ṣəyon's family, suspended a picture of Our Lady Mary with her Beloved Son above his head before sleeping. When the pilgrim resumed his journey, he gave Mäba' Ṣəyon the picture of Mary, and the child hung it around his neck. The gift appears to have been a folding parchment painting like one in the collections of the Institute of Ethiopian Studies at Addis Ababa University. The latter is 8.3 by 7.4 centimeters when folded; it may have been worn or carried within a parchment or fabric envelope. When opened to its full length of 67.2 centimeters, it could have been suspended, as the pilgrim had done, above its sleeping owner.

On certain occasions, an icon of Our Lady Mary in the treasury of a church might be removed. This practice is attested in an inscription on a triptych of Our Lady Mary in the Museum of the Institute of Ethiopian Studies (fig. 2.12) that reads:

This picture belongs to Dama Krəstos and his wife Amata Hawaryat who purchased it as a cure for their souls. Let those who erase this [inscription] be warned that their name shall be condemned; whosoever may remove it from the church for a solemn oath [mahala] let him be cursed; we trust that those who may pray to it [the image] will not forget us.[4]

In times of distress such as drought or locusts, the people of a church or a village perform the Mehella solemn procession of popular prayers.

FIG 2.11
Ethiopian Orthodox, *Sensul,* Gondär, Ethiopia, late 17th century. Hide and parchment, each panel: 3 ⅝ × 3 ⅛ inches (9.2 × 9 cm). Walters Art Museum, museum purchase with funds provided by the W. Alton Jones Foundation Acquisition Fund, 1996, 36.1V

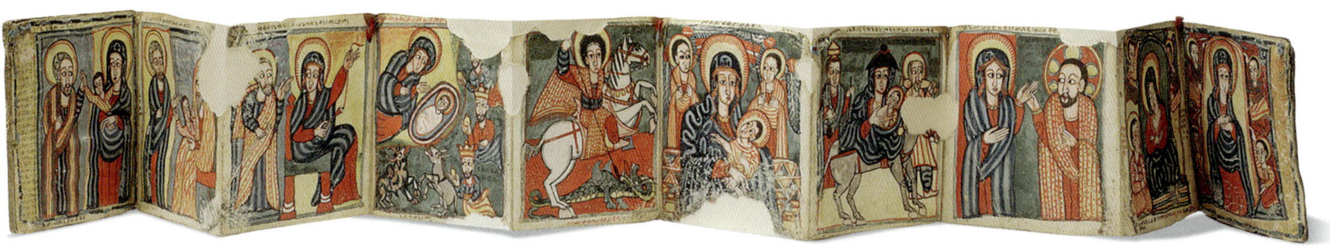

Crowned Virgin and Child and
Twelve Apostles, Resurrection,
Covenant of Mercy, Saint George,
Crucifixion, Four Saints, Including
Abuna Gäbra Mänfäs Qəddus,
mid- to late 17th century.
Tempera on gesso-covered
panels, open: 13 ⅛ × 15 ⁵⁄₁₆ × ⁹⁄₁₆
inches (33.3 × 38.9 × 1.5 cm).
Institute of Ethiopian Studies,
no. 4755

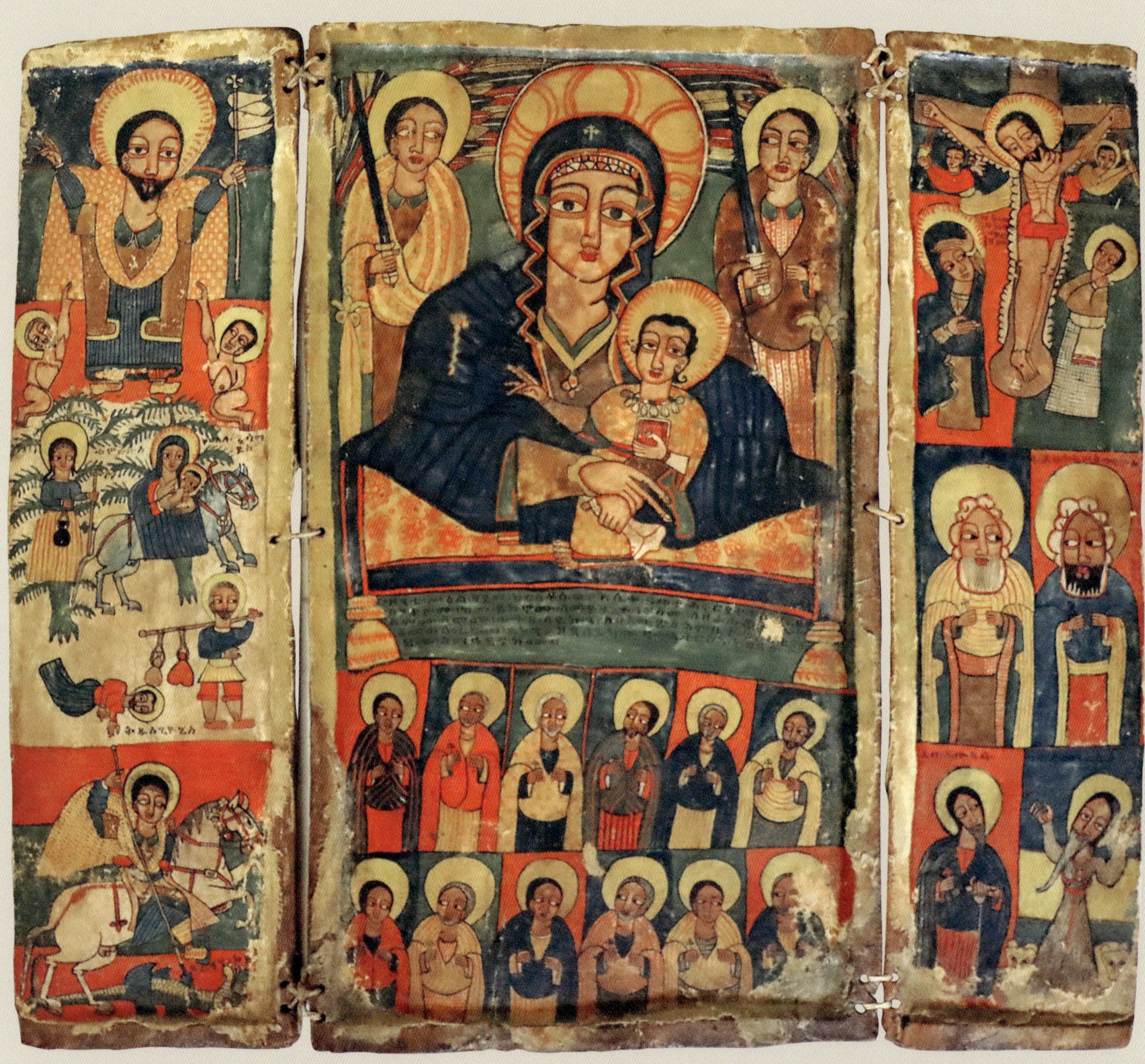

     ETHIOPIAN DEVOTIONS

CONCLUSION

The impact of Zär'a Ya'əqob's introduction of the cult of Our Lady Mary into the Ethiopian Orthodox Church and the icons created for the cult established a pattern of iconography that remained visible in Marian icons from the fifteenth to the twentieth century. Especially prevalent was the portrait of Our Lady Mary with her Beloved Son flanked by the Archangels Gabriel and Michael. In many icons, Mary is accompanied by the twelve apostles, symbolizing the Orthodox Church. Beside or beneath many Ethiopian icons of Our Lady Mary, Saint George appears riding a white horse, in reference to the emperor's victory over Sultan Badlay, ruler of the neighboring Muslim state of 'Adal, on Christmas day in 1445. Zär'a Ya'əqob attributed this victory to Our Lady Mary and thereby arranged that this victory would be celebrated annually at Täklä Haymanot's monastery of Däbrä Däbrä Metmaq, later remaned Däbrä Libanos Šäwa. Sometime later, certainly by the eighteenth century, the story of Saint George's victory over the dragon that would eat the princess of Beirut was translated into Gə'əz. Images of Saint George slaying this dragon may be seen in later Marian devotional images (fig. 2.13).

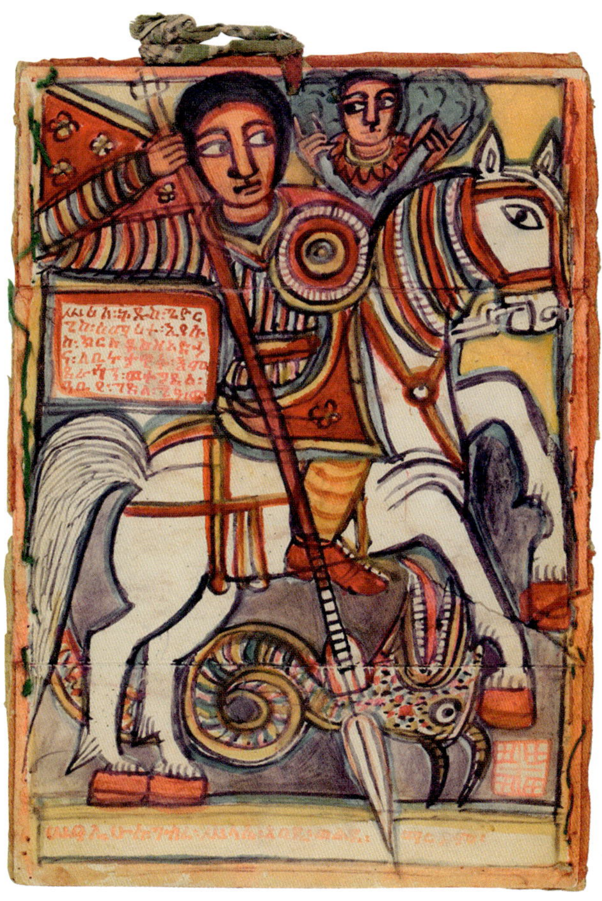

FIG 2.13

Aläqa Gabra Selasse (ca. 1900–86, b. Ethiopia), Saint George Slays the Dragon and Rescues the Princess of Beirut, ca. 1973. Tempera on cardboard, 14 ¾ × 10 ¼ inches (37.5 × 26 cm). Photograph by Franko Khoury, Smithsonian Institution, National Museum of African Art, Gift of an anonymous donor in memory of Louis Gilden, 2006-3-13

Ethiopian Orthodox, Saint George, late 18th century. Wood and paint, 9 ¾ × 13 ¹¹⁄₁₆ × ¹⁵⁄₁₆ inches (24.7 × 34.7 × 2.4 cm). Photograph by Franko Khoury, National Museum of African Art, Smithsonian Institution, Gift of Ciro R. Taddeo & family in memory of Mrs. Jean Taddeo-Ruiz of Brooklyn, New York, 2010-19-1

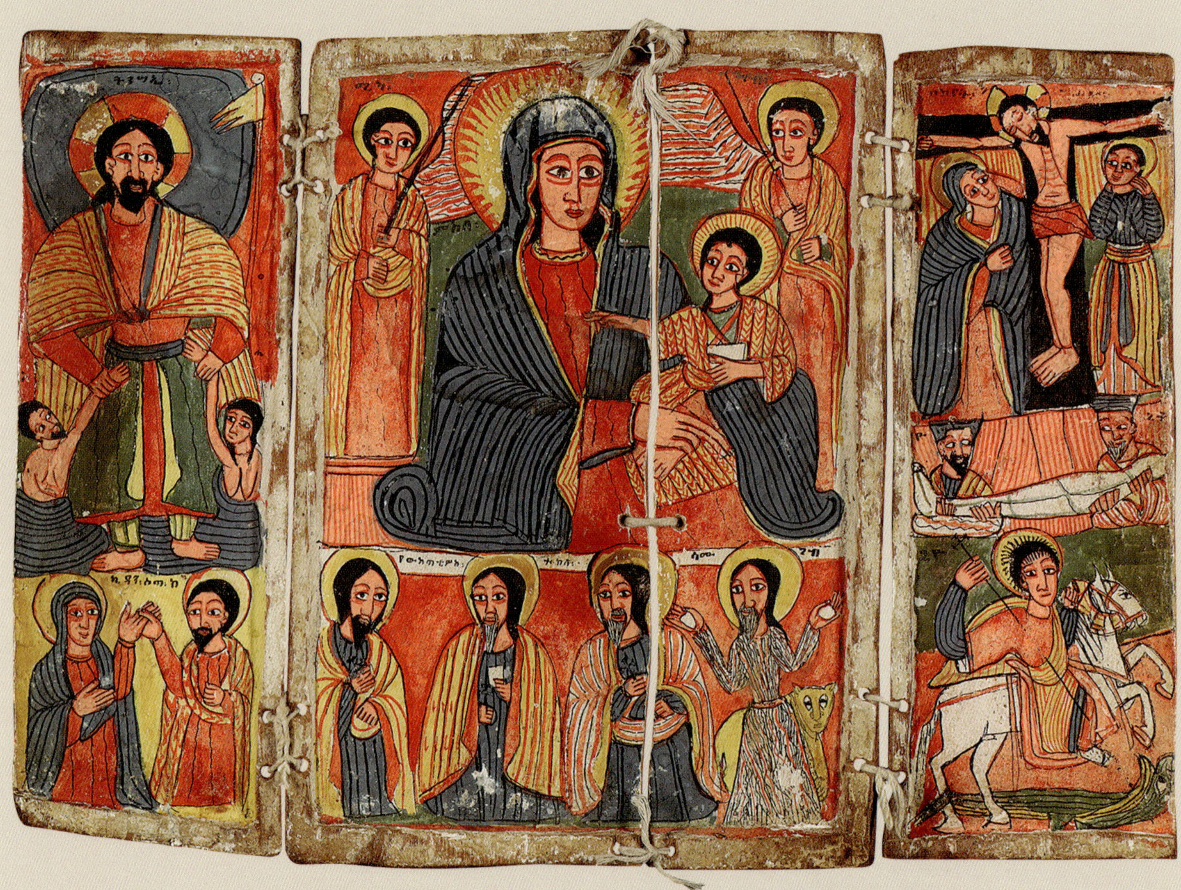

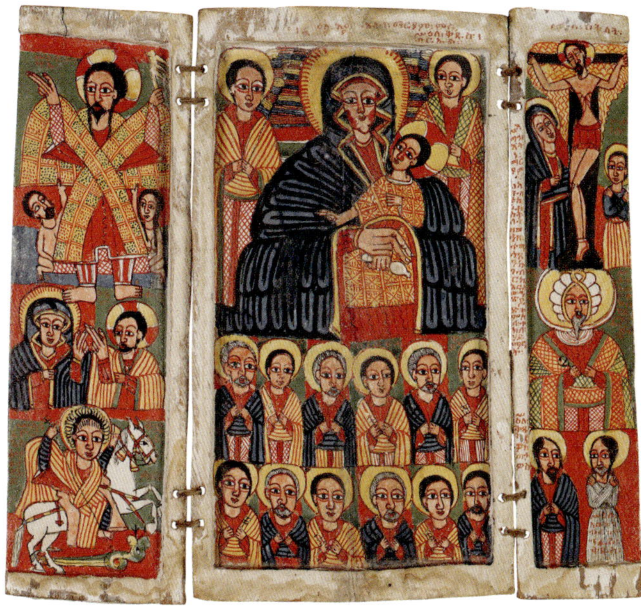

Marian icons from Ethiopia sometimes include a pair of Ethiopian monastic saints, Täklä Haymanot and Ewosṭatewos, usually on Mary's left or the viewer's right. A monastic leader in northern Ethiopia who embraced the Old Testament command to celebrate the Saturday Sabbath, Saint Ewosṭatewos wished to celebrate both the Saturday and the Sunday Sabbath. Because this dual celebration was rejected by other Ethiopian monastic leaders, Ewosṭatewos went into exile, probably in what is present-day Syria, and never returned to Ethiopia. Nevertheless, his followers established monasteries in northern Ethiopia, among the most famous being Däbrä Bizan.[5]

Another major example of Zär'a Ya'əqob's impact on the Ethiopian Orthodox Church is the inclusion of Christ's Crucifixion with the mourning figures of Our Lady Mary and Saint John the Beloved at the base of the cross (figs. 2.14 and 2.15). The Crucifixion is usually placed to the left of Our Lady Mary (on the viewer's right). On Mary's right (our left) there appears an image of the resurrected Christ standing in victory in triumph over death. Adam and Eve rise up at his hem, signifying the Christian belief in the resurrection of the body and the life everlasting.

Emperor Zär'a Ya'əqob's devotion to Our Lady Mary shaped Ethiopia's veneration rituals to her in ways large and small. He established a court church in her honor, along with the visual language for its decoration, where scribes and editors created collections in her name: the Miracles of Mary. Churchgoers—effectively everyone in Zär'a Ya'əqob's realm—participated in rites at altars dedicated to Mary and readily adapted devotional arts in her honor to their lives and needs. Zär'a Ya'əqob's policies and processes ensured that the cult of Our Lady Mary would thrive.

Our Lady Mary

MARILYN E. HELDMAN

Devotional images of Our Lady Mary painted on wood panels emerged in Highland Christian Ethiopia during the 1440s, when Emperor Zär'a Ya'əqob mandated the use of an icon of Our Lady Mary for display. These images were the foci of special ceremonies to venerate her image during the Sunday service and on the celebration of Marian feast days in her honor that were introduced to the calendar of the Ethiopian Orthodox Church. The typical imagery of the early Marian icons relates to the emperor's homilies on Mary.[1] Her half-length portrait with the Christ Child, inscribed "Picture of Our Lady Mary with Her Beloved Son" (fig. E2.1), is accompanied by portraits of the apostles, a few local saints of the Ethiopian Orthodox Church, and several equestrian saints (Saints Theodore, Victor, and George, the latter identified by his white horse). Because the emperor attributed his decisive victory over Sultan Badlay of 'Adal in 1445 to the intercession of Our Lady Mary and the intervention of Saint George, Ethiopian icons usually show Saint Mary accompanied by George (figs. E2.2, and fig. E6.1).

During the late fifteenth and early sixteenth centuries, the growing popularity of the cult of Our Lady Mary inspired the creation of devotional images of the Holy Family. An unusual icon celebrating the Holy Families includes portraits of the priest Zacharias, his wife, Saint Elizabeth, their son, Saint John the Baptist (Luke 1:5–25), as well as Salome (sister of Elizabeth), Mary and Jesus, Joseph, and Saints Täklä Haymanot and Ewosṭatewos. The last two figures are recognized as the founding fathers of Ethiopian monasticism. Saint Täklä Haymanot (d. 1313) founded the monastery of Däbrä Asbo (renamed Däbrä Libanos), in the southern region of the Highland Christian kingdom. Saint Ewosṭatewos (d. 1352) was the founder of a monastic movement in the northern region.

The portraits of the two founders were often identical—each carrying a book and a prayer staff (*maqwamiya*) and wearing a small monastic cap (*qob*). By the seventeenth century a standard pattern for their depiction had been established—Täklä Haymanot was portrayed with white hair and beard, and Ewosṭatewos with dark hair and a beard (fig. E2.3). This pattern not only established their individual identities, it also indicated that the abbots of Täklä Haymanot's monastery had the greater authority. By the eighteenth century if not earlier, Täklä Haymanot was given a more distinctive portrait,

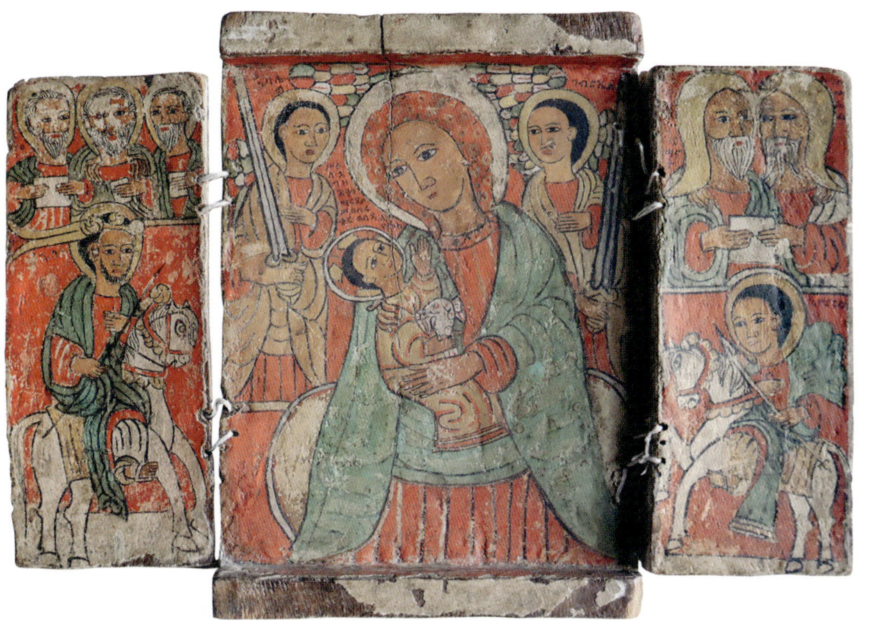

Ethiopian Orthodox, Abraham, Isaac and Jacob, Lalibela, Virgin and Child, Saints Michael, Gabriel, Täklä Haymanot, Abuna Samuel, and George, Central Ethiopia, second half of the 15th century. Icon. Tempera on gesso-covered wood panels, open: 12 ³⁄₁₆ × 17 ⁵⁄₁₆ inches (31 × 44 cm). Institute of Ethiopian Studies, no. 3450

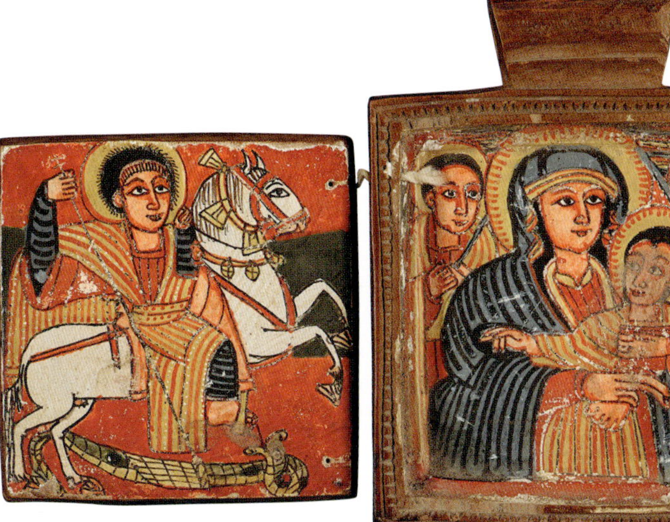

Ethiopian Orthodox, Saint George; Virgin and Child, Saints Michael and Gabriel, 17th century. Icon. Tempera on gesso-covered wood. National Museum of African Art, Smithsonian Institution, Gift in memory of Nancy E. MacDonald, 2015-7-9

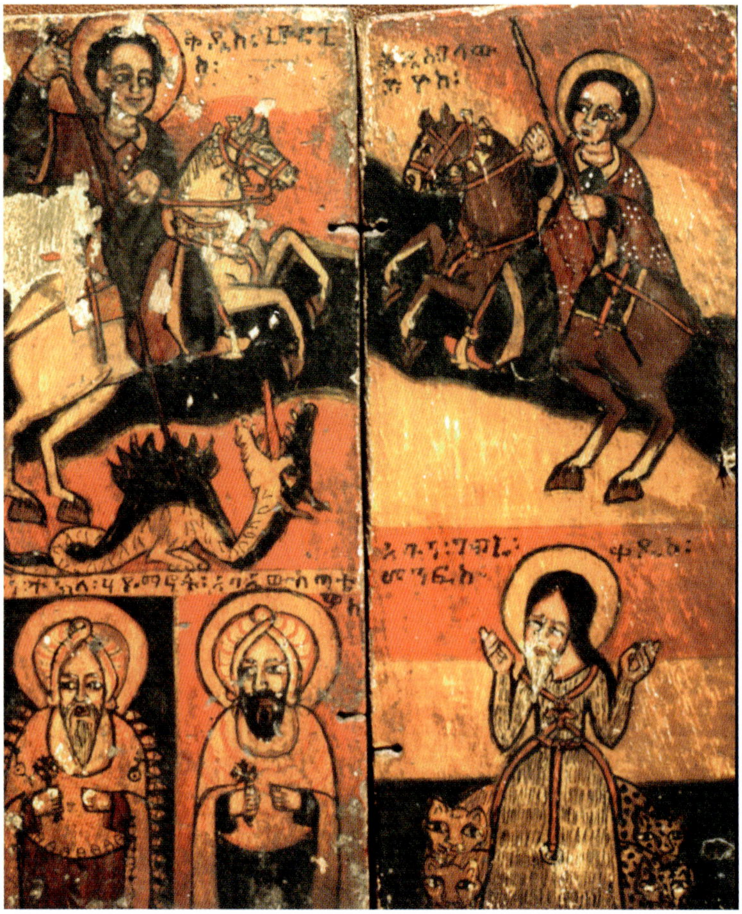

FIG E2.3

Ethiopian Orthodox, Saints George and Gälawdewos (top), Täklä Haymanot, Ewostatewos and Gäbrä Mänfäs Qəddus, (bottom), Gondär, Ethiopia, late 17th or early 18th century. Icon. Wood, gesso, and tempera, closed: 4 1/16 × 3 9/16 × 7/16 inches (10.3 × 9 × 1.1 cm). Institute of Ethiopian Studies, no. 3531

displaying his self-mortification—standing for so long on one leg that the other leg fell off. A third saint, Gäbrä Mänfäs Qəddus, a holy hermit, also had a unique iconography: depicted with God-sent holy hair covering his body and sometimes accompanied by several lions, tamed by his sanctity (fig. 4.4).

Three annual liturgical feasts of Saint Mary inspired new imagery for Marian icons during the late sixteenth and early seventeenth centuries. The celebration of the Covenant of Mercy (Kidana Məhrat) on 16 Yekatit (23 February) was introduced to the revised Synaxary of 1581. The composition that signifies this feast shows Mary and Jesus joining hands, a gesture that signifies Christ's promise he will answer prayers made in her name.

The feast of the Dormition (Eräfta) is celebrated on 21 Tərr, while the feast of Mary's Assumption (Felsäta) is celebrated on 6 Nahasse. An unusual early seventeenth-century diptych (fig. E2.4) combines the prevalent image of Mary and Jesus with representations of her Dormition and Assumption. The image of the Dormition, Mary on her deathbed with apostles at each side, relates to an unidentified engraving based on a woodcut by Albrecht Dürer (fig. E2.5).

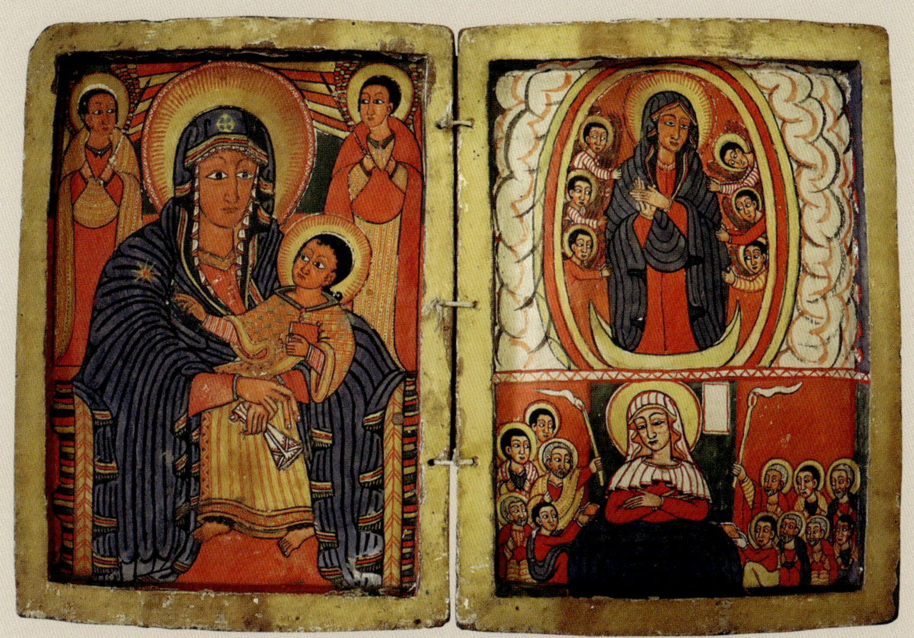

FIG E2.4

Ethiopian Orthodox, Virgin and Child, Saints Michael and Gabriel; the Dormition and Assumption of the Virgin, 17th century. Icon. Wood, gesso, and tempera, open: 10 ⅜ × 15 ¹⁄₁₆ × ¹³⁄₁₆ inches (26.4 × 38.2 × 2.1 cm). Institute of Ethiopian Studies, no. 4656

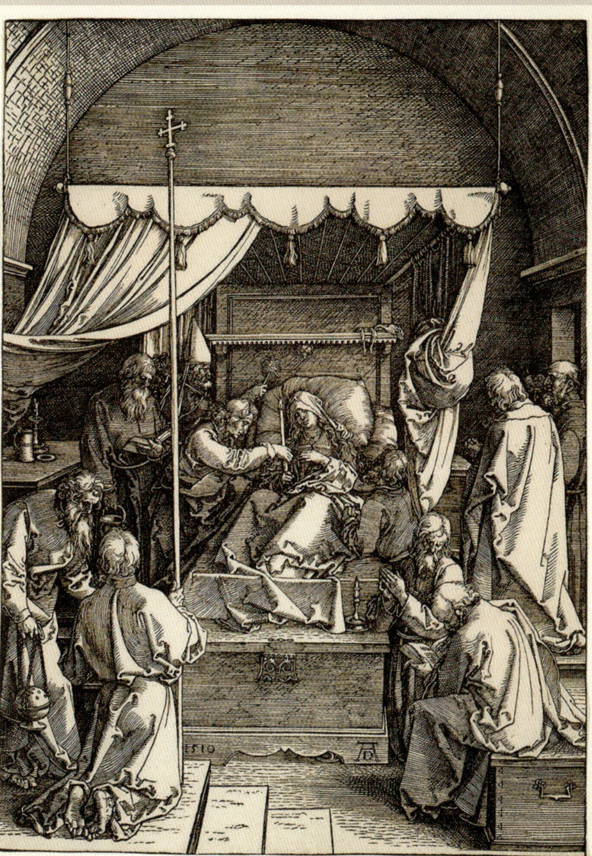

FIG E2.5

Albrecht Dürer, German, 1471–1528, *The Death of the Virgin*, 1510. Woodcut, 11 ⁷⁄₁₆ × 8 ⅛ inches (29.1 × 20.6 cm). Minneapolis Institute of Art 2013.24, Gifts of funds in memory of John E. Andrus III, 2013.24

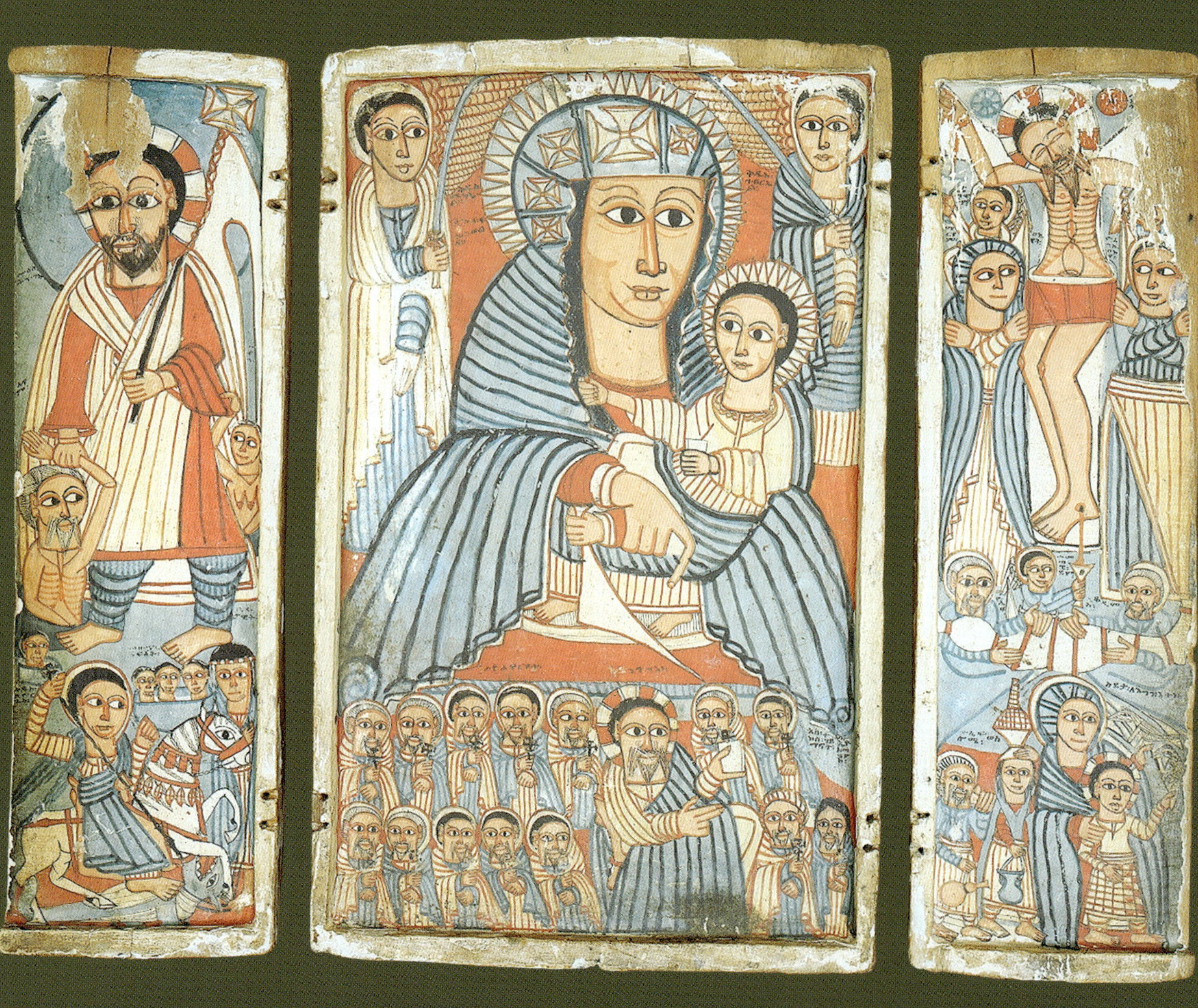

Chapter 3

The Blessed Virgin: Inspiration for Ethiopian Artists

GETATCHEW HAILE

Mary, the Mother of God, has a special place in the hearts of the faithful of the Ethiopian Orthodox Church, who believe she has a place for them in her heart. The source of this imaginary familial relationship is the unbroken *Kidan* (Covenant or Pact) given to her by her beloved Son on the sixteenth day of the Ethiopian month of Yäkkatit. She once asked him to give her a country for her tithe *('aśrat)*. "Let the nation of Azeb be yours," he replied. "Are they Christians?" she asked. "No, not yet," he replied, "but they will be, and their faith will shine like the sun, and a church will be built in your name in a place called Aksum."[1] Azeb is the Gəˤəz equivalent of "south," named in the Gospels as the direction in which the presumed kingdom of the Queen of Sheba lies.[2] For Ethiopians, however, "Azeb" is another name for "Ethiopia" rather than the cardinal direction.[3] Ever since the inception of the Covenant, Ethiopia has been a property of the Blessed Virgin. Ethiopia is Mary's country, a "Maryland." The relationship between Mary and her people is clearly summarized in the *Kidan*: Her Son will forgive the sins of anyone for whom she intercedes—those who build a church and dedicate it in her name, and who observe her holy days with festive food and drink for the poor and the clergy.

This covenant, which she used to benefit those who adore her, earned her the name of the covenant itself: *Kidanä Məḥrät*, or "Covenant of Mercy" (fig. 3.1). With this moniker, she becomes another Mary, observed on the sixteenth day of every Ethiopian month and annually on the sixteenth day of Yäkkatit. Churches are dedicated in the name of *Kidanä Məḥrät* as much as in the name of Mary. The *Kidan* was repeated and expanded when Mary prayed to her Son for more wishes on one of the *Kidan*'s anniversaries.

The Son appeared (in response to her prayer) and asked her what she wanted Him to do for her. She said, "It concerns whomever makes my memorial, builds a church in my name, clothes the naked in my name, visits the sick, feeds the hungry, gives water to the thirsty, comforts the grief-stricken, gives joy to the distressed, copies the book of my praises, names his children in my name, and chants hymns in my name on my holy days: Give him, O Lord, a generous reward 'which the eye has not seen, the ear has not heard, and has not been conceived in the heart of man.[4] I petition you, O Lord, and supplicate you for everyone who believes in me. Make them free of Hades, in remembrance of the hunger and thirst and all temptations that I endured while with you." Our Lord Jesus Christ answered, saying, "Let it be done as you said. I shall fulfill all your wishes. Was I not incarnated for this? I swear to you by myself lest I deny my covenant."[5]

In recognition of Mary's popularity, the *däbtära* (lay clergy)[6] have introduced to the *Kidan* a reward for those who recite the three apotropaic prayers: the *Ləfafä Ṣədq* (or "Bandlet of Righteousness") and the two untitled prayers ascribed to Mary—the ones she recited at Bartos and at Golgotha.[7] The *Ləfafä Ṣədq* has even become part of the funerary ritual. According to its introduction, it is "a book of life and salvation which the Father wrote with his own hands and gave to Mary (through Christ) after her Son was born on the 29th day of the month of Taḫśaś. It is to be a guidebook to the Kingdom of Heaven." In response to her prayer for this additional promise, "Our Lord said to her, 'I give you my word (*ma'əkwät*), that whoever observes my memorial and trusts in this book, and carries it, hangs it on himself, keeps it in his house, carries it on his neck, and is baptized in water prayed on it with (this prayer) or drinks it in faith, no harm will ever befall him.'"[8]

Mary's petitions show that she is a caring and forgiving Mother of faithful Ethiopians. *Rəḥrəḥtä Ḥəllina* ("tender-hearted"), the appellation given to her by Ethiopians, reveals the primary reason for their Marian devotion. In contrast to God, who is "Our Father in heaven," Mary is "Our Mother on earth," near to her people. In Ethiopian tradition, fathers are just but also strict and fearsome because of their role as disciplinarians, while mothers are understanding and find excuses to overlook their children's mistakes. There are instances of her intervention in the Marian literature, wherein the Blessed Virgin obliges her Son to change his mind from giving sinners the punishments they deserve. One well-known example is the story of the cannibal of Qəmmər (*bäla'e säb'*), a rich man who killed many people, including members of his family, due to his hunger for human flesh. Because he had aided a thirsty man who begged for water in her name, he was saved from eternal damnation when Mary interceded on his behalf.[9]

On the other hand, as a monastic source indicates, the Blessed Virgin could be equally vengeful if treated unfairly.[10]

There was a man who criticized Our Lady Mary in public. [Mary] came to him (in a dream) on one night and said to him, "O man, what contact have I had with you? And what did I do to you to make you criticize me? The man woke up from his sleep and increased the criticism. [Mary] appeared to him again and said to him, "Do not do that; you will lose yourself." But he did not heed her warning. So, she came (to him) at midnight while he was asleep and paralyzed his arms and legs. The wretched man woke up from his sleep and saw that his arms and legs were as if they were cut off from his body. He admitted in public, saying, "This happened to me because I scolded St. Mary."

Ethiopian teachers believe that the motherhood of Mary, Maryam Ṣəyon, had been predicted by the psalmist King David when he stated in Psalm 87:5 / LXXXVI, *"Ǝmmənä Ṣəyon yəbl säb', wä-bə'əsi täwäldä bä-wəsteta"* ("People say, 'Zion is Our Mother; a man [Christ] was born of her'").[11] One of the communal prayers starts with: "O Lord, have compassion on your land [Ethiopia]. Hallelujah. May your heart rejoice, O Virgin, and may your horn be exalted in glory, O Second Heaven. The world was saved because of you, and there is peace through your Son. Mary (you are) Our Mother and the Mother of Our Lord. Pray for us (to your Son) so He may have mercy and compassion upon us. May He bestow His goodness upon us."

The introduction to one of her Miracles states, "The Virgin and the pure John Son of Thunder (St. John the Evangelist) shout, saying 'for that bride shone much brighter than the morning star.' This is Zion, the new City of Our God, in which the joy (Christ) of all the holy prophets dwelled." The introduction of every prayer that is also the brief opening to any work includes the name of the Blessed Virgin along with the Trinity: "In the name of the Father and the Son and the Holy Spirit, one God. Believing in, and taking refuge with the Holy Trinity, I renounce you, Satan, before this Mother of mine, the Holy Church, which is my witness, Maryam Ṣəyon, forever and ever. Amen."[12]

The Blessed Virgin has been revered in all apostolic churches since the early history of the church. In 430 CE, Patriarch Nestorius of Constantinople was deposed from the throne because of his heretical stance against her—he held that she was not the Mother of God. The following year at the Council of Ephesus, Mary received the title *Theotokos* (The One Who Bore God). The Ethiopian Orthodox Church shares the tradition of holding her in an elevated position, raising her even beyond that level.

Emperor Zär'a Ya'əqob's (r. 1434–68) role in the Ethiopian promotion of the cult of Our Lady Mary in the mid-fifteenth century is well documented, although he may not have been the first to initiate its development. Zär'a Ya'əqob's chronicle begins the record of the emperor's achievements with the monarch's instructions on how to be a good Christian. In this decree, he commanded his subjects, the entire Christian population of his kingdom, to inscribe on their left hands the statement "I am the servant/slave of Mary, Mother of the Creator of the whole world."[13] The emperor expanded this order with the following command:

Listen, all you, people of Ethiopia, men and women, you are the captives of Mary whom she received from her Son to be her tithe. Take refuge always with her, for she is capable of delivering you from all evil. Make your children also take refuge with her, so that she may help them grow in good (health) by her prayer. If children are born to you before [the day] of the [monthly] feast of Mary, give offering to the priests on the feast day of Mary in the month during which they are born.[14]

The clergy was instructed to venerate the text of the Miracles of Mary (fig. 3.2) with the same reverence given to the four Gospels. Those who violated the emperor's command faced the threat of excommunication. Her Miracles were read during the Mass services

FIG 3.2
Ethiopian Orthodox, Tä 'ammärä
Maryam (Miracles of Mary),
Gondär, Ethiopia, 1667–1706.
Parchment, ink, tempera, wood,
leather, cotton, and string, 14 ½
× 12 ½ × 3 ¾ inches (36.8 ×
31.8 × 9.5 cm). Art Institute of
Chicago, 2002.4, Ada Turnbull
Hertle and Marian and Samuel
Klasstorner endowments

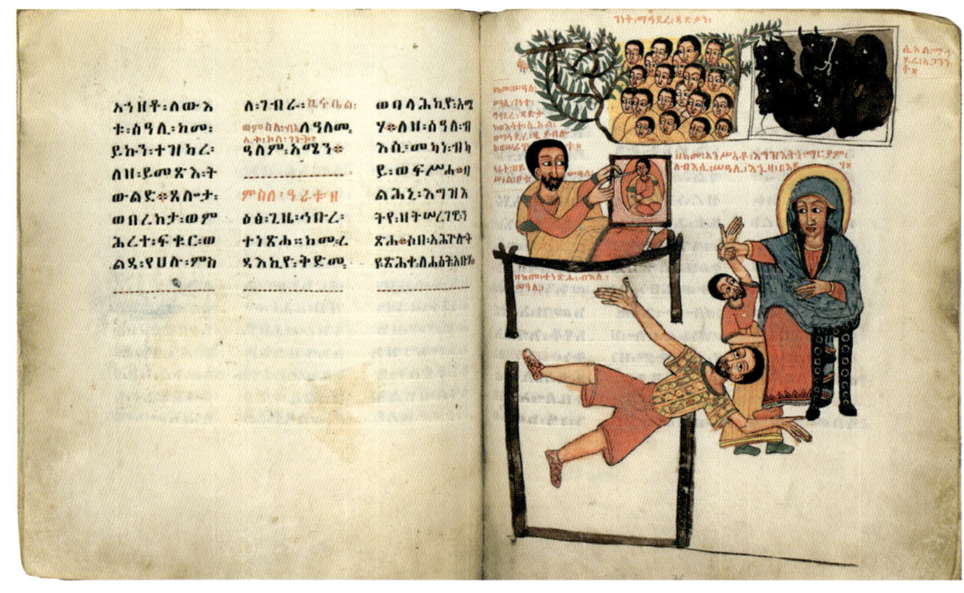

FIG 3.3
Frē Ṣəyon, Ethiopian, Our Lady
Mary and the Christ Child,
Apostles, Saints George and
Theodore, 1445–80, Central
Ethiopia. Icon. Tempera on
gesso-covered wood panels,
closed: 17 ⁵⁄₁₆ × 12 ⁵⁄₁₆ inches (44 ×
31.1 cm). Institute of Ethiopian
Studies, no. 3980

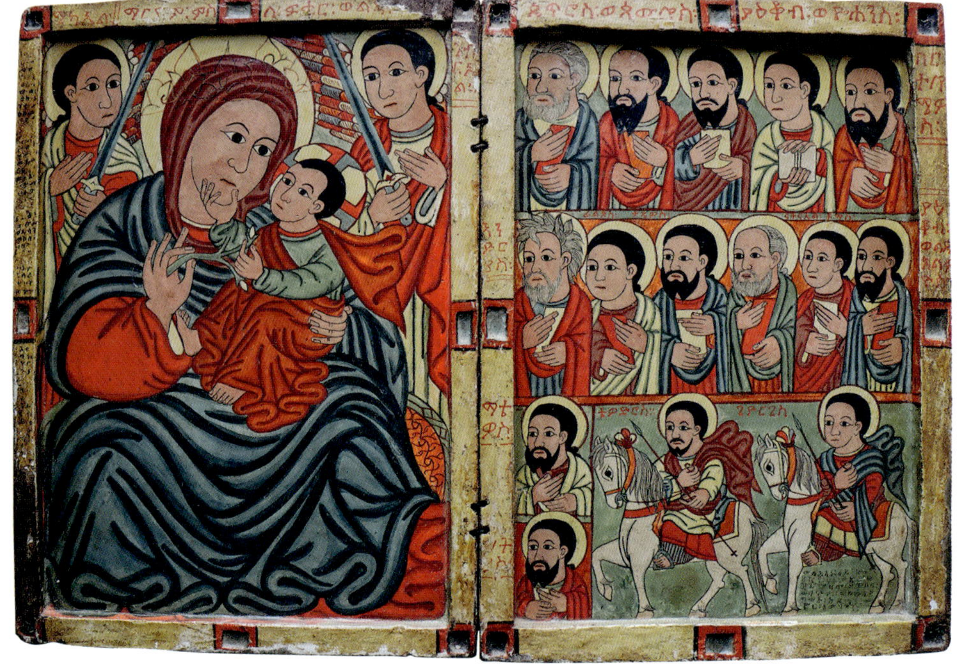

following the well-defined ritual of the Gospel reading. Zär'a Ya'əqob's command to honor the icons of the Blessed Virgin with bows to the ground before her icon has been obeyed by the Ethiopian faithful with fervent hope for the Virgin's help for an ever-needful population whose history has never been free of suffering from drought, famine, pestilence, and infant mortality. The clergy composed heartbreaking hymns with pleas for her help. The need for her icons encouraged the development of great artists, such as the fifteenth-century painter Frē Ṣəyon, who worked at the court of Zär'a Ya'əqob (fig. 3.3).[15] Most painters, however, have remained anonymous for the same reason authors of religious books do so—both out of modesty as well as because their creations are for the glory of God, not earthly fame.

Obedience to the emperor's decrees was not total. The monks of the monastery of Gundä Gunde in Ṭəgray who refused to worship man-made objects defied the emperor's command with unprecedented courage. Led by the indomitable Äbba Ǝsṭifanos, they refused to bow to none but God the Father, the Son, and the Holy Spirit. This included their refusal to bow to the Madonna and to the monarch before whom his subjects were to fall to the ground. The monks' inflexibility, which the emperor mistook for disrespect to his status, forced them to abandon their fundamentalist stance and ultimately cost them their lives. The Ǝsṭifanosites, as these monks are called by historians, were accused of being anti-Mary, but there is no evidence to support this claim. Their writings reveal, rather, that they were only against bowing to pictures and to human beings, as they considered those a form of worship. As to the person of the Blessed Virgin, they did not deny her the reverence she deserved as the Mother of God and intercessor for the faithful. Along with the rest of the clergy, they recited her praises, the *Wǒddase Maryam* and the *Anqäṣä Bərhan* (Gate of Light), and solicited her intercession when they embarked on any work, including the copying of books : "I start [copying] with the goodwill of the Father and the Son and the Holy Spirit. And I proceed with the intercession of Our Lady Mary."[16] In fact, many of the Gundä Gunde manuscripts contain miniatures of the Madonna and Child, the Crucifixion, and portraits of monastic leaders painted in the distinctive Gundä Gunde style that had been developed at the monastery (figs. 3.4 a and b).[17]

A church becomes a holy place (*Betä Krəstiyan*) when a ritually blessed *tabot*, an altar tablet of wood or stone,[18] is ceremoniously placed within the sanctuary. An icon of the Virgin is then installed in the sanctuary, and the walls painted with murals of the life of Jesus and the saints. The constant need for the creation of icons, murals, and illuminated manuscripts gave rise to a continuous development of painting styles and new iconography in Ethiopian religious arts (fig. 3.5). The rationale for revering icons and *tabots* is that one honors not the painting and its wood panel but the person depicted therein. Pictures are holy because they represent the holy Mother of God, the crucified Christ, and the tortured martyrs, just as the Holy Bible or other sacred texts are holy for having the holy name of God written within them. The teachers remind their critics of the Letter of Saint Paul to the Philippians (2:10), which states, "so that at the name of Jesus Christ every knee should bend, in heaven and on earth and under the earth."

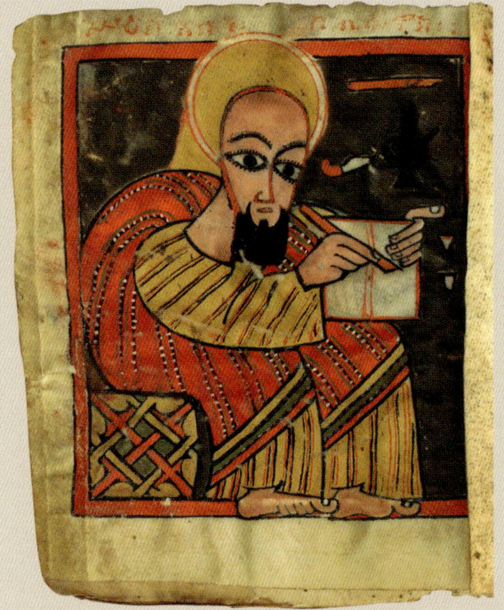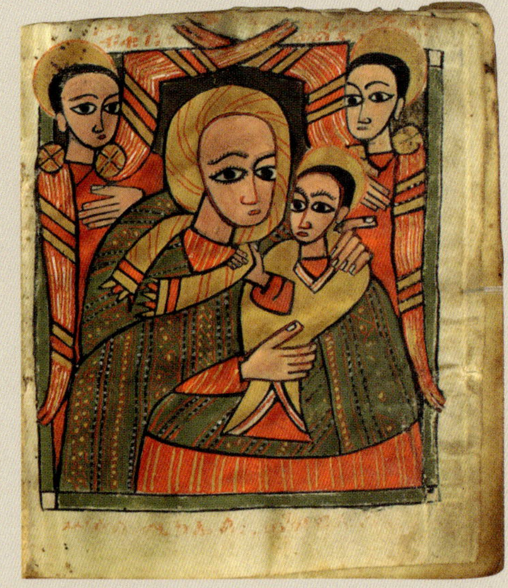

FIG 3.4 A AND B

Ethiopian Orthodox, Wəddase Maryam (Praises of Mary and other Marian texts), 1700–1999. Vellum, 7 ½ × 6 ⅞ × 3 ⅛ inches (19 × 17.5 × 8 cm). Gundä Gunde Manuscript Collection, Michael Gervers, Balicka-Witakowska, Columba Stewart, University of Toronto Scarborough, Toronto, GG-078

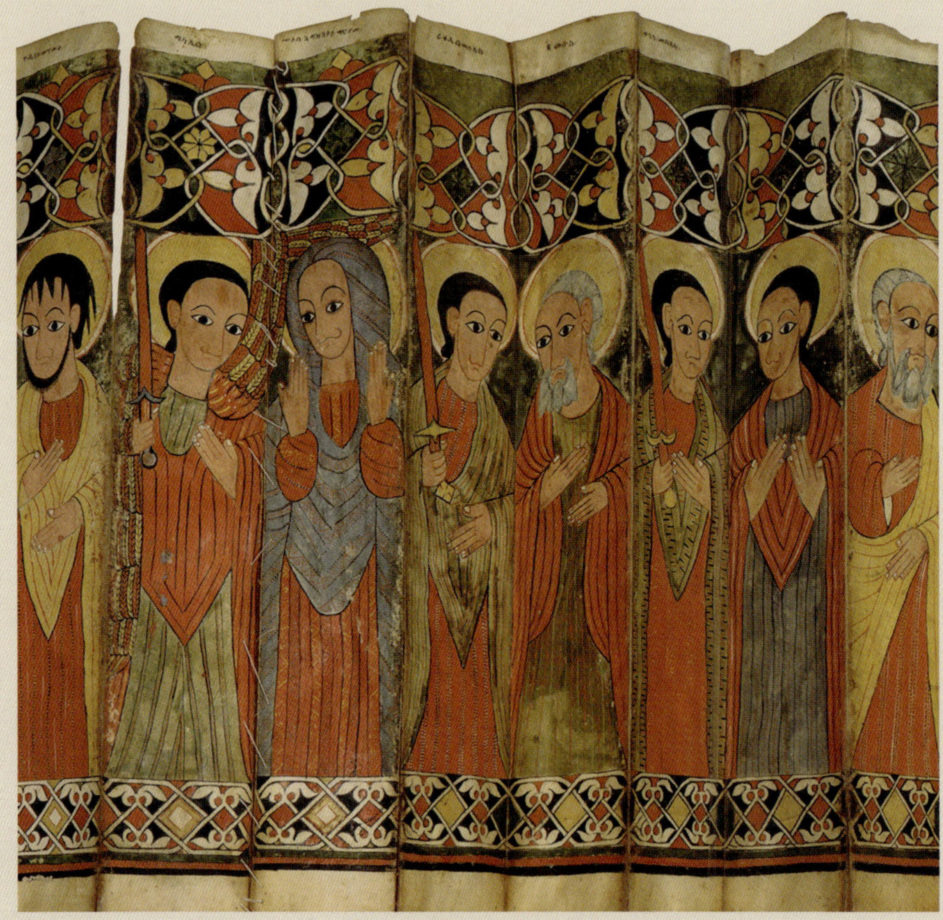

FIG 3.5

Ethiopian Orthodox (Stephanite), folding processional icon in the shape of a fan, late 15th century. Tempera with ink on parchment and wood handles, open: 24 ¼ × 154 ⅛ × 4 ¾ inches (61.6 × 391.4 × 12 cm); panel: 24 ¼ × 4 ⅟₁₆ inches (61.6 × 10.3 cm). Walters Art Museum, no. 36.9, museum purchase with funds provided by the W. Alton Jones Foundation Acquisition Fund, 1996

Furthermore: "There are holy names on the icons and on the *tabot*s before which every head should bow." To show the extreme level of respect an icon deserves, they quote from the book *Gännätä Mänäkosat* (Paradise of Monks): "If anyone stones the picture of a king and there is someone who stands by his side while he stones the picture of the king, both are to be put to death."[19]

By the early sixteenth century, negative attitudes toward the use of icons had virtually disappeared. Indeed, during the iconoclastic invasion of the Highland Christian kingdom of Ethiopia (1527–43 CE), most churches were burned and their contents, including manuscript libraries and icons, destroyed amid a jihad led by Ahmad b. Ibrahim, the charismatic leader of the client state of 'Adal. The survival of the Ethiopic religious manuscripts and icons created prior to 1527 is credited to the bravery of the unnamed Christian faithful who risked their lives to save them.

The Virgin is worshipped through her icons. The standard inscription for the iconic portraits of Our Lady Mary with the Christ Child is *məslä fəqur wälda*, "with Her Beloved Son," rather than "with His Beloved Mother." The faithful focus their eyes upon Mary rather than the Child. The introduction to the Miracles of Mary states: "Trust in her with all your heart, without any doubt, because she is your salvation. Prostrate yourselves before her icon. And may he who does not prostrate himself before her be obliterated [from the earth], and may the memory of his name enter into oblivion. May all the angels in heaven say Amen."

Ethiopian Orthodox churches follow the practice of placing an icon of the Madonna and Child in a prominent position before the faithful (fig. 3.6). During the celebration of the Mass, this icon rests on the altar, where the Eucharist is placed and broken, and is continuously incensed. It is carried during processions and accompanies the monarch on his military expeditions. When Emperor Iyyasu I (r. 1682–1706) prepared to fight the invading Oromo in Wällo in 1683, he first solicited Mary's help. Presumably kneeling before her icon, he prayed: "O My Lady, you are my shield in time of war, and my refuge against violent people. And now, strengthen my expedition, and grant me the power of victory against my foes and enemies who kill the laity and clergy, and who burn churches in which the holy body of your Son, the God of heaven and earth, is sacrificed and his honored blood is poured. Make me not an object of derision or scorn by my enemies who worship burning the fat."[20]

Icons have life in them. The Virgin speaks through them.[21] She may express her milk through icons by which the blind are cured.[22] The life-giving nature of the Virgin's milk was recognized by the Egyptian Coptic Church as early as the third century. Pilgrims' accounts of the so-called Icon Incarnate, the icon of Mary at Saidnaya (a town near Damascus), began to appear in the late twelfth century. They describe the miracle of this icon and the oil that dripped from her breasts into an alabaster basin; the oil had a fragrance sweeter than all perfumes. Pilgrims, of all Christian creeds as well as Muslim, visited this icon. Consider the following quotation from a recently discovered Miracle of Mary in a manuscript belonging to the monastery of Zämäddo Maryam, in Lasta (Wällo):

The governor of the district had the custom of coming to the Monastery of Saidnaya every year for the feast on the 20th of Maskaram [around September 17th] and would remain a while in the vicinity of Saidnaya, giving orders to make the following announcement three times per day: "No one of the population should enter the church and argue with (the community) regarding the incarnated icon, or do anything evil against the church." This governor [of the district] came to the head governor and kissed his foot. The head governor said to this governor, "Please, protect this monastery and the Christians who are in it as well as those who come to visit it." Then he said to the Christians, "As of now, do not worry, because this place is within my protectorate. If the Muslims give you difficulties, come and tell me, and I will avenge you." He said this and left. And I returned (to Saidnaya) and entered the church. On that same day, Ethiopians arrived—twelve priests and many deacons—in order to be blessed by the icon of Our Lady. We welcomed them warmly in a spirit of Christian fellowship and were blessed by them. When they entered the church and they saw the holy icon incarnate, they started praising it in their native language with a sweet song, clapping their hands and tapping their feet. They went round the icon of Our Lady Mary with glowing hearts and joyous minds, skipping before it like a calf.[23]

When the Mass of the Jacobites and the Mass of the Melkites [Christians of the Eastern Byzantine rite] are both over and the people have received the Holy Mysteries, the Melkites have the custom of preparing (a meal) at the conclusion, serving it before the church in order to feed the people who came for their feast. The Melkites thought that the Ethiopians were in unity with them, (so) they invited them, saying, "Come over; let us dine together." The Ethiopians replied, saying, "How could we partake (a temporal meal) with you, when we do not partake with you of the meal that will live in the everlasting life? God forbid it for us! We do not live with you nor will we ever be united."

FIG 3.6

Acolytes holding lit candles during a Maundy Thursday ceremony at Yohannəs, Addis Ababa, Ethiopia. Photograph by Marilyn E. Heldman, 1974. National Museum of African Art, Smithsonian Institution, Eliot Elisofon Photographic Archives, EEPA 2013-013-0170

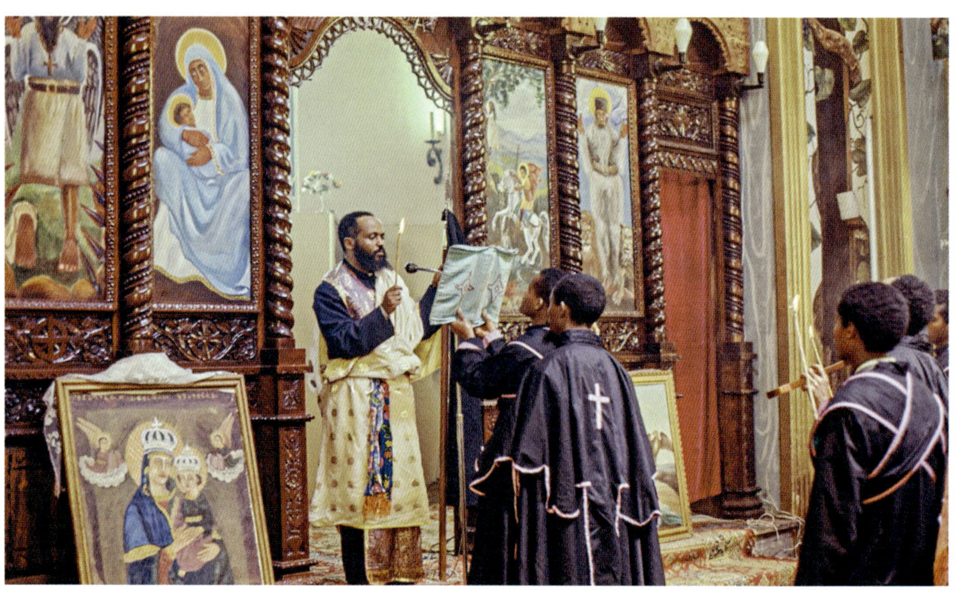

However, we, the Jacobites, have a five-story hall, where we prepared a meal and ate with the Ethiopians. We spent the night together with joy and merriment, giving thanks to Our God for the good things He has done for us. The next day, we left from there and headed for Damascus with the Ethiopians in spiritual love, singing and saying, "Behold, it is good and pleasing when brothers live together."[24]

The author of this account is evidently a Jacobite pilgrim, a member of the Miaphysite Orthodox Syrian Church of Antioch.

One of Mary's Miracles in the Zämäddo monastery's manuscript collection includes an account of the theft of an icon that was in the house of Martha at Saidnaya.[25] A *frängawi* (European) pilgrim attempted to steal the icon. During his attempt to remove what is believed to be the Lady Mary Incarnate, the thief ripped the icon. He was caught (a miracle), and his life was subsequently saved by the Blessed Virgin through her object because the motive of the crime was his love of her icon.

We brought this news to you. Receive it with your ears and put it in your heart. If you believe in Our Lady Mary, that it is possible for her to do all this and that (if) you take refuge with her help, you will be saved from all destruction, O worldly man. When Our Lady Mary shows all these miracles, she has no desire to benefit herself, but trust that her power is only to save people.[26]

The monastic community of Zämäddo Maryam attributes their icon of Our Lady Mary to the hand of Saint Luke the Evangelist and believe it is the same Incarnate Icon of Saidnaya. There are other Ethiopian monasteries that claim they, too, possess icons painted by the hand of Saint Luke[27] because the icons are not typically Ethiopian in style. Indeed, some of these are post-Byzantine icons from Crete purchased for Emperor Ləbnä Dəngəl (r. 1508–40) and thus datable to the early sixteenth century (fig. 3.7). Not all of the emperor's imported icons are believed to have profound spiritual power, even though copies of a Saint Luke icon may derive a limited measure of spiritual power from the original. Icons attributed to Saint Luke's hand were given meaningful names that are sometimes related to miracles that Mary worked through them (fig. 3.8). The monastic community of Däbrä Zämäddo gave their miracle-working icon from Saidnaya several monikers—including Gəbṣawit ("Egyptian") and Adnanitä ʿOm ("Bender of Tree")—because it saved their church by redirecting a tree poised to fall on it.

Mary's ultimate help is related in another of her Miracles, which asserts that her church at Mount Zion will turn into a boat or ark, like Noah's Ark, and will help the faithful sail across the sea of fire to reach paradise. One Miracle states:

Now listen, O my brothers, to this mystery, an amazing and astounding account which our fathers told us as they had found it written in the sacred books. They say that when Our Lord comes at his Second Coming in great glory, escorted by his angels and powers and the blowing of the horn, he will sit upon the throne of his glory at Mount Zion (Däbrä Ṣəyon)

Ethiopian Orthodox, Elousa
(Virgin of Tenderness), 15th to
16th century. Panel painting,
framed: 28 ½ × 22 ½ × 1 inches
(40.1 × 24.2 × 4.4 cm). Institute
of Ethiopian Studies, no. 4231.
National Museum of African
Art, Smithsonian Institution,
Chojnacki Collection, EEPA
2007-001, 003

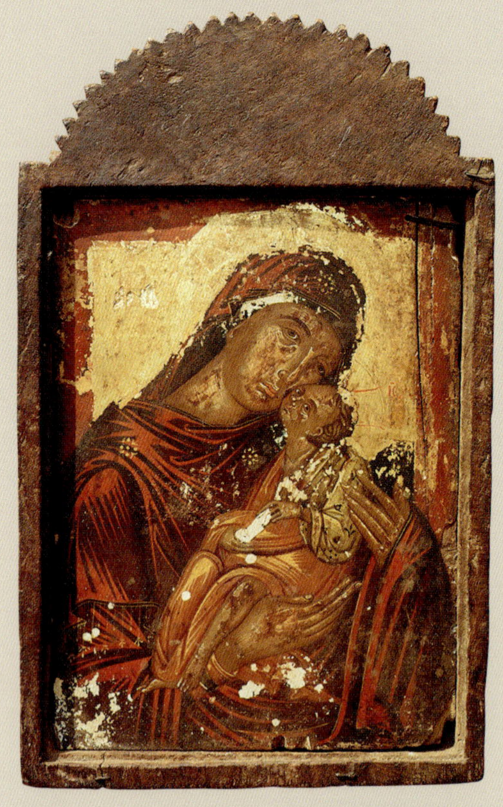

Ethiopian Orthodox, Saint Luke,
late 17th to early 18th century.
Icon. Distemper, gesso, and
cloth on wood, 13 ⁷⁄₁₆ × 18 ½ ×
6 ¹¹⁄₁₆ inches (34.2 × 47 × 17 cm).
National Museum of African Art,
Smithsonian Institution, Gift of
Ciro R. Taddeo, 98-3-2

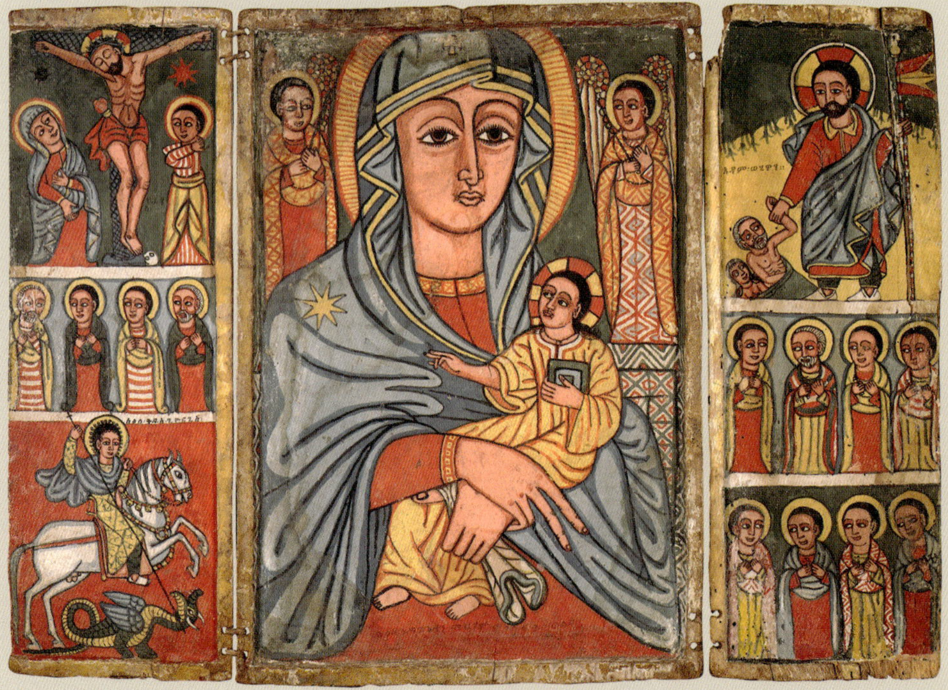

    ETHIOPIAN DEVOTIONS

to judge the whole world. The heavenly Jerusalem will come down with all the saints in it and settle upon Mount Zion and Jerusalem, facing the Mount Olive (Däbrä Zäyt). There is, between them, a wide and deep valley called the Field of Josaphat where a church was built on the tomb of Our Lady Mary. They said that when Our Lord comes (the church) will become a boat (ḥamär)[28] and it will bring all Christians who observed the holy days of Our Lady Holy Mary, Virgin in Two Ways (i.e., in body and thought) who treated the poor and the wretched mercifully in her name across (the sea of fire) so that they may rejoice with her in the Kingdom of Heaven and inherit everlasting life.[29]

Ethiopian poets and artists owe gratitude to the saints of the Church, especially the Blessed Virgin, for inspiring their creative talents in writing and painting. There are many anonymously composed hymns in praise of her, prayers to Mary and her icon,[30] four Anaphoras (Eucharistic prayers) in her honor,[31] and a wide range of illuminated manuscripts that record the Miracles of Mary, as well as countless Marian icons.

Holy Manuscripts

MARILYN E. HELDMAN

With the exception of Aksumite ceramic bowls decorated with impressed raised crosses, two illuminated liturgical Gospel books in Ethiopic (Gəʿəz) copied in the sixth century and currently at the Äbba Gärima monastery are the earliest extant examples of Christian religious arts in Ethiopia. Known as the Gärima Gospels (fig. E3.1), they are among the few pre-fifteenth-century manuscripts that have survived use and destruction by natural disaster or war.

Every Ethiopian Orthodox church requires a liturgical manuscript of the Four Gospels, preferably illuminated. Richly illuminated Gospel manuscripts of the late fourteenth and fifteenth centuries may feature an introductory frontispiece with as many as sixteen full-page miniatures dedicated to scenes of the life of Christ, ranging from Gabriel's Annunciation to Mary (fig. E3.2) to the Ascension of Christ (fig. E3.3). The wood endboards of these deluxe liturgical Gospels were covered with gold plates that have long been removed and recycled. The only remnant of this practice is the term *Wängelä Wärq* (Golden Gospel).[1]

The Gospel book is not only the source of liturgical readings but also represents Christ's presence among the congregation, as in the Gospel of John 1:1—"In the beginning was the Word, the Word was with God, and the Word was God." The Acts of the Apostles, the Pauline Epistles, the Psalms of King David, and the Ritual for Passion Week, with biblical readings primarily from the Psalms from Palm Sunday until the twelfth hour of Easter, are also essential texts. Each of these may be embellished with simple, interlaced designs or a full-page author portrait (fig. E3.4). A recently identified late fifteenth-century manuscript of the Acts of the Apostles and the Pauline Epistles was created at the monastery of Däbrä Libanos of Šäwa for the wealthy monastery's new church of Our Lady Mary, founded by its abbot, Märḥa Krəstos. The abbot's name appears in short prayers within the manuscript, which can be identified as having been copied and illuminated at his monastery's scriptorium. Two initial pages (called "incipit" pages in medieval manuscripts) are decorated with simple designs that are similar to the Ritual for Passion Week manuscript, also commissioned by Märḥa Krəstos for his new church (fig. E3.5 shows an example of an incipit page from the same period). The latter manuscript is in the collections of the British Library (MS Oriental 597).[2] According to the Life of Märḥa Krəstos, the abbot also presented

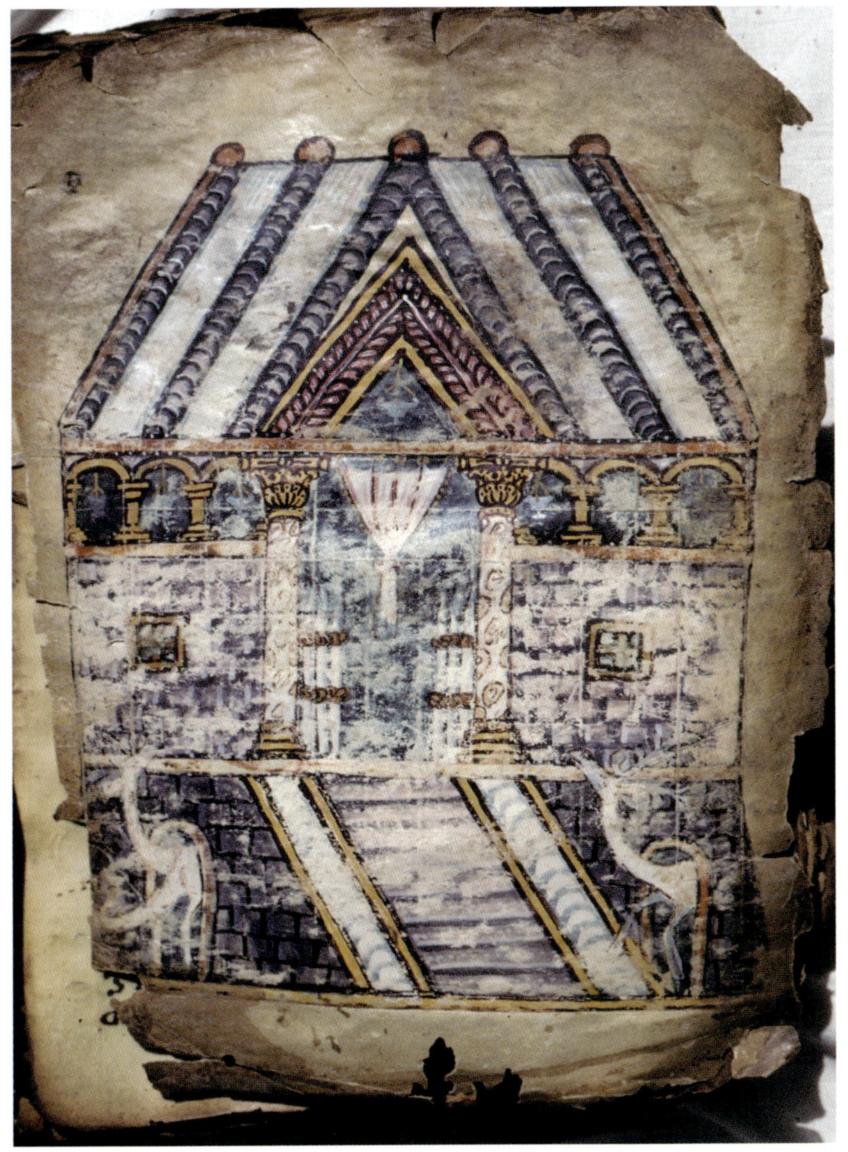

FIG E3.1
Ethiopian Orthodox, Gärima
Gospels, Äbba Gärima,
Ṭǝgray, Ethiopia, 6th century CE.
Parchment (vellum), acacia wood,
tempera, and ink. Photograph by
Michael Gervers, 2000

Ethiopian Orthodox, Gabriel's Annunciation to Mary, illuminated Gospel, Amhara region, Ethiopia, late 14th to early 15th century. Parchment (vellum), acacia wood, tempera, and ink, 16 ½ × 11 ¼ × 4 inches (41.9 × 28.6 × 10.2 cm). Metropolitan Museum of Art, Rogers Fund, 1998.66

Ethiopian Orthodox, Ascension of Christ, illuminated Gospel, Amhara region, Ethiopia, late 14th to early 15th century. Parchment (vellum), acacia wood, tempera, and ink, 16 ½ × 11 ¼ × 4 inches (41.9 × 28.6 × 10.2 cm). Metropolitan Museum of Art, Rogers Fund, 1998.66

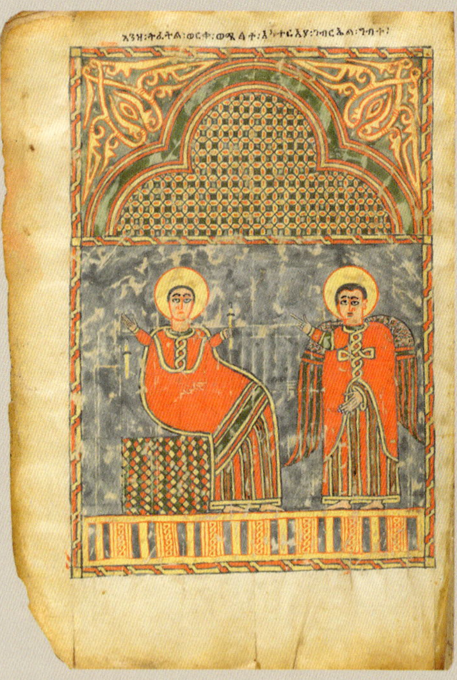
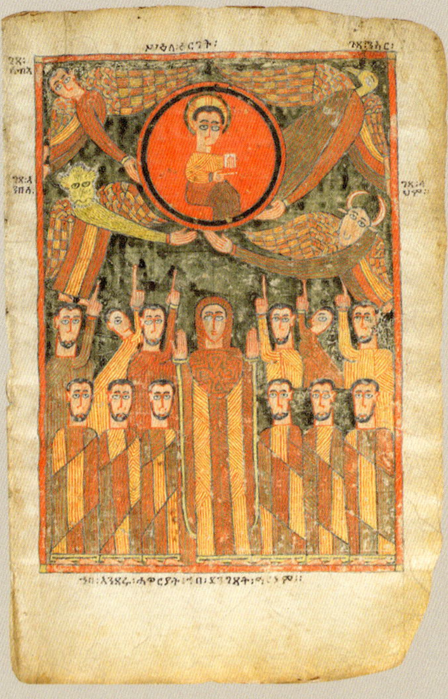

Ethiopian Orthodox, portrait of the Evangelist Luke, 1500–50. Ink and paint on heavy, thick parchment, 11 ¹³⁄₁₆ × 9 ⅝ inches (30 × 24.5 cm). Walters Art Museum, museum purchase with funds provided by the W. Alton Jones Foundation Acquisition Fund, 1998, W.850.96V

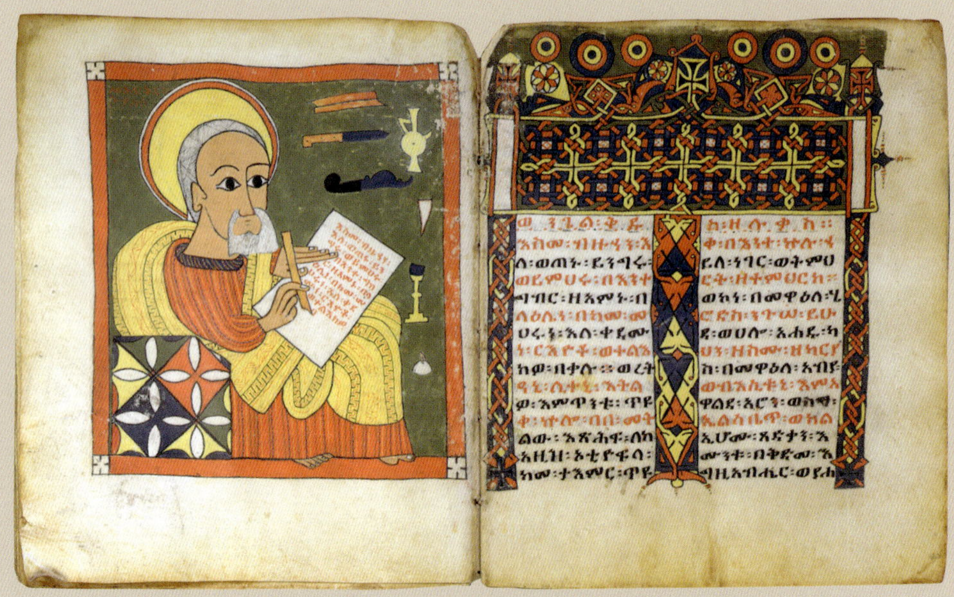

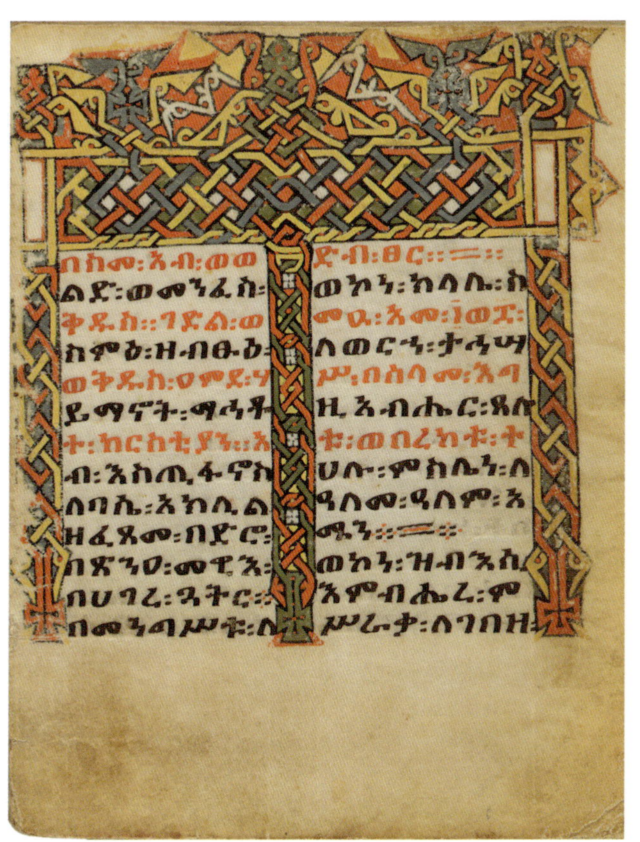

FIG E3.5
Ethiopian Orthodox, decorated
incipit page, ca. 1504–5. Tempera
on parchment, 13 9/16 × 10 7/16
inches (34.5 × 25.6 cm). The J.
Paul Getty Museum, Los Angeles,
Ms. 102 (2008.15), fol. 144

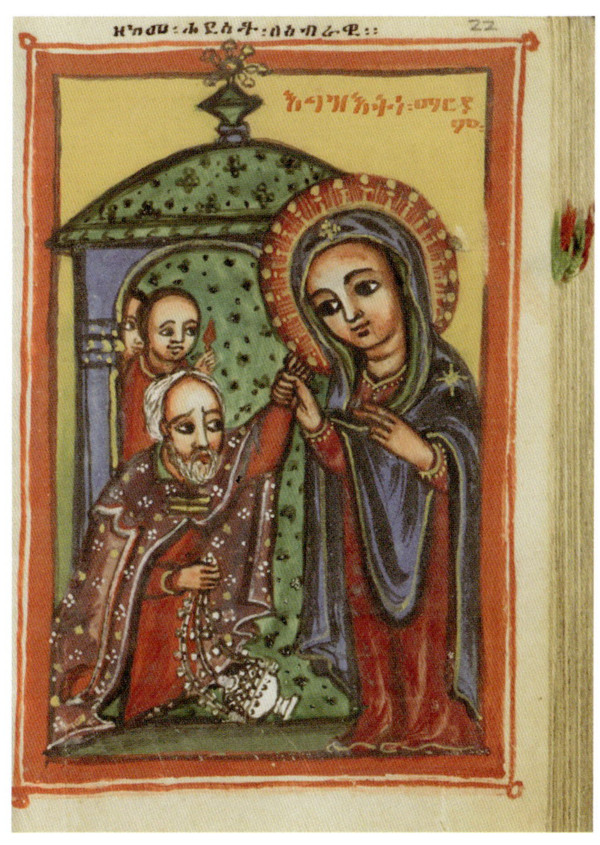

FIG E3.6
Ethiopian Orthodox, Miracles
of Mary with Three Miracles of
Saint George, mid-18th century,
3 15/16 × 6 3/16 inches (10 × 15.7
cm). Princeton University Library
Special Collections, Princeton
Ethiopian Manuscript no. 57 f.22r

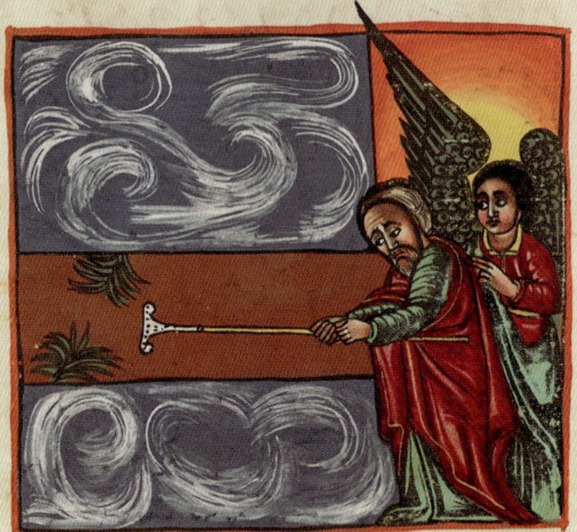
በ ኤሜ፡ዘበጣ፡ሙሴ፡ሳባሕረ፡ኤርትራ፡በበትሩ፡ወአፌለጋ።
ሳኖተ የ⬦ወ እቱ፡እ ምሳ ኪ፡የ፡ወእ
ሴ ብ ሐ⬦እ ምሳ ከ፡እ ቡ፡የ፡ወ እ ሴ
ዕሎ⬦እ ግ ዚ እ ብ ሐ ር፡ዩ ቀ ጠ ቅ
ኁበ፡
ጥ፡ወእ ግ ዚ እ ብ ሐ ር፡ስ መ⬦ዕ ስ
ረ ገ ሳ ቲ ሁ፡ስ ፌ ር እ ን፡ወ ሠ ራ ዊ

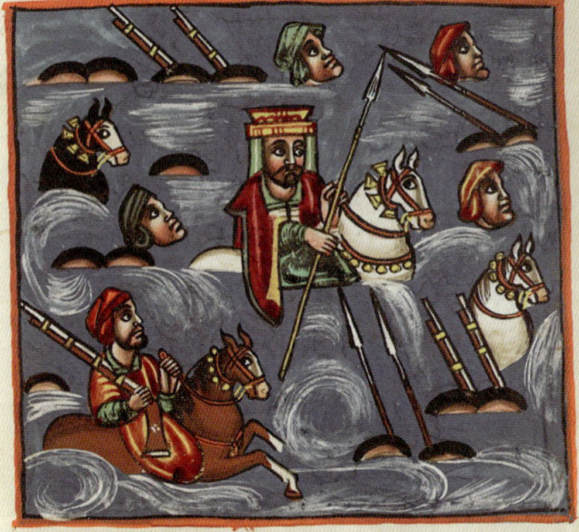
ዘ ኤሜ፡ተ ስ ዋ ሙ፡ፌ ር እ ን፡ ም ስ ስ ⬦ሠ ራ ዊ ቱ።
ት፡ወ ረ ወ፡ው ስ ተ፡ባ ሕ ር⬦ሳ ሩ ሃ ኒ
ወ መ ስ ተ ዕ ዕ ና ፤፡በ መ ስ ል ሥ ተ⬦
ወ ተ ሰ ጥ ሙ፡ው ስ ተ፡ባ ሕ ረ፡ኤ ር ት
ራ⬦ወ ደ ፌ ኖ ሙ፡ማ ዕ በ ል⬦ወ ተ
ሰ ጥ ሙ፡ው ስ ተ፡ቀ ላ ይ፡ከ መ፡ዕ ብ

a manuscript of the Holy Gospels with golden end covers to the church of Däbrä Libanos.[3] When the monastery was destroyed by invading Muslim troops in 1532, the abbot and many monks were killed,[4] but acts of profound courage saved these two manuscripts from destruction.

Numerous post-sixteenth-century manuscripts, such as the illuminated Miracles of Mary (Tammera Maryam), Homilies and Miracles of the Archangel Michael (Dersana Mikael), and a handful of illuminated Gospels, contain various miniatures that are essentially narrative in content (figs. E3.6 and E3.7 a and b). Monarchs and other members of the ruling class commissioned such manuscripts from scriptoria (located at Gondär) as gifts to the many local churches and for their private devotion. Indeed, it was the daily custom for the family's priest to read aloud a passage from the illuminated *Dersana Mikael* or the *Tammera Maryam*, a practice that reflects both a great respect for texts written in Gəʻəz and a love of the beauty of the oral recitation of this liturgical language. These extensively illustrated manuscripts also fulfill the goal of interpreting the narrative imagery. The miniatures may not tell the full story, but they effectively project the essence of the plot of each miniature.

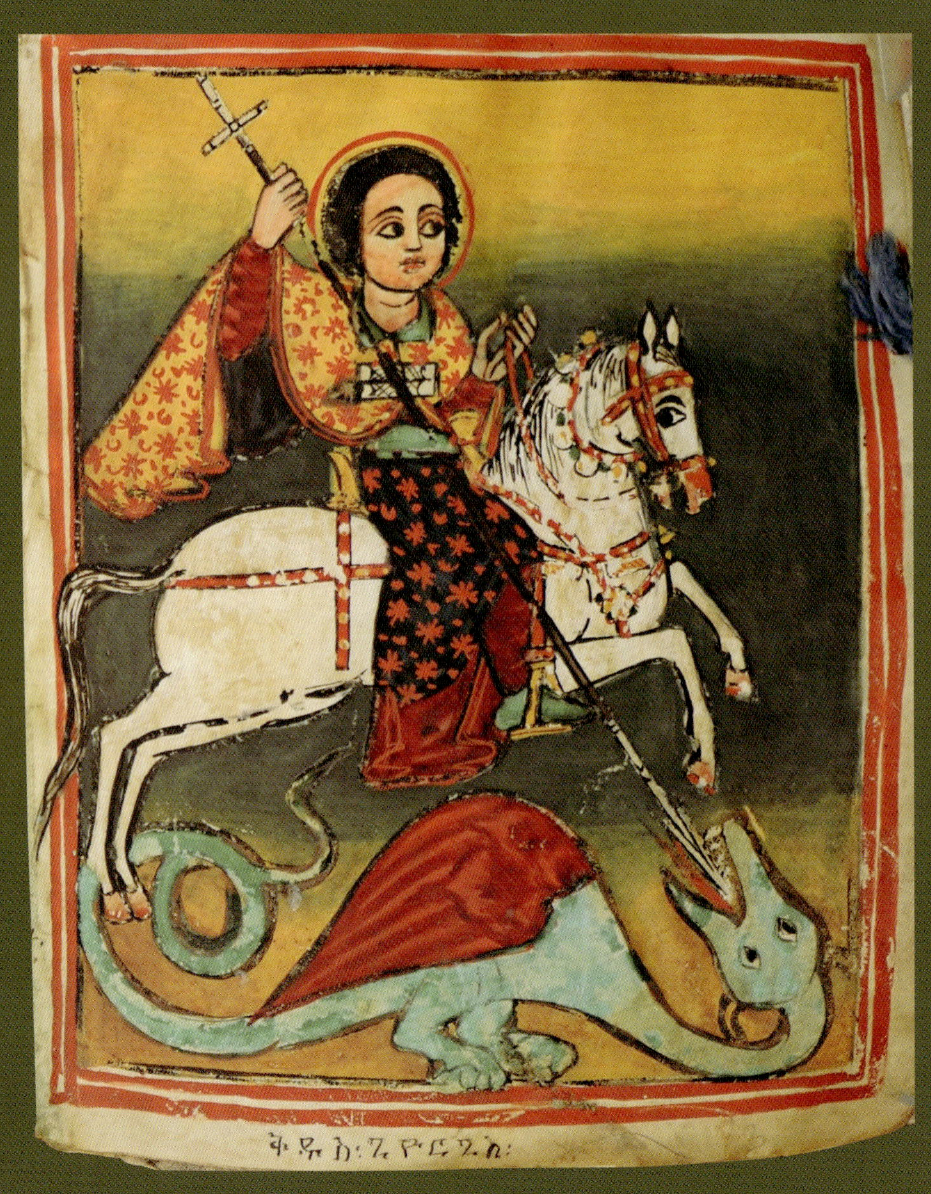

ቅዱስ፡ጊዮርጊስ፡

Chapter 4

Ethiopic Hagiography: History, Saints, and Texts

DENIS NOSNITSIN[1]

As in many other religious traditions, the Ethiopian Orthodox Church venerates as saints charismatic individuals renowned for achieving an extraordinary degree of righteousness, possessing spiritual powers of intercession, and working miracles. Ethiopic hagiography—literary works about these holy persons composed in Ethiopic (Gəʿəz), the language of literature and the liturgy of the Ethiopian Orthodox Church—was crucial for the expansion of the saints' cults and for their enduring popularity.

The creation of hagiographies has been one of the most seminal undertakings in the history of the Ethiopian civilization. In the context of the Christian Orient and sub-Saharan Africa, Ethiopic hagiography represents a remarkable literary and cultural phenomenon that merits close attention. The number of Acts of the local saints far exceeds two hundred, and from time to time previously unknown works are still being discovered.[2] Many dozens of Ethiopic hagiographic texts (primarily Acts) have been edited and translated by scholars, and a number of them have been published by the Ethiopian Orthodox Church. Hagiographic literature remains a constituent part of Ethiopian Orthodox culture. Although on a more limited scale than before, the old way of copying hagiographic texts by hand on parchment continues.[3]

The present chapter seeks to provide a summary of the history and geographical distribution of Ethiopic hagiography and highlights some of its leading characteristics.[4] An overview of the earliest indigenous and translated hagiographic works will be followed by a presentation of the hagiographic literary forms, a survey of the main works (Acts) focusing on the period of the fifteenth to the eighteenth century, when the bulk of Ethiopic hagiography is believed to have been created. At the end of the essay, some aspects of the creation and circulation of hagiographic works will be discussed.[5]

EARLY WITNESSES

Sometime in the second quarter of the fourth century CE, King ʿEzana of Aksum accepted Christianity as the official religion of his kingdom. Aksum was a mercantile state with economic and cultural ties, and henceforth also religious ties, to the Mediterranean world. From the very beginning, the Church at Aksum was officially under the authority of the Coptic Patriarchate of Alexandria, from which an Egyptian monastic priest was sent to serve as the bishop of Aksum (later the metropolitan, the head of the Ethiopian

FIG 4.1
Ethiopian Orthodox, George of Lydda Killing the Dragon, late 18th to early 19th century. Parchment codex, 11 7/16 × 9 3/16 inches (29 × 23.4 cm). Miniature from MS Tänsəhe Kidanä Məhrät, Təgray (Ethiopia), TKMG-001, "Miracles of Mary," fol. 2v. Photograph by Ethio-SPaRe

Church). Little is known of the forms of saintly veneration in the Ethiopian-Eritrean Highlands at this time; probably only a few saints and martyrs were initially known there, likely those revered in the Christian Middle East. During the first centuries after the adoption of Christianity, several hagiographic texts were translated from Greek into Gəʿəz, which at that time was the spoken language of the people of the Aksumite realm.[6]

The earliest indigenous hagiographic texts—composed in the Ethiopian-Eritrean Highlands, in Gəʿəz—are brief panegyrics identified by their authors as *dərsan*, "homily, sermon, panegyric," intended for reading on the commemoration days of particular saints. *Dərsan* are included in large collections, together with other homilies for other church feasts. The hagiographic homilies are dedicated to a few saints of the Aksumite period, such as the sixth-century monk Mättaʿ (also known as Libanos), composed by Elyas, bishop of Aksum; the fifth- or sixth-century monks Gärima, Guba, and Yəm'ata, three of the so-called Nine or "Roman" Saints;[7] Frumentius (Fəremnaṭos), the fourth-century evangelizer and the first bishop of Aksum;[8] the mid-sixth-century Kaleb (Ǝlla Aṣbəha), king of Aksum; and Yoḥanni of Däbrä Sina (in present-day Eritrea). These homilies extoll the saints but contain little information on their lives. The exact time and place when these works were composed is unknown, but they are certainly earlier than the fourteenth century, as they are found in several ancient manuscripts.[9]

Antiphons or—liturgical chants dedicated to saints, attested in several ancient manuscripts or their fragments—comprise a special segment of early Ethiopic hagiographic texts.[10] These chants are non-narrative sources and, like homilies, contain little tangible information on the saints. But both liturgical chants and homilies seem to constitute the earliest stratum of Ethiopic hagiography and preserve the earliest retrievable elements of the saints' legends.

There are a handful of hagiographic works—such as the Acts of Saint Yared, regarded as the founder of Ethiopian church music, or of the saintly brother-kings Abrəha and Aṣbəha—whose protagonists are placed in the Aksumite period, but the antiquity of these texts cannot be proven, at least for the moment.[11] Instead, the style of the hagiographic texts points to the medieval period or even to more recent times. There is often no clear evidence of the older form of these allegedly ancient texts; if they ever existed, their originals may have been lost long ago or absorbed into later compositions.

TRANSLATED HAGIOGRAPHIES OF EARLY CHRISTIAN SAINTS

As late as the beginning of the fourteenth century, Ethiopic hagiographic literature was dominated by translated works, organized and circulated in extensive collections. The primary type of such collections is known as the Acts of the Martyrs (*Gädlä säma ʿtat*), to which several versions attest. Acts are very large compendia of texts mainly devoted to martyrs and saintly monks from Egypt and the Middle East, arranged according to the day and month of their commemoration in the Church. Although several of these saints' Acts were translated from Greek during the Aksumite period,[12] the majority were translated at a later time from Copto-Arabic hagiographies.[13] Among many dozens of such texts, the Acts of Azqir and the Acts of Ḥirut (Arethas) should be mentioned as the foundation of the Ethiopic hagiographical "Cycle of Naǧrān" that includes both translated works and those locally composed (see below).[14] Another translated hagiographic collection, which was widely disseminated in Ethiopia, is the apocryphal Acts of the Apostles (*Gädlä ḥawaryat*). This collection includes dozens of texts, translated into Gəʿəz primarily from Arabic and occasionally from Greek, on the preaching and martyrdom of the apostles.[15] The translated texts are thought to have influenced the nascent Ethiopic hagiography.[16]

After the fifteenth century, the circulation of the Acts of the Martyrs and the apocryphal Acts of the Apostles greatly diminished. Yet, certain saints and Early Christian martyrs, such as George of Lydda (fig. 4.1), Cyriacus (Qirqos) and his mother Julitta, John the Baptist, Gäbrä Krəstos (also known as Saint Alexius, "the Man of God"), and Minas continued to enjoy a long-lasting popularity in Ethiopia, and their Acts were later circulated separately.

LITERARY FORMS

Over the centuries, Ethiopic hagiography adopted a system of literary forms similar to those of the other Eastern Christian and Western traditions but with its own distinctive features.[17] Passions (Gəʿəz *səmʿ*)—narratives of the deeds and death of Early Christian martyrs—were widely known, but this form was hardly applicable to the Ethiopian context, even though a handful of Ethiopian saints ended their lives as martyrs. After the fourteenth century, the form of hagiographic homily was rarely used. Instead, a type of narrative work known as Acts, Vita, or Life (Gəʿəz *gädl*), telling the life story of a saint from their birth to their death, became the dominant form of Ethiopic hagiography.[18]

The hagiographic Miracles (Gəʿəz *täʾammər*) became another important form; Miracles are short stories dedicated to a single (usually posthumous) miraculous feat of the saint. The hagiography of most saints includes a collection of their Miracles, which are commonly appended to the Acts in manuscripts. The Miracles were generally composed somewhat later than the Acts. (The Acts do include accounts of miracles performed by the saints, but the establishment of the Miracles as a distinct category of Ethiopic hagiography may have been suggested by the earliest translated collections of the Miracles of Mary.) The Miracles usually concern situations in everyday life, stressing the efficacy of saintly intervention on behalf of their believers but also the severity of the punishment that the saints may impose. Among the most prevalent subjects of the Miracles is miraculous healing, along with salvation of the believers' property and life in perilous situations.

In addition to Acts and Miracles, Ethiopic hagiography includes a short form of Acts gathered in the Synaxary, a book of brief commemorative accounts of saints' lives arranged in calendrical order. At least one saint is commemorated on each day of the Ethiopian Orthodox Church calendar. The Ethiopic Synaxary was derived from the Copto-Arabic Synaxary versions; in the sixteenth century, it was revised to accommodate additional readings for Indigenous Ethiopian saints.[19] Most of the notices are fairly short, abridged versions of the respective Acts. As it has been available in almost every ecclesiastic library in Ethiopia, the Synaxary has been immensely important for popularizing the saints' stories and expanding their cults across regional borders.

In addition to hagiographic literature in prose form, Ethiopia has an extensive tradition of hagiographic poetry. One of the most widespread poetic genres is the *mälkə'* (literally "image, likeness"). A *mälkə'* commonly consists of approximately forty-four stanzas that praise the parts of the saint's physical body in an established sequence, relating each of these parts to the saint's spiritual merits.[20] By the seventeenth or early eighteenth century, the *mälkə'* had become a popular literary form.[21] And from that time on if not earlier, a hagiographic collection copied into a single manuscript would frequently include such main elements of the "hagiographic dossier" as the Acts of the saint followed by their Miracles, the *mälkə'*-poem, and occasionally other minor texts. There are other secondary hagiographic forms in both poetry and prose, such as *'arke*- and *sälam*-hymns, monastic genealogies, and narratives concerning saintly relics.

Liturgical chants dedicated to saints comprise another important aspect of Ethiopic hagiography. They were not gathered in special hagiographic collections, but they constitute a substantial portion of the main chant books of the Ethiopian Orthodox Church.[22]

HAGIOGRAPHY IN NORTHERN ETHIOPIA AND ERITREA

The (re)establishment of the so-called Solomonic dynasty by Yəkunno Amlak (r. 1270–85 CE) and the reinvigoration of the monarchy in the fourteenth century was followed by the rapid expansion of monasticism from the core territory of northern Ethiopia to other areas in the west, the south, and the east.[23] Monasteries became leading centers of literacy and manuscript production where hagiographic texts were composed and multiplied. Thereafter, Ethiopian monks were the primary authors of the Acts of Ethiopian saints. The monastic communities felt a particular need to establish and popularize the veneration of their saintly founders and community leaders, for which hagiography was an important vehicle.

Northern Ethiopia, the domain of the ancient Aksumite kingdom and the region of the earliest literary activity, remained a hub of hagiographic creation and a repository of hagiographic literary traditions. The Acts of Ṗänṭälewon are arguably among the oldest Acts of the local saints of northern Ethiopia.[24] The work recounts how Ṗänṭälewon, the son of a nobleman related to "the King of Rome," entered monastic life at an early age and later left his country, journeying to Ethiopia with his companions. After spending some time at Aksum, he settled as a hermit on a steep hill not far from Aksum, where an old church now known as Däbrä Ṗänṭälewon is located. His Acts narrate an episode from the Ḥimyarite war describing how Ṗänṭälewon blessed King Kaleb's military campaign in Yemen and brought about the king's miraculous victory in the crucial battle.

The Acts of another of the Nine Saints, Gärima, date to the fifteenth century. Exceptionally, we know the name of its author—Yoḥannəs, bishop of Aksum. Gärima, like Ṗänṭälewon a son of the "King of Rome," succeeded his father on the throne, but a few years later he abandoned his worldly existence and followed Ṗänṭälewon and the other "Roman" saints to Aksum, where they fought and killed the local "dragon-king." Shortly thereafter, the pious King Kaleb ascended to the throne. Gärima later moved to the locale called Mädära, where he founded the famous monastery Ǝnda Äbba Gärima.

The Acts of Arägawi, or Zä-Mika'el Arägawi, another of the Nine Saints, are datable to the early sixteenth century. The saint has enjoyed great fame as the founder of the monastery of Däbrä Dammo, among the oldest and most important of the Ethiopian monastic centers. His Acts describe how Arägawi—a son of a noble family from "Rome"—joined Pachomius the Great at Thebes but then left Egypt for Ethiopia. His Acts include a legend that recounts how Arägawi, with the help of a snake, reached the top of an *amba*, a flat-topped mountain, which was too steep to be scaled. This is the site of Däbrä Dammo. His Acts also elaborate upon the story of Kaleb's campaign in Yemen but without mentioning Ṗänṭälewon, instead ascribing to Arägawi the essential role in Kaleb's victory.

Two remarkable hagiographic traditions arose in northern Ethiopia, those of the so-called Ewosṭateans and Stephanites. Ewosṭateans, or the members of the Ewosṭatean movement, were the followers of the monk Ewosṭatewos (ca. 1273–1352); they adhered to the keeping of the Saturday Sabbath as well as the Sunday Sabbath, as prescribed by their spiritual leader.[25] Several versions of the Acts of Ewosṭatewos are known, all from the fifteenth century, describing his struggles with adversaries, his journey to the court of Patriarch Benjamin II in Egypt and further to the Middle East, his miraculous crossing of the Mediterranean Sea on his monastic vestment, and other wonders. Ewosṭatewos died in self-imposed exile in Cilicia (Lesser Armenia).[26] Some of his direct disciples and followers became heads of Ewosṭatean monasteries in what is present-day Eritrea. These monks, commemorated with Acts of their own, included Märqorewos of Däbrä Dəmaḥ; Absadi, Täwäldä Madḫən, and Fiqṭor of Däbrä Maryam Qoḥayn; Filəṗṗos and Yoḥannəs of Däbrä Bizän (the leading center of the Ewosṭateans); Bəṣu'a Amlak of Ǝnda Śəllase; Yonas of Däbrä Dəḫuḫan; Dəmyanos of Däbrä Sina; and Ananya of Däbrä Ṣärabi (northern Ethiopia).[27] An inscribed seventeenth-century devotional icon (fig. 4.2) presents a rare pictorial monastic genealogy, portraying Ewosṭatewos with his disciples.[28]

The so-called Stephanite movement—inspired by the monk Ǝsṭifanos (ca. 1397/98–1444)—generated an extensive body of hagiographic writing. Ǝsṭifanos was critical of the "excessive veneration" of Saint Mary and the Holy Cross mandated by fifteenth-century Ethiopian kings and he demanded from the monastic communities strict asceticism and independence from the worldly authorities. The monastery of Gundä Gunde became the major bulwark of the movement and the locus of its hagiographic tradition. The Acts of Ǝsṭifanos and his close disciple Abäkärazun were composed in the late fifteenth century.[29] They embody the rich Stephanite hagiographic tradition and prolific production of illuminated manuscripts (figs. 4.3 a and b).

The Acts of the subsequent heads of Gundä Gunde, including those of Gäbrä Mäsiḥ, ʿƎzra, Isayyəyyas, and later abbots down to the eighteenth century, were likely written not long after their deaths and circulated in several monasteries. Apart from

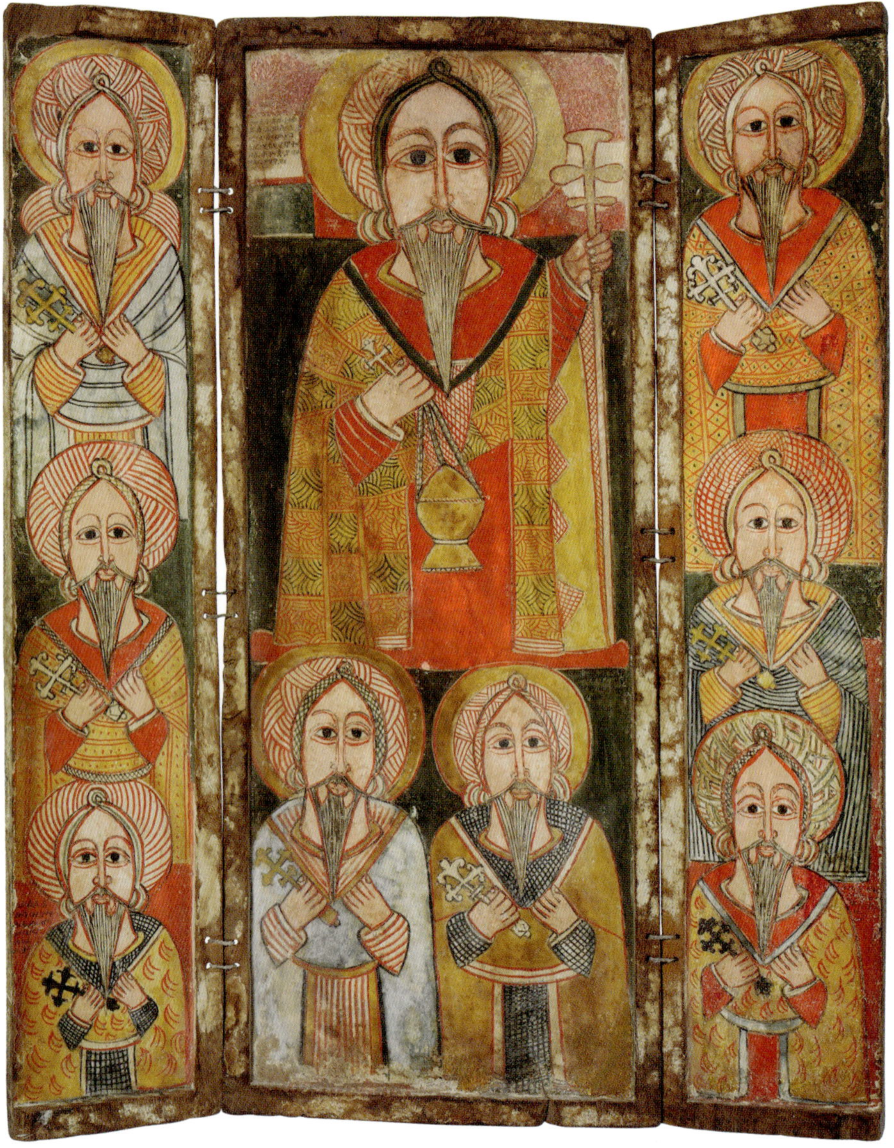

FIG 4.2
Ethiopian Orthodox,
Ewostatewos and Eight of
His Disciples, Amhara region,
Ethiopia, late 17th century.
Icon. Wood, tempera, and cord,
triptych: on mount: 27 9/16 ×
22 3/16 × 4 ¾ inches (70 × 56.3 ×
12.1 cm). Metropolitan Museum
of Art, Louis V. Bell Fund,
no. 2006.98

Acts of individual saints, the collective memory of the fifteenth- and early sixteenth-century persecutions of the Stephanite martyr-monks generated hagiographical works dedicated to them as a group. Only a handful of these works became more prevalent, such as the Acts of Ǝstifanos and especially the Acts of Mäzgäbä Śǝllase, the prominent late seventeenth- to early eighteenth-century head of Gundä Gunde.[30]

Other local hagiographic traditions were established and flourished in northern Ethiopia from the late fourteenth to the seventeenth or eighteenth century, among them the Acts of Samu'el of Däbrä Halelluya (near Aksum); Samu'el of Wali or Waldǝbba (fig. 4.4), one of Ethiopia's most famous saints; 'Abiyä Ǝgzi' of Däbrä Mädḥanit; Mädḥanina Ǝgzi' of Däbrä Bänkʷal; Dani'el of Qorqor Maryam, who was the

     ETHIOPIAN DEVOTIONS

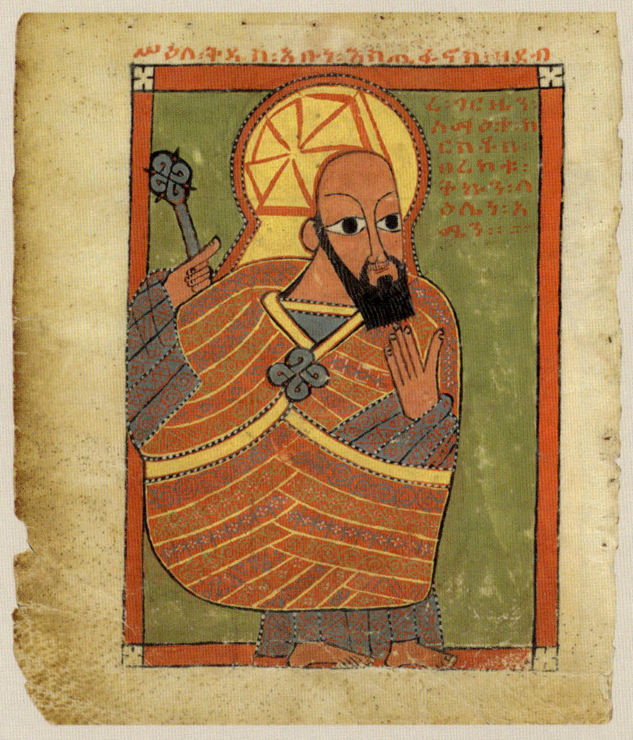

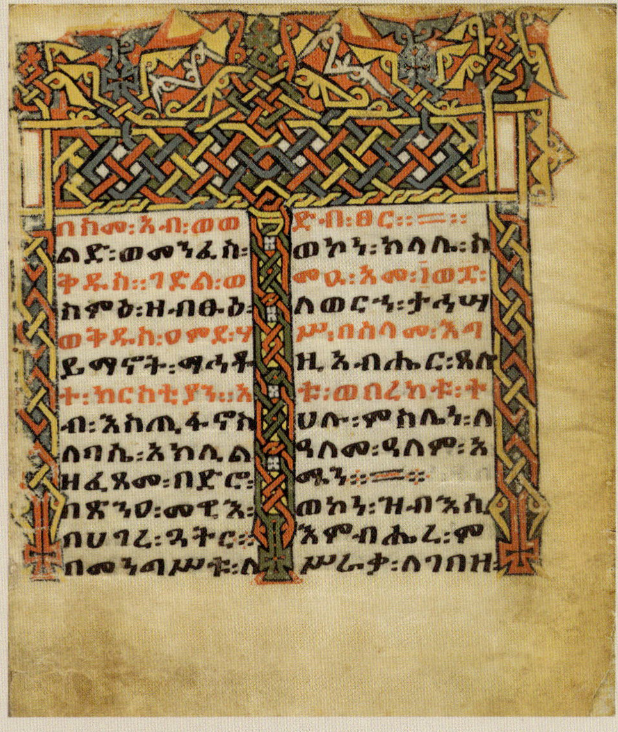

FIG 4.3 A AND B
Ethiopian Orthodox, Acts of
Ǝsṭifanos and Abäkärazun,
(a) frontispiece of the Acts of
Ǝsṭifanos, fol. 4v, (b) first text
page of the Acts of Ǝsṭifanos
decorated with a headpiece,
fol. 5r, after 1480 to early
or mid-16th century. Parchment
codex, 10 ¹⁄₁₆ × ⅝ inches (25.5 ×
15.5 cm). New York Public
Library, Spencer Collection,
Ethiopic MS 7

FIG 4.4
Ethiopian Orthodox, Samu'el
of Waldǝbba Riding on a Lion,
late 18th to early 19th century.
Parchment codex, 11 ⁷⁄₁₆ × 9 ³⁄₁₆
inches (29 × 23.4 cm). Miniature
from MS Tänsǝhe Kidanä Mǝhrät,
Tǝgray (Ethiopia), TKMG-001,
Miracles of Mary, fol. 3r.
Photograph by Ethio-SPaRe

spiritual father of Ewosṭatewos; Tadewos of Däbrä Bärtärwa; Filmona of Däbrä Aysama; Yoḥanni of Däbrä ʿAśa; Bänadlewos of Ǝnda Bänadlewos; and Mäzraʾtä Krǝstos of Ahsäʾa.

HAGIOGRAPHY IN CENTRAL AND SOUTHERN ETHIOPIA

Numerous hagiographic traditions arose in the central part of Ethiopia, roughly corresponding to the historical provinces of Amhara, Wällo, and Šäwa. Hagiography from this area is not as well-known and has not been as carefully studied as that of northern Ethiopia. This group includes the Acts of Aron of Däbrä Däret; Bäṣälota Mikaʾel of Däbrä Gol; Gäbrä Ǝndrəyas of Däbrä Qozät; Mälkəʾa Krǝstos of Gəšäq; Giyorgis of Sägla (Gassəča); and Akalä Krǝstos of Mədrä Zoga, a nephew of King Fasilädäs (r. 1632–67). The hagiographic tradition of the island monastery of Däbrä Ḥayq Ǝsṭifanos, founded by Iyäsus Moʾa in the mid-thirteenth century, is potentially very important, but thus far the only known examples are limited to the Acts of the founder, Iyäsus Moʾa, and the Acts of Bəstawros, a seventeenth-century abbot of Ḥayq Ǝsṭifanos.

During the thirteenth and early fourteenth centuries, Ethiopian kings expanded their rule over the region south of Amhara, a vast province that later became known as Šäwa, and to areas farther south. There, in the early fourteenth century, a monastery initially known as Däbrä ʿAsbo was founded by Täklä Haymanot (d. ca. 1313; fig. 4.5), a monk who took his monastic vows in the community of Bäṣälota Mikaʾel of Däbrä Gol. He lived in monasteries in Amhara and Ṭəgray before returning to his native region to establish a monastery of his own—Däbrä ʿAsbo, later renamed Däbrä Libanos of Šäwa. This monastery became the hub for the evangelization of the entire region and would later play a dominant role in the religious and political affairs of the Ethiopian kingdom.

A substantial amount of hagiographic literature was produced at Däbrä Libanos and at associated monasteries. Although the Acts of Täklä Haymanot exist in several versions, the standard version, composed in 1515 CE, became one of the most widely disseminated hagiographic works in Ethiopia.[31] The well-known hagiography of later abbots of Däbrä Libanos include the Acts of the fourteenth-century Filəppos, the fifteenth-century Märḥa Krǝstos (d. 1497), and the sixteenth-century ʿǝnbaqom and Yoḥannəs.

 From the fourteenth to the sixteenth century, many Acts of local saints were composed in the vast region around Däbrä Libanos, to the north as well as far to the south, beyond the location of the contemporary capital, Addis Ababa. These include the Acts of the fifteenth-century hermit Habtä Maryam, associated with Däbrä Libanos, and Iyasu, the sixteenth-century founder of the monastery of Ǧar Śəllase; Samuʾel, the founder of Däbrä Wägäg or Däbrä Asabot, the monastery in the Chercher Mountains; Täklä Ḥawaryat of Däbrä Gäbärma; Färe Mikaʾel of Wäräb; and Mäbaʾ Ṣəyon of ʿǝndägäbṭän, an abbot as well as a painter.[32] A number of later Acts of saints from Šäwa indicate close literary links to the hagiography of Täklä Haymanot, for instance, the

Acts of Zena Marqos of Däbrä Bəśrat; Qawəsṭos of Nəbge Maryam; and Yoḥannəs (Məśraqawi) of Mänz.

An important hagiographic tradition dedicated to Gäbrä Mänfäs Qəddus (fig. 4.5) emerged in southern Šäwa in the fifteenth century and then circulated, like the Acts of Täklä Haymanot, throughout the Highland Christian kingdom. The main sanctuaries of Gäbrä Manfas Qəddus are located at Mount Zəqʷala (south of Addis Ababa, in present-day Oromia) and Mədrä Käbd (Soddo, in today's Southern Nations, Nationalities, and Peoples' Region).

The study of hagiographies from the historical region of Šäwa and southern Ethiopia is particularly difficult because the historical context and the bulk of the man-uscript evidence disappeared long ago as a result of wars and population movements.

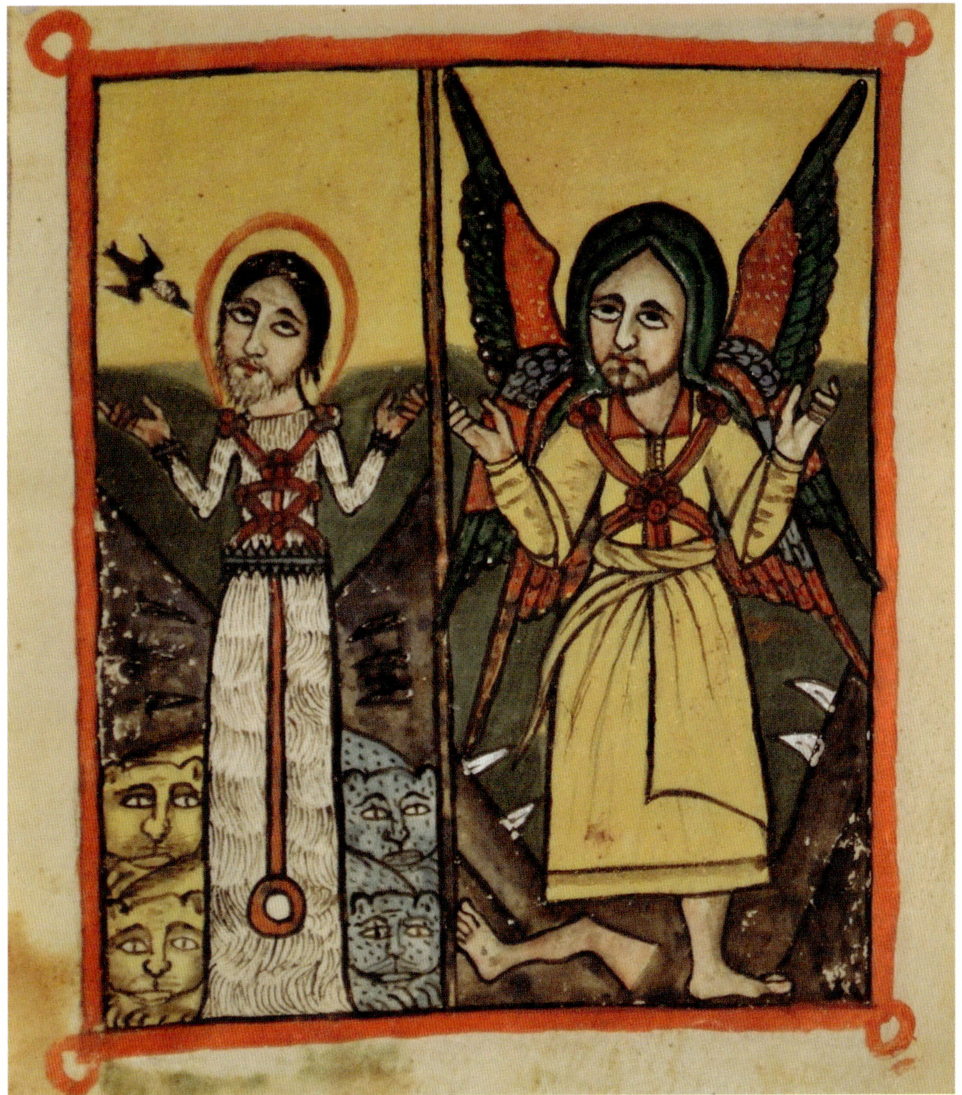

By the fifteenth century, another important area of hagiographic production began to emerge in the region around Lake Ṭana, reaching southward to the historical province of Goǧǧam and northward to the vicinity of Gondär (established as the royal capital in 1636 CE) and beyond. Although important lake monasteries such as Däbrä Daga Ǝsṭifanos, Ṭana Qirqos, and Kǝbran Gäbrǝ'el were established in the fourteenth century, local hagiographic production apparently did not begin there until the fifteenth century or later with such works as the Acts of Za-Yoḥannǝs of Kǝbran, the Acts of Yafqǝrännä Ǝgzi' of Ṭana Qirqos, and the Acts of Bäträ Maryam of Zäge Giyorgis. What appears to be the earliest known Acts of an Ethiopian female saint was produced in the area: the Acts of Krǝstos Sämra of Gʷangʷǝt, from the late fifteenth or the early sixteenth century.[33] A number of hagiographic traditions exist in the large region of the historical Bägemdǝr (today's North and South Gondär), but only a few are well-known, such as the Acts of the female saint Zena Maryam of Ǝnfraz and the Acts of Akalä Krǝstos of Däbrä Maḥǝw, a nephew of King Fasilädäs.

The establishment of the permanent royal capital at Gondär led to an unprecedented surge in literary activity and manuscript production, including the creation of extensively illuminated deluxe manuscripts. Several hagiographic narratives were enhanced at that time with lavish miniature cycles, such as the Acts of Wälätta Ṗeṭros, the famous female anti-Catholic saint; the Acts of Täklä Haymanot of Däbrä Libanos and his successor, Filǝṗṗos; and, later, the Acts of King Lalibäla. In a rare case, King Iyasu I Adyam Sägäd (r. 1682–1706), killed by his adversaries, was proclaimed a saint, and his Acts were compiled, in addition to his Chronicle.

The province of Goǧǧam, located south of Lake Ṭana, is home to numerous monastic communities also renowned as places of literary activity. Various local saints are venerated there, but these hagiographic traditions have not been extensively studied. The Acts of Särṣa Ṗeṭros (from the late fourteenth to the mid-fifteenth century) are preserved at Däbrä Wärq, the monastery with which this saint is associated. The Acts of Takaśta Bǝrhan are housed at Däbrä Dima Giyorgis, the monastery that he founded, as are the Acts of its sixteenth-century abbot Täklä Alfa. The Acts of Sinoda are preserved at Däbrä Ṣǝmmuna. Perhaps the most famous hagiography from Goǧǧam is the eighteenth-century collection of the Miracles of Zär'a Buruk, the saint whose main sanctuary is located at the source of the Abbay (Blue Nile) River. Due to his cult's popularity, the Miracles of Zär'a Buruk are found throughout the Christian Highlands including the present-day state of Eritrea.

HAGIOGRAPHY IN EASTERN ETHIOPIA: LASTA

Several unique hagiographic traditions emerged in the historical region of Lasta, the region famous for the rock-hewn churches of Lalibäla. There, the primary subjects of Acts are saintly kings, the rulers of the Zagʷe dynasty, which rose to power sometime in the early second millennium and was overthrown in 1270 CE by the abovementioned Yǝkunno Amlak. Although some historical sources present the Zagʷe kings as "usurpers," the Ethiopian Orthodox Church regards some Zag^we sovereigns as saints, namely Lalibäla, Ḥarbay, Yəmräḥannä Krəstos, and Nä'akk^wəto Lä-Ab. The context and reasons behind the creation of their Acts are still insufficiently understood but they constitute our main written sources on the Zag^we era.[34] With the exception of the more widely known Acts of Lalibäla, the circulation of these Acts was primarily limited to Lasta and neighboring Wäg, where local rulers claimed their origin from the Zag^we royal line. A few more hagiographical works from that area dedicated to local monks have been recently published, such as the Acts of Bärtälomewos and the Acts of Yoḥannəs of Däbrä Zämäddo (the famous church known today as Ǧammädu Maryam).

COMPOSING HAGIOGRAPHIC NARRATIVES

Historically, the composition of a hagiographic work, or Acts dedicated to a monk, nun, abbot, or hermit, signified the recognition of that person's sanctity. The formalized process of canonization did not exist in medieval Christian Ethiopia. Rather, considering someone a saint was the result of spontaneous popular veneration and appreciation of the person's charisma and piety. Popular recognition was in itself no small matter, as we do not see unlimited multiplication of saints in medieval Ethiopia. The proper liturgical veneration started when a *tabot*[35] was consecrated in the name of a saint. The conse-cration could be performed only by the metropolitan, the highest Church authority. Thereafter, a regular liturgical veneration pivoting on the saint's commemoration feast was initiated. Some hagiographical compositions, especially the Acts, were indispensable for that. Therefore, the respective community would seek ways to commission a learned ecclesiastic to compile a story of the saint's life.[36] The elevation of the saint frequently marked a change in status of their community that would, in turn, become the saint's sanctuary.[37] Thus, the reasons behind the creation of hagiographic works were both devotional and practical. There is no doubt that the growth of hagiographic literature and the multiplication of hagiographic works went hand in hand with the spread of the saints' liturgical veneration.[38]

When a hagiographer embarked on the task of writing Acts, oral accounts in vernacular languages were frequently the first sources he had at hand. In rare cases, the hagiographer knew the saint personally; sometimes he had at his disposal accounts from the saint's contemporaries, but in most cases the composition of the Acts was under-taken long after the saint's death, by which time concrete information had faded into vague legend.[39] When compiling a narrative, Ethiopian hagiographers adhered to some kind of traditional literary conventions for the text's format and content.[40] The basic pattern of the narrative was defined, more or less, by the saint's vocation: whether the saint was an evangelizer and monastery founder, one of the monastery's successive heads, a hermit, a saintly king, a holy nun, and the like. In most Acts, the saint's life story is tripartite: the birth, the active life (presented as a chain of miraculous episodes), and the death of the saint; sometimes, this structure is accompanied by an elaborate prologue or epilogue.

A number of topoi, or "commonplaces,"[41] provide a narrative framework of sorts for the story as a whole. The hagiographer may further develop the narrative, drawing upon a repertoire of recurring motifs. For example, the saint's parents are frequently described as pious, noble, and wealthy. Many saints are said to have been of foreign origin. The birth of the saint frequently follows a long period of their parents' infertility. Parents of saints are often said to impart wisdom and the fear of God to their children. Saints are very serious and mature in mind already in their infancy; they complete the usual course of learning in an unusually short period of time; their exceptional qualities are blessed by high-ranking ecclesiastics.[42] At a certain moment, the saint abandons the worldly life, doing so following a vision, having been called by a "voice," or after an accidental encounter with an unknown monk, frequently on the eve of or right after marriage, sometimes against the will of the family. Upon entering a monastic community, the monastic vow may be preceded by years of rigorous apprenticeship. The monastic ritual is frequently mentioned, with the name of the saint's "spiritual father" recalled. Many Acts conclude with the saint's celestial journey and an episode in which Jesus Christ grants to the saint a solemn promise of the heavenly reward.[43]

Commonly for a medieval literary tradition, Ethiopian hagiographers made extensive use of material originating from various Gəʿəz texts, both hagiographical and other.[44] Biblical quotations are the most typical components of all Acts. Very popular, for instance, is Matthew 5:14–16 (from the Sermon on the Mount), which appears in some Acts in reference to a situation where the sanctity of a saint can no longer be concealed. Also popular are Matthew 16:24–26 ("You are the light of the world …"), Psalms 67:36 ("God is wonderful in his saints …"), and Luke 9:25 ("What does benefit man …"). Nearly every Act contains a varying amount of Ethiopic textual material originating from different texts that constituted the hagiographer's source material. Many recurring images and metaphors in the hagiographies are drawn from the Bible and other Christian texts. The protagonists of the Acts are frequently depicted as "imitating" other holy personages such as Jesus Christ, the apostles, prophets, or other saints. On the whole, rendering new meanings with the help of already existing texts was a common narrative strategy of the hagiographers.[45] Folklore accounts in vernacular languages (for example, Amharic or Tigrigna) comprised another type of source; closely related to local cultures and identities, these sources are frequently difficult to identify and understand.

The use of standard phrases and expressions, recurring quotations, and stereotypical behavior was intended to elevate the style of the Acts, but it was not only a matter of style. Such devices were also intended to make the essence of the narratives more easily understood, as they were employed to emphasize analogies between events in the life of the saint and corresponding situations described in the Holy Scriptures (and other religious texts). The process of writing a hagiographic text was thus much more than telling a story. The hagiographer had to interpret the history in order to reveal the divine meaning of the events in the saint's life. His primary concern was not an accurate rendering of these events; rather, his task was to craft a narrative that conveys the concepts of virtue and sanctity and demonstrates how God directs the life of His elect.

The hagiographer was not considered the creator of the text in the full sense but rather as a "mediator" inspired by the Holy Spirit. Within this framework, the hagiographer's aims could also include the sanctification of some persons and institutions, the justification of events, or the legitimation of claims.[46] Overall, it is difficult to see the hagiographers as merely inventing their narratives, even though some of them may appear purely fictional. Historical or realistic elements were not necessarily excluded from the Acts, but they were not indispensable and actually less important than the eternal example of the saint's pious life.

Despite the fact that some saints' hagiographies may resemble one another in narrative structure, content, and style, the Acts cannot be reduced to a set of topoi, motifs, and standard imagery. Many of them are highly specific. Composing a hagiographic text was not a codified procedure, and hagiographers differed greatly in their literary skills and approaches. They selected various motifs, arranging and elaborating on them in various ways, and leaving traces of their individuality in the texts. Some Acts appear very authentic and individual, quite dissimilar to other works of the genre. Others feature accounts that appear puzzling and resist interpretation. Yet others contain strikingly realistic episodes and historical details. Some Acts are remarkable due to their vivid style or sophisticated composition.

The prevalence of some Acts indicates, among other things, that they were greatly appreciated by a readership across regional and ethnic borders. It should be added that hagiographic works were normally "open traditions"; as such, they could be repeatedly reworked and revised over time, adapted to new requests and changing historical circumstances. As a result, there often exist various versions of the Acts of various saints, such as Täklä Haymanot, Gäbrä Mänfäs Qəddus, Ewosṭatewos, Iyäsus Mo'a, Mäṭṭa'/ Libanos, and Lalibäla. This existence of these multiple versions contributes to the complexity and richness of Ethiopic hagiographic literature.

CONCLUSION

Having briefly explored the history of Ethiopic hagiography, its main forms and some of the principles underlying the hagiographer's work, we may grasp some of the challenges of researching hagiographic texts. Only after prolonged study, cross-reading of many hagiographic works, and deep understanding of local traditions and historical geography will the student of hagiography be able to discern layers and nuances in the narratives and find their way into the Ethiopic "world of hagiography." More than 140 years have elapsed since the first complete publication of the full-fledged Acts of an Ethiopian saint.[47] Since that time, critical studies of Ethiopic hagiography have resulted in numerous editions and translations. The process of recording hagiographic traditions, gathering hagiographic manuscripts, and editing hagiographic texts continues, but perhaps the time has come to pay greater attention to the style and language of Ethiopic hagiography, and to offer a deeper and more systematic interpretation of its contents.[48] We need to understand hagiographic texts, as we will turn to them again and again in our efforts to understand the history and culture of the region, and the worldview of its people.

Narrative Imagery

MARILYN E. HELDMAN

Visual narratives come in many formats: mural cycles in circular churches with a central sanctuary, icons, and illuminated manuscripts, to name a few. This diversity speaks to the popularity of Ethiopian Christian narrative imagery, which was largely developed during the seventeenth century.

The most highly evolved form in Ethiopian Christian art is the continuous narrative, which was introduced to large triptychs as the focus for devotions in private chapels or oratories. Painted narratives, such as the Nagara Maryam (Scenes from the Story of Mary), recounting the Holy Family's trials in Egypt, are arranged in a grid pattern (fig. E4.1). Vertical rows are read from left to right (as Gə'əz and Amharic are written), and each cell in the vertical row is read from top to bottom. The narratives as arrayed in horizontally arranged cells are read from top to bottom. Each single-image cell works as a mnemonic, prompting recollections of particular events in the pious tale (fig. E4.2). The beautiful designs painted on the exterior of the lateral panels are visible when the triptych is closed at the conclusion of the devotions.

Mural decorations of post-sixteenth-century churches display narrative sequences. In centrally planned churches, they feature easily identifiable representations of popular saints on the external walls of the freestanding rectangular sanctuary, the so-called embedded sanctuary (figs. E4.3–4.4). The large narrative triptychs were evidently inspired by contemporary layouts of mural decoration in Ethiopian royal churches.[1] Oratories and chapels do not have *tabots* (altar tablets), but must have icons. In fact, they are each called "House of Icon" (*Śə'əl Bet*) rather than "House of Christians" (*Betä Krəstiyan*), a building with an altar and an altar tablet for the celebration of the Eucharist.

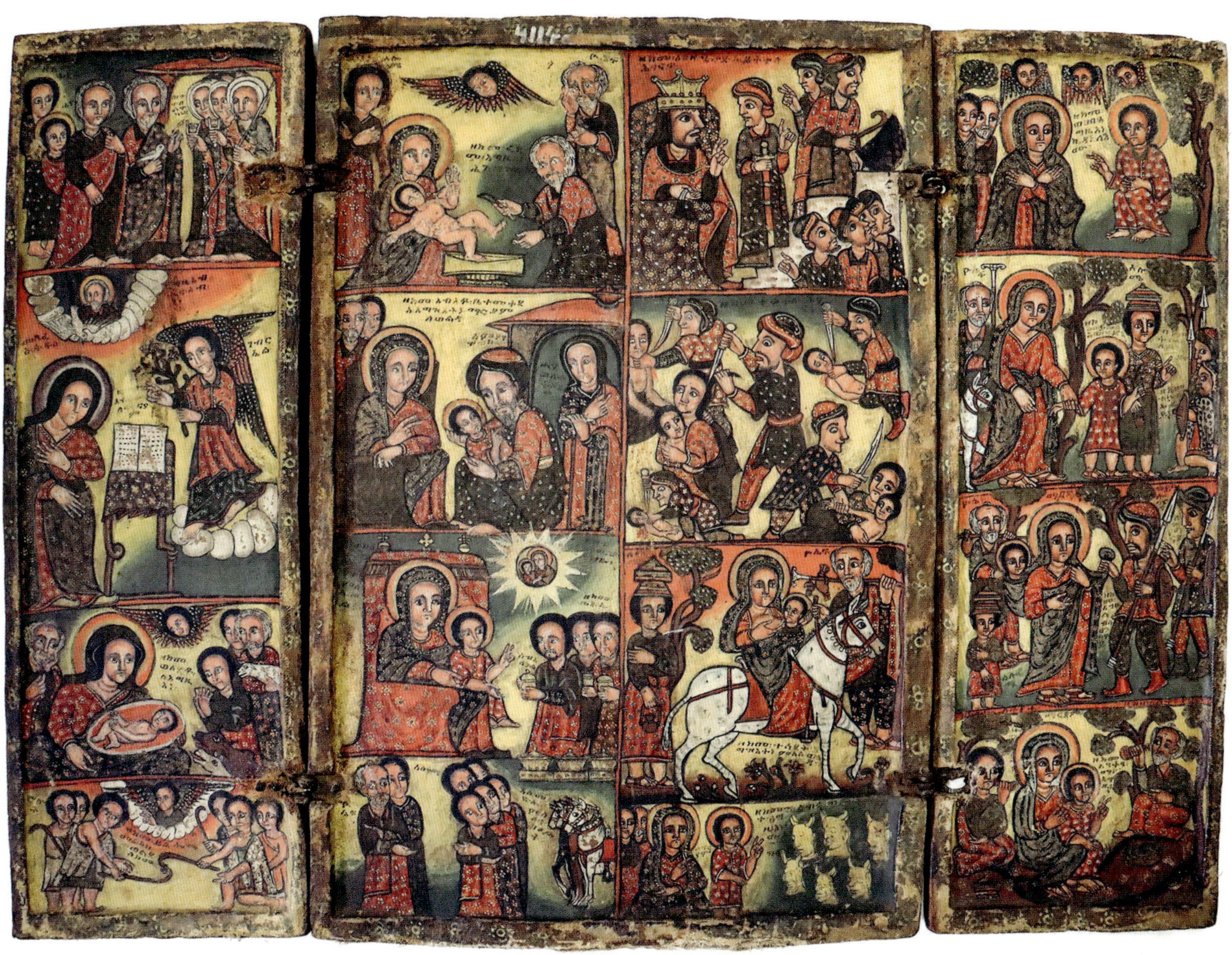

FIG E4.1
Ethiopian Orthodox, Nagara Maryam (Scenes from the Story of Mary), ca. 1730–55. Icon. Tempera on gesso-primed cotton on wood, including frames, open: 23 ⅜ × 30 ¾ × 1 inches (59.4 × 78.1 × 2.6 cm). Institute of Ethiopian Studies, no. 4187

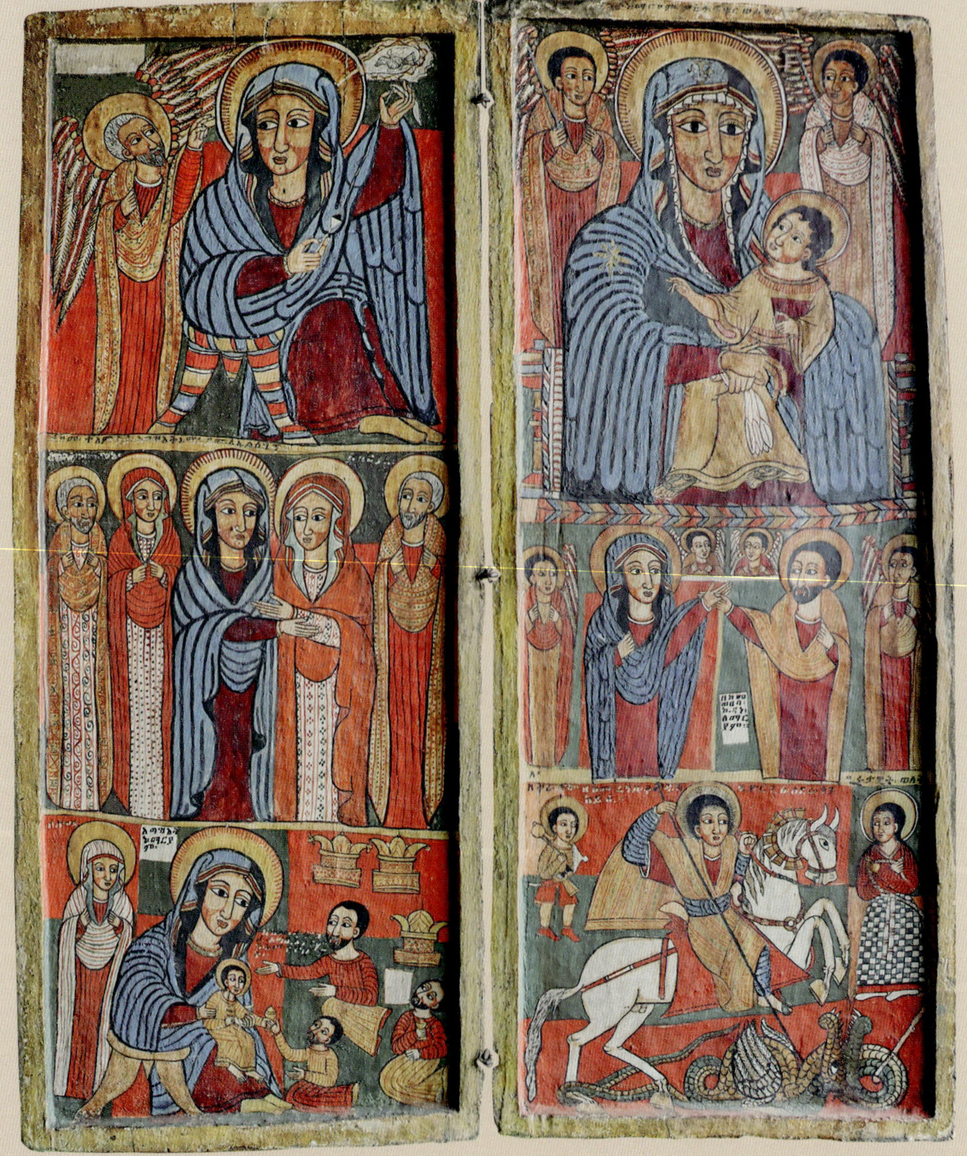

     ETHIOPIAN DEVOTIONS

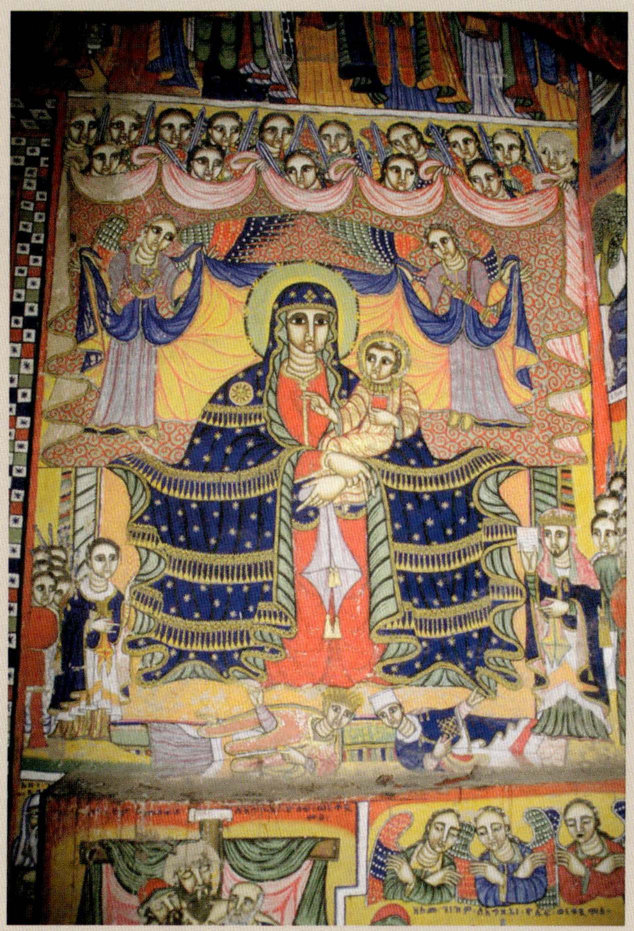

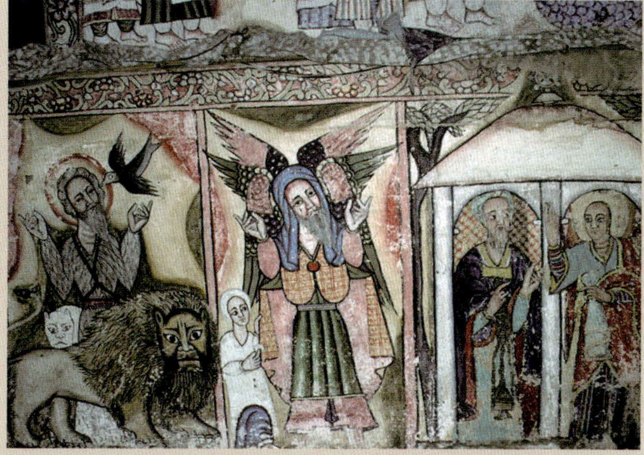

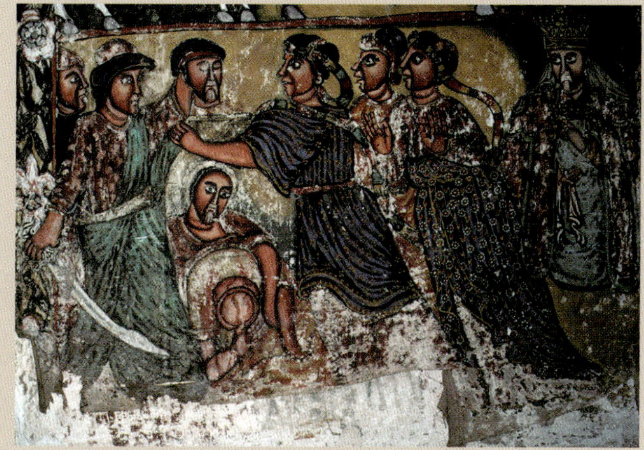

FIG E4.3
Aläqa Estazya (1872–1942,
b. Ethiopia), Ethiopian, Enthroned
Virgin Mary with Child Flanked
by Two Angels and Two Donors;
Two Donors in *Proskynesis* (below);
Choir of Angels (above). St. George,
Ruba Kusa, Tämben, Təgray region,
Ethiopia. Photograph by Michael
Gervers, 2002

FIG E4.4
Ethiopian Orthodox, Saints
Gäbrä Mänfäs Qeddus and
Täklä Haymanot; and Two
Ecclesiastics, Mikael-Gabriel,
Säqota, Wällo, Ethiopia,
second half of the 19th
century. Photograph by Michael
Gervers, 1993

FIG E4.5
Ethiopian Orthodox, Decollation
of Saint John the Baptist,
Zuramba Arägawi, Gayent,
Begemder region, Ethiopia,
18th century. Photograph by
Michael Gervers, 2005

ወፈርህ፡ወኢኮ...ኩ፡ገጽ፡
ውስተ፡ምድር፡ወይቢል
ምን፡ምንት፡ተኃሥሣ፡
ለሕያው፡ምዉታን፡ተን
ሠአ፡ኢ፡ህሎ፡ዝየስ፡ተዘ
ክሩ፡ዘይቤ፡ለክን፡በገሊ
ሉ፡ህለዉ፡ለወልደ፡እጓለ
እመሕያው፡ይግባእ፡ወ
ክቱ፡እይሰብ፡እ፡ኃጥአ
ን፡ወይስቀልዎ፡ወይቀቱ
ልዎ፡ወይትንሣእ፡በሣል
ስት፡ዕለት፡ወተዘከራ፡ቃ
ሉ፡ወአቲምን፡እም፡ነቦ
ም፡ልቀብር፡ነገራ፡ሆሙ፡በ
ሠርቱ፡ወአሐዱ፡ወለቢ
ጸሙ፡ለሦሱ፡ዘንቱ
ወጽጋንቲሱ፡ግርየም፡ወ
ግደለዊት፡ወየሐና፡ወግ
ርያእ፡ቶኩ፡ወቢ
ጸንሂ፡አለ፡ምስሊ፡ሆን
ነገራ፡ሆሙ፡ለሐዋርያት፡
ዘንተ፡ወአነ፡ዝንቱ፡ነገ

ሞዋ፡ሐብሕቲ፡ቸ፡ናቦ
ወአተ፡ወ፡እንዘ፡ያንክረ
ዘኮነ፡ወወ፡እተ፡ዕባተ
እንዘ፡የሐውሩ፡አኤ
እምውስቲ፡ቸሙ፡ሀጊ
ንተ፡ርሕቅት፡እም፡ኢየሩ
ክሌም፡መጠነ፡ስስ፡ምዕ
ራፈ፡እንተ፡ስግ፡አግሐስ
ወይትናገሩ፡በበይናቲሆ
ሙ፡በባሕቲቶሙ፡በእንተ
ሦሉ፡ዘኮነ፡ወይትናገርሙ
ወይትናሠሡ፡ለዝንቱ
ወቀርቦሙ፡ኢየሱስ፡ወሐ
ረ፡ምስሌ፡ሆሙ፡ወተአ
ዘ፡አዕይንቲ፡ሆሙ፡ወአይ
ኑ፡ክሉ፡ኢየ፡አምርሙ
ወይቤሎሙ፡እግዚእ
ምንተኑ፡ዝንቱ፡ነገር፡
ትትናገሩ፡በበይናቲኩ
ሙ፡እንዘ፡ተሐውሩ፡ወ
ቆሙ፡ትኩዘ፡ሆሙ፡ወ
አውሠአ፡አሐዱ፡እም
ሉ፡ወይቤሎ፡ዘክሉ፡ቀበለ፡የ

ቀዳሚሁ፡ቃሉ፡ወ
አቱ፡ወወ፡እቱ፡ቃ
ሉ፡ኀቡ፡እግዚአብ
ሐር፡ወ፡እቱ፡ወእ
ግዚአብ፡ሐረ፡ወ
አቱ፡ቃሉ፡ወኵሎ
ሁ፡አምቀደሉ፡ኮበ
እግዚአብ፡ሔረ
ወ፡አቱ፡ወሣሉ፡ኮቱ
አኩ፡ወዘእንከሊ
ሁኩ፡አልቦ፡ዘኮነ
ወኢምንተኒ፡ወ
ዘኮ፡አኩበእንቱ
አሁ፡ኮቱ፡ሕይወ
ት፡ወአቱ፡ወሐይ
ወትኩ፡ብርሃኑ፡
ለእጓለ፡እመሕያ
ው፡አቱ፡ወብርሃ

አሐዱ፡ብእሲ፡ዘተ
ፈነወ፡እምኀበ፡እ
ግዚአብሔር፡ዘስ
ሙ፡ዮሐንስ፡ወው
እቱ፡መጽአ፡ስምዕ
ተ፡ይኩን፡በእንተ
ብርሃን፡ወብርሃ
ኑ፡ዪቅሱ፡ዘ፡በር
ሁ፡ለሠሉ፡ኩ፡በእዝ
ይመጽእ፡ውክተ፡ዓ
ለም፡ወውክተ፡ዓለ
ም፡ህሱ፡ወዓለም፡ኢ
በቱ፡አኩ፡ወዓለሬ፡ኢ
የእመር፡ወክተ
ዘአሁ፡መጽአ፡ወ
እለአሁ፡ሱ፡ኢተወ
ክፍዱ፡ወእለኩ፡ተ
ወለፍዩ፡ሦሉ

Chapter 5

*The Ethiopian State and the Religious Centers
from the Thirteenth to the Sixteenth Century*

MARIE-LAURE DERAT

A common theme in the writing of Ethiopian history is the close relationship between the monarchs of the Christian kingdom of Ethiopia and its religious centers, especially the monastic communities.[1] This is primarily due to the types of historical sources employed in reconstructing the history of the Highland Christian state. Hagiographies (lives of saints) and royal chronicles, as well as records of land donations, emphasize this close relationship. Although there were sometimes conflicts between the monks and the kings, there was often harmonious accord, as manifested by royal patronage in the founding of churches and the commissioning of manuscripts and paintings. Indeed, the expansion and control of the territories of the Christian kingdom are the result of the close association between royal power and the Ethiopian Church. This nested history can be tracked between the late thirteenth century—when a new Christian regime, the Solomonic dynasty, was established by King Yəkunno Amlak (r. 1270–85)—and the early sixteenth century. Beginning in 1527, the war between the Christian kingdom and the neighboring Islamic sultanate of ʿAdal (or Barr Saʿdaddīn) caused the destruction of Ethiopian religious centers, the decline of the kingdom, and changes in the Christian state.

To better understand the relationship between the monks and the kings, three historical turning points will be examined. The first focuses on the reign of the first Solomonic king, Yəkunno Amlak, and his role in the establishment of churches and the monastery of Däbrä Ḥayq, a monastic community that would become a cultural and artistic center. The second turning point is the founding of Däbrä Libanos, a center of evangelization that during the fourteenth century became the nucleus of a monastic network in the newly conquered territories of the Ethiopian rulers in the region of Šäwa. The community of Däbrä Libanos was among those to seek and maintain some independence in relation to royal authority, but was ultimately forced to cede this independence, becoming the religious arm of the sovereign. The third centers on the figure of King Zärʾa Yaʿəqob (r. 1434–68), whose reign embodies the culmination of this process of reconciliation between the Ethiopian Church and the kingdom as well as the tensions within the Church resulting from this rapprochement.

King Yəkunno Amlak is known to us through his role as patron. He was the founder of the church of Gännätä Maryam, encouraged the founding of other religious monuments, and promoted the development of the monastic center of Däbrä Ḥayq. These acts of patronage allow us to reconstruct significant aspects of his reign.

Yəkunno Amlak became king in 1270 and established the rock-hewn church now known as Gännätä Maryam (Paradise of Mary). Gännätä Maryam is located in the region of Lasta not far from the churches of Lalibäla, the center established by a ruler of the Zagʷe dynasty at the turn of the thirteenth century (fig. 5.1). Locating Gännätä Maryam in this region was presumably intended to affirm the authority of the new Solomonic dynasty in territory previously ruled by the Zagʷe.[2] A pier in the church features a donor portrait of Yəkunno Amlak flanked by two monks identified as Nəḥyo Bäkrəstos and Mäḥari Amlak. The two monks evidently occupied important positions during the emperor's reign. The inscription identifies the king as well as the two monks:

In giving thanks to God. It is I who has (this church) built, (I), Yəkʷənno Amlak whom God made king by his (good) will. My father, Nəḥyo Bäkrəstos, was an agent for me for to have this church built in the name of Mataʾ. May God have mercy upon me in the Kingdom of Heaven with my fathers Mäḥari Amlak and Nəḥyo [Bäkrəstos]. Amen.[3]

Mäḥari Amlak is also represented in a mural in another local church in Waša Mikaʾel, of which he was reportedly the founder. In the inscription accompanying the painting, he is designated as *ṣäware narge* of the kingdom (holder of the container for medicine).[4] He was thus an important figure in Yəkunno's entourage, being one of the dignitaries present at the royal ceremony of anointing the king with the precious perfume.[5]

The narthex of Gännätä Maryam features painted portraits of members of the royal family; they include a "king's son" called Kʷäleṣewon with his mother, Təḥrəyännä Maryam. The latter is also seen in a wall painting in Ǝmäkina Mädḥane ʿAläm, a cave church on Mount Mäkina above Gännätä Maryam (fig. 5.2). Təḥrəyännä Maryam may have been the founder of Ǝmäkina Mädḥane ʿAläm[6] and was possibly the wife of Yəkunno Amlak.

These fragmentary pieces of evidence, which constitute the majority of the historical sources relating to Yəkunno Amlak's reign, highlight both the importance of this region, today known as Lasta, and its importance for the new sovereign. He evidently attempted to impose his authority by founding churches and encouraging his entourage to do the same, thereby leaving his mark upon the territory while contributing to the development of the Ethiopian Church.

Elsewhere, Yəkunno Amlak supported the development of a monastic center of the charismatic abbot Iyäsus Moʾa, who was recognized as a saint shortly after his death. Relatively little is known about Iyäsus Moʾa, because the writing of his hagiography was not undertaken until the late seventeenth century.[7] The hagiography is partly based on

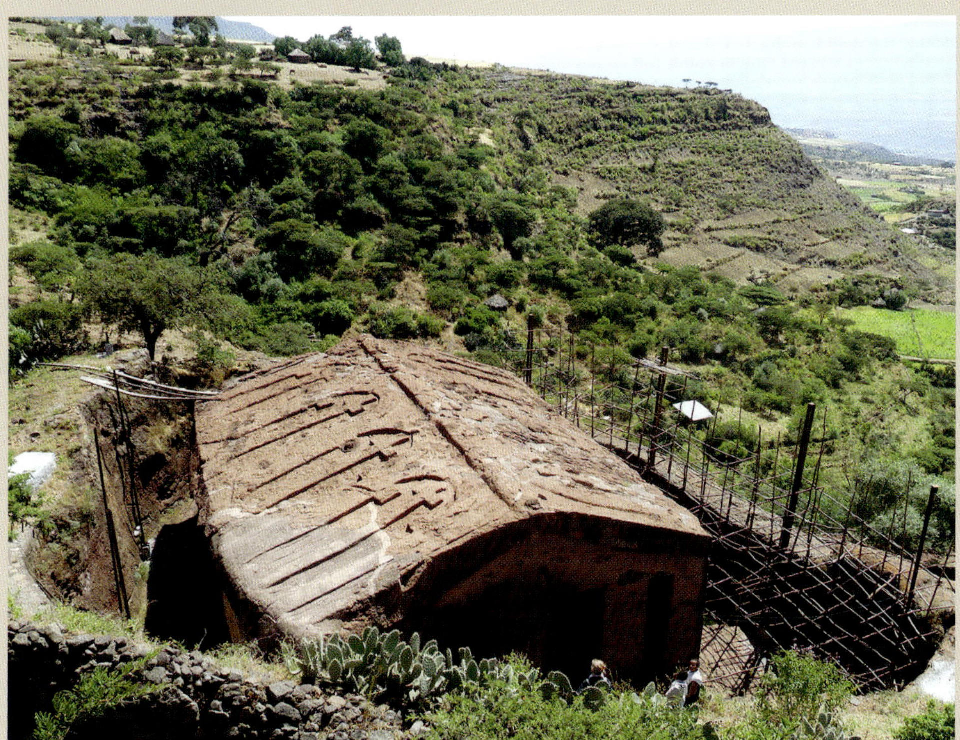

FIG 5.1
Exterior of Gännätä Maryam,
Lalibäla, Ethiopia, 13th century.
Photograph by Marie-Laure
Derat, Mission Lalibela, 2017

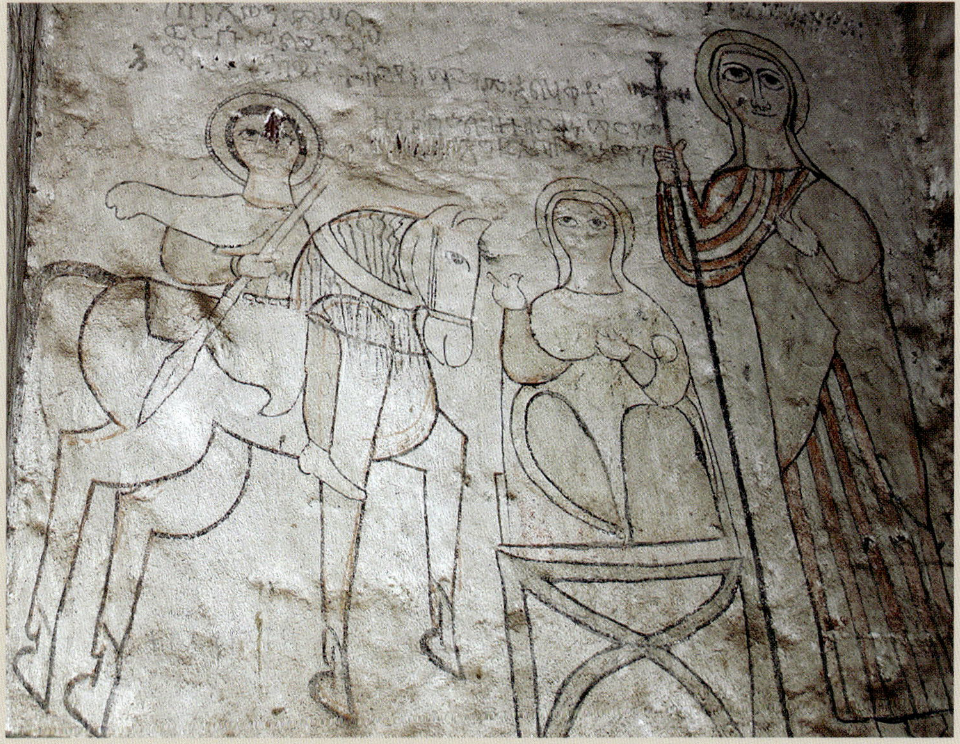

FIG 5.2
Ethiopian Orthodox, Täḥräyännä
Maryam with her son
Kʷäleṣewon, Gännätä Maryam,
Lalibäla, Ethiopia, 13th century.
Photograph by Claire Bosc-
Tiessé, 2012

old documents preserved in manuscripts in Däbrä Ḥayq, the monastery of which he was founder and abbot, established on an island in Lake Ḥayq. Among these documents, the most important are the notes copied into the illuminated liturgical Gospel Book that Iyäsus Mo'a had given to the monastery.[8] One document enumerates the eight-five volumes books the abbot donated to his community prior to his death,[9] indicating that he was a scholar monk who collected many books, not only liturgical and biblical texts but also hagiographic and patristic literature. This book donation marks the initial development of Däbrä Ḥayq as an intellectual and cultural center that would be expanded by Iyäsus Mo'a's successors.

A fifteenth-century inventory recorded in the same Gospel Book numbers 202 books,[10] attesting to the growing importance of the community library. Among those preserved at Däbrä Ḥayq are the Gospels (fig. 5.3) Iyäsus Mo'a donated to the monastery. After the book was granted, King Yagba Ṣəyon (r. 1285–94), son and successor of Yəkunno Amlak, stated that he "adorned with gold and silver this gospel" in 1293–94.[11] Other additions to the manuscript at this time may include a full-page portrait of Iyäsus Mo'a inscribed, "Saint Iyäsus Mo'a," attesting to the recognition of the abbot's sanctity not long after his death. With this added portrait and the gift of the golden covers, the Gospel Book became the Gospels of Saint Iyäsus Mo'a—a dramatic visual transformation promoted by the Ethiopian monarchy that illustrates not only the power of royal patronage in this monastic community but also the link between the saint and the king, a link established during Yəkunno Amlak's reign.[12]

A note in the Gospel Book suggesting a pact between Abbot Iyäsus Mo'a and the king indicates that women were prohibited from the island of Ḥayq; that only monks could build houses in the monastery; and that a monk, once invested with the monastic habit in Ḥayq, could not receive another monastic investiture with a different abbot.[13] The exact terms of the exchange between Yəkunno Amlak and Iyäsus Mo'a are not given,

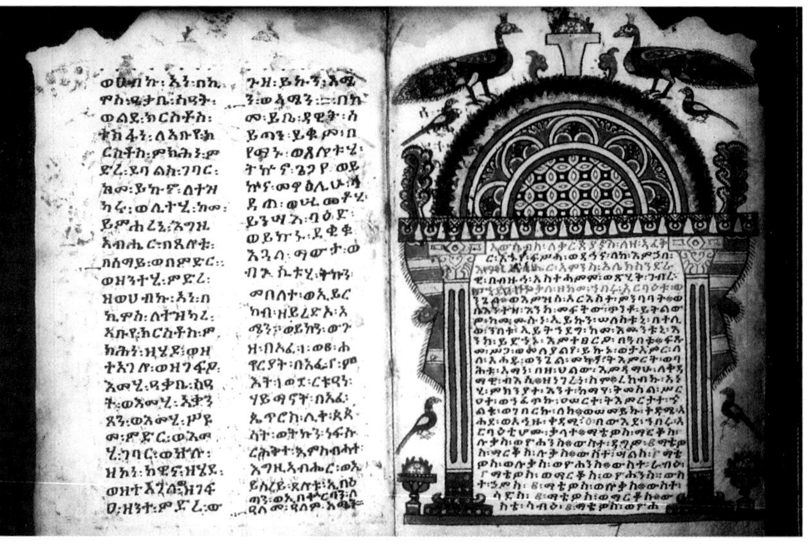

Ethiopian Orthodox, Gospel Book given by Iyäsus Mo'a Hayq Estifānos Monastery, Wällo Province, Ethiopia, 13th century. Parchment, 10 ¹³⁄₁₆ × 6 ⅞ inches (27.5 × 17.5 cm). Virtual Hill Museum & Manuscript Library Reading Room, EMML 1832

but the text specifies that these rights were conferred on the monastery by the king, who in return likely obtained the abbot's support for his reign, support that was periodically renewed with donations of land or liturgical objects, paintings, and manuscripts.

Royal patronage of Däbrä Ḥayq was also manifested by conferring on the abbot the special office of *'aqqabe sä'at*, or "the guardian of hours."[14] The title *'aqqabe sä'at* was not new; the abbot of the older community of Däbrä Libanos in Šämäzana (present-day Eritrea, also known as Ham) held this office at the same time. Abbot Zä'iyäsus (successor to Iyäsus Mo'a) was the first to hold the office, whose exact functions are rarely described in the historical sources. Yəkunno Amlak evidently wished to duplicate the existing ecclesiastical organization in the older northern region of the kingdom in Däbrä Ḥayq in the province of Amhara.[15] A copy of a mid-fifteenth-century letter from *'aqqabe sä'at* Amḫa Lä Ṣəyon of Däbrä Ḥayq to the abbot of Däbrä Kärbe, a monastery located near Aksum, discloses that the *'aqqabe sä'at* exercised his authority over all the monks of the kingdom.[16]

The *'aqqabe sä'at* of Däbrä Ḥayq ultimately became a close advisor to the Ethiopian monarchy while continuing to exercise his authority over the monastic communities of the realm. At times, the abbot of Däbrä Ḥayq and the *'aqqabe sä'at* were two different individuals: there was an abbot who remained in the community and there was the *'aqqabe sä'at*, appointed from among the monks of Däbrä Ḥayq, who resided at the royal court.

DÄBRÄ LIBANOS:
THE DEVELOPMENT OF MONASTIC NETWORKS AND THE SHIFTS OF POWER

Shortly after the founding of Däbrä Ḥayq, another monastic community was established in Šäwa, an area in a southern region, by followers of the teachings of Täklä Haymanot (d. 1313), who was recognized as a saint by the Ethiopian Church (figs. E2.3, 4.4, and 5.4). Initially named Däbrä Asbo, this community was renamed Däbrä Libanos (as it continues to be known) in the mid-fifteenth century by King Zär'a Ya'əqob. There are no contemporary historical sources on Täklä Haymanot. The story of his life, written for his commemoration as a saint, was originally composed a century after his death. At least three other versions of his life were written,[17] in which the hagiographers reworked the text to connect the story of the saint's life to the story of his monastic community. For example, in one of the first versions of the Life of Täklä Haymanot, from the early fifteenth century, he received his monastic habit from a monk named Bäṣälotä Mika'el. A century later, an author revised the text to incorporate the leading religious and intellectual centers and ecclesiastic figures of the time. In this version, Täklä Haymanot's monastic training occurred at Däbrä Ḥayq, where he received instruction from Abbot Iyäsus Mo'a. The fictionalized link between Täklä Haymanot and Iyäsus Mo'a could have rendered the monastery of Däbrä Libanos an auxiliary community, dependent on Däbrä Ḥayq. For this reason, in the sixteenth-century iteration of the Life of Täklä Haymanot, this tradition was supplemented by extensive references to Täklä Haymanot's visit to the monastery of Däbrä Dammo, the ancient monastery in northern Ethiopia that Iyäsus Mo'a had attended, and where Täklä Haymanot received the full

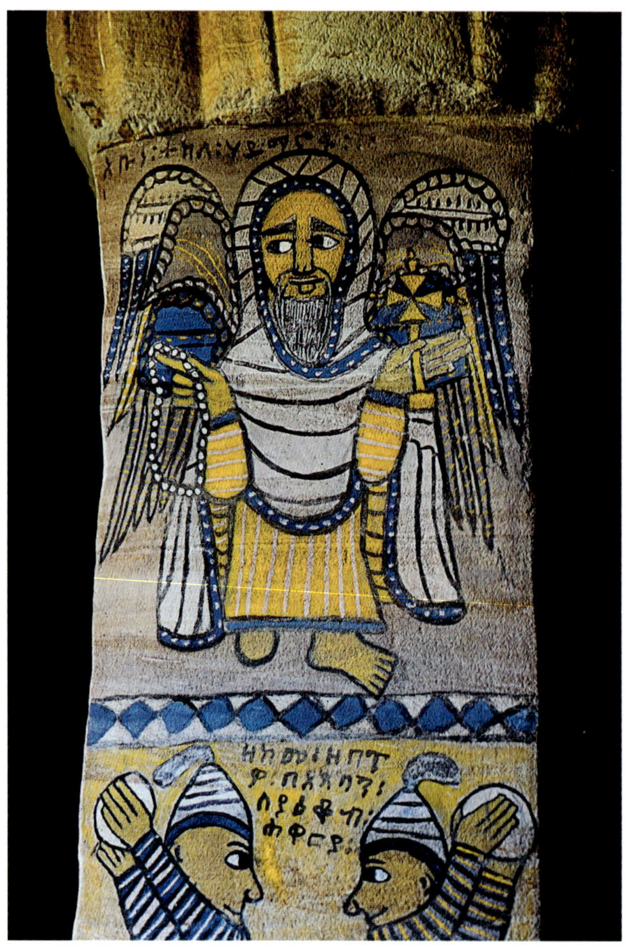

monastic habit. Täklä Haymanot is thus depicted as a disciple of both Yoḥanni, abbot of Däbrä Dammo, and Iyäsus Mo'a.[18] These revisions of his hagiography reflect the nascent rivalry between the monastic houses of Däbrä Ḥayq and Däbrä Libanos.

Däbrä Libanos developed rapidly, in a very different manner than Däbrä Ḥayq. Whereas Däbrä Ḥayq was distinguished as an intellectual center, Däbrä Libanos was primarily devoted to the evangelization of the Šäwa region and the founding of monastic communities by followers of Täklä Haymanot throughout Šäwa and its outskirts.

When Täklä Haymanot was preaching, Šäwa was beyond the control of the Christian kingdom. Indeed, much of the region was under the rule of the Damot kingdom, which seems to have been powerful enough to prevent the spread of the Christian kingdom as well as the Muslim sultanate of Šäwa. This political dynamic shifted during the reign of the Christian king Amda Ṣəyon (r. 1314–44).[19] Famous for his military conquests, his victories are recorded in a historical note copied in the Gospel Iyäsus Mo'a gave to Däbrä Ḥayq: "God gave me all the people of Damot into my hands, its king, its princes, its rulers, and its people, men and women without number, whom I exiled into another area."[20]

Amda Ṣəyon achieved this victory early in his reign, before other areas submitted to his authority and when other eastern regions were under the domain of the Muslim sultanate of Ifat.[21] Thus, the evangelization of the Šäwa region by the sermonizing of Täklä Haymanot and his disciples preceded and later accompanied the territorial conquest. Once the soldiers left, the monks symbolized both the Christianization of the region and its control by Christian rulers. Nevertheless, for many years, the monastery of Däbrä Libanos and its monastic network sought to escape royal hegemony and regularly came into conflict with the monarchy. They denounced royal polygamy and refused any form of royal gifts that might have limited their freedom of speech. Two abbots of Däbrä Libanos, Filəppos and Əndrəyas, led the opposition to the king and faced royal reprisals. One was exiled, the other jailed, and both died far from their communities. Their bodies were transferred to Däbrä Libanos when relations between the monastery and the monarchy improved under Zär'a Ya'əqob (r. 1434–68).

During Abbot Märḥa Krəstos's tenure at Däbrä Libanos, the community of Täklä Haymanot experienced profound changes that resulted in a harmonious relationship between the Ethiopian monarchy and his abbot. This gave the abbot a more powerful position in the kingdom such that the abbot of Däbrä Libanos was able to compete with the abbot of Däbrä Ḥayq. This profound shift was evidently due to Zär'a Ya'əqob's rulership. It was he who appointed Märḥa Krəstos the new abbot of Däbrä Libanos following the death of the imprisoned Abbot Əndrəyas, who had objected to the observance of the Saturday Sabbath in addition to that on Sunday. Zär'a Ya'əqob ruled in favor of Sabbath observance and imposed this reform on the kingdom, forcing the Egyptian metropolitans to write a letter in which they recognized this observance as Orthodox.[22] Zär'a Ya'əqob's endorsement of this reform put an end to decades of conflict between the supporters of this observance and the proponents of Alexandrian Orthodoxy who rejected it. The latter included the Egyptian metropolitan bishop and a large segment of the clergy of the southern portion of the kingdom, especially the abbots of Däbrä Ḥayq and Däbrä Libanos.

Zär'a Ya'əqob secured the loyalty of the monastery and its monks with the renaming of the community of Täklä Haymanot as Däbrä Libanos (1449), the death of Abbot Əndrəyas (1463), the selection of a new abbot (Märḥa Krəstos), and the permanent placement of two monks from the community to his court.[23] The king's guardianship brought about consequential changes for the community, as reflected in the new tone of the monks' texts. Prior to this alliance, the monks could slip some harsh criticism of the monarchy into the life stories of the holy abbots, as in the early fifteenth-century Life of Abbot Filəppos, who died in exile.[24] Such was not the case with Abbot Märḥa Krəstos, whose texts composed in Däbrä Libanos reflect the harmonious relationship between the king and the monastery. The early sixteenth-century Life of Abbot Märḥa Krəstos portrays the abbot as the guarantor of the continuity of the monarchy, a pillar of power.[25] He is credited with producing many manuscripts and writing numerous texts for the monastery (fig. 5.5).[26] The monastery's change in attitude toward royal authority is evident in the position conferred on Märḥa Krəstos and his successors within the network of royal churches and monasteries.[27]

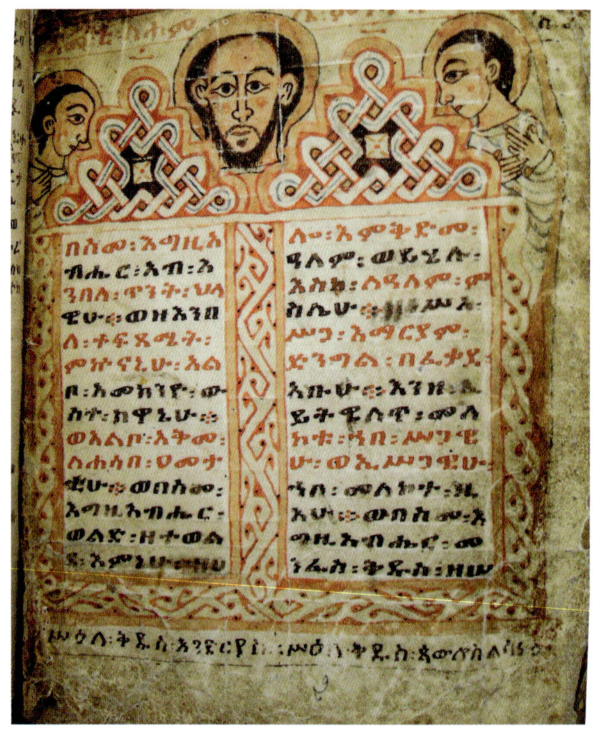

Beginning with Yəkunno Amlak, founder of the church of Gännätä Maryam, Ethiopian monarchs exercised their role as patron, building churches and monasteries primarily in central regions of power such as Amhara, where Däbrä Ḥayq was established, and Šäwa, where Däbrä Libanos was located. Churches and royal monasteries played an increasingly important role in the kingdom, serving as residences for the royal mobile court, meeting places for the great councils, and tombs for kings: institutions that once again illustrate the close association between the Church and the kingdom.[28] From the time of Zär'a Ya'əqob, royal monasteries were placed under the authority of the abbot of Däbrä Libanos. By the end of the fifteenth century, the abbot was the head not only of his monastic community but also of the network of monastic houses founded by the disciples of Täklä Haymanot and of the royal monasteries, where he held the sole authority to bestow the monastic habit on novices.[29]

The church of Məsḥalä Maryam was among the royal churches and monasteries established by the Ethiopian monarchs under the authority of Däbrä Libanos. Founded by Bä'ədä Maryam (r. 1468–78), son and successor of Zär'a Ya'əqob, Məsḥalä Maryam was located in northern Šäwa in the region of Mänz. This church is known to us largely because of the Gospel Book given by the sovereign to the church at the time of its founding. Now in a private collection, the volume (fig. 5.6), contains records of donations and historical notes that document royal patronage and the church's role in the network of royal churches and monasteries.[30] Of note in the Gospel of Məsḥalä Maryam is the account of a land grant renewed by King Ǝskəndər (r. 1478–94). The thus-far unidentified recipient of the land grant evokes the presence of witnesses who are the guarantors of this donation, the religious leaders of three royal churches founded by Zärʾa Yaʿəqob: Məshalä Maryam, Däbrä Bərhan in Amhara,[31] and Däbrä Mətmaq in Šäwa. The recorder of this note is none other than the official spokesman of the king (*afä nəguś*), a priest from the royal church of Atronsä Maryam in Amhara, also founded by Bäʾədä Maryam. As such, this document attests to the important role played by ecclesiastical leaders of the royal churches. They formed a sort of college tending to the sovereign and representing him in his absence.

The church of Məshalä Maryam was part of the larger political and religious project to establish royal symbols of authority in the central regions of Amhara and Šäwa in order to remind the inhabitants they were governed by a Christian monarch whose power was ever present, even if he was not always physically present. These royal symbols also forged links between the different regions where royal church-es were established. These relationships were vividly manifested at major ceremo-nies, where the clergy from each royal church was assembled.[32] The document in the Gospel of Məshalä Maryam lists four ecclesiastical dignitaries as witnesses, including the head priest of Məshalä Maryam and the spokesman of the king from the royal church of Atronsä Maryam; from this we may infer that a grand ceremony was held there. Another document in the Gospel notes that Bäʾədä Maryam had made the journey to the church for the founding ceremony. We may imagine the splendor of this event, with the royal entourage and with the presence of the abbot of Däbrä Libanos, whose authority extended over all the monks attached to the royal monasteries.

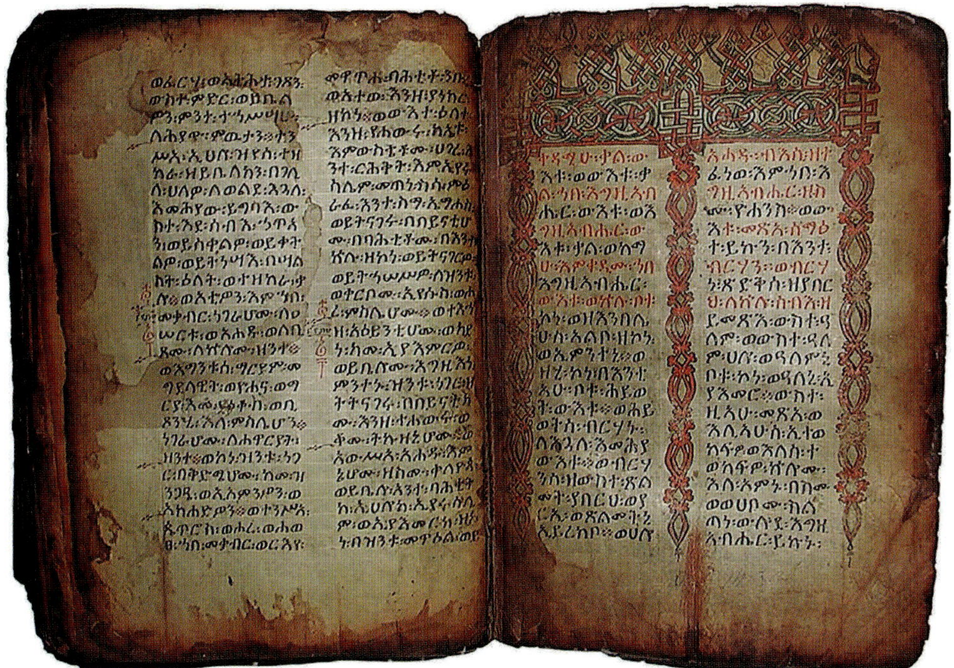

Ethiopian Orthodox, Gospel Book given by king Bäʾədä Maryam to the church of Məshalä Maryam, 15th century. Vellum. Schoyen Collection, MS 2850

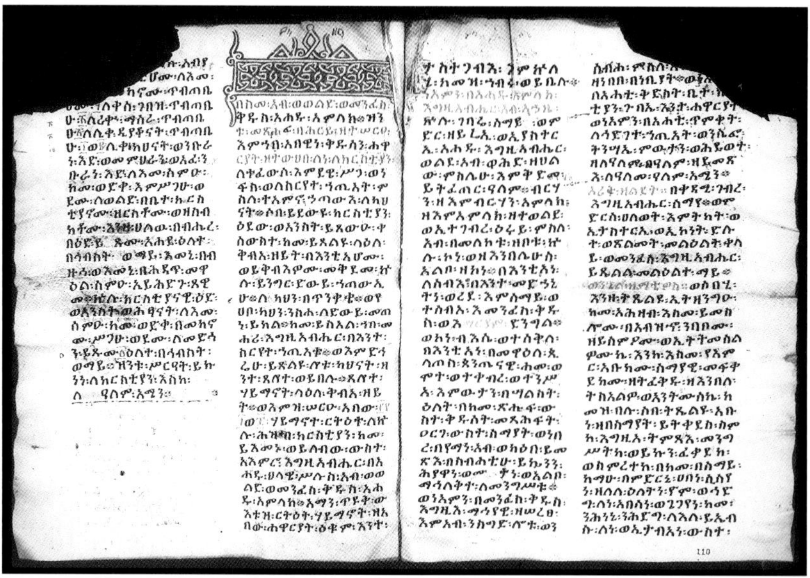

THE REIGN OF ZÄR'A YA'ƎQOB

Zär'a Ya'əqob is among the figures who best embodies the union between the monastic centers and royal sovereignty. Son of King Dawit (r. 1379/80–1412), whom he succeeded after several of his brothers had been in power, Zär'a Ya'əqob followed in his father's footsteps. Like his father, his regnal name was Constantine and he was designated the "Orthodox King." Dawit had translated the Book of Miracles of Mary from Arabic into Gə'əz; Zär'a Ya'əqob completed the work by adding local stories to the book, which was then disseminated throughout the kingdom.[33] But whereas Dawit had allowed the supporters of Sabbath observance to follow their own dogma, Zär'a Ya'əqob, as noted above, forced the observance of Saturday Sabbath upon the entire Ethiopian Church.[34]

Zär'a Ya'əqob's reign undoubtedly marked a seminal moment in the history of the Christian kingdom of Ethiopia. A pious scholar, Zär'a Ya'əqob encouraged the writing of many homiletic works, some of which he himself probably wrote.[35] He also denounced his adversaries, such as a dignitary accused of plotting against the king.[36] Many individuals—including his own children—who manifested the slightest opposition to his reforms were depicted as heretics and sentenced to death for heresy.[37]

The texts Zär'a Ya'əqob sponsored served a dual function: they allowed the sovereign to make known and then implement his religious reforms. For example, he mandated that thirty-three feasts of Mary were to be observed throughout the liturgical year. Toward this goal, he worked to complete the readings in celebration of these new feasts, which included passages he wished to be disseminated throughout the kingdom. Texts produced under his direction were copied and widely disseminated throughout the realm for public reading on special feast days. Each church was to have a copy, although there is no proof that this was indeed the case.

    ETHIOPIAN DEVOTIONS

A large manuscript (fig. 5.7) containing many homilies written under Zär'a Ya'əqob's supervision speaks to how texts written in the royal court were distributed to the monasteries. It was discovered at Däbrä Maryam of Qwäḥayn, a church located in the kingdom's northern territory (present-day Eritrea).[38] Däbrä Maryam of Qwäḥayn evidently occupied a special position. One of its monks, an ecclesiastic of the court, served at the royal Church of Mary during Zär'a Ya'əqob's reign.[39] The story of his life was added to the homilies in this manuscript, perhaps to emphasize the role the church had played in the drafting or distribution of the king's texts.[40]

One homily written under the king's supervision included text celebrating his military victory over the Muslim sultan of 'Adal in the Battle of Gomit in 1445.[41] A passage from correspondence between the *'aqqabe sä'at* of Däbrä Ḥayq and the church of Däbrä Karbe near Aksum, the text belongs to a collection of homilies known as the *Book of the Nativity* (*Mäṣḥafä Milad*).[42] Like other homilies, it was to be read at church during Mass on the anniversary of the victory, particularly at Christmas. It was also appended to the Miracles of Mary.[43] When Zär'a Ya'əqob's son, Bä'ədä Maryam, founded the royal church of Məṣḥalä Maryam, he donated many manuscripts to the new institution, including two works by his father: the *Book of the Nativity* (*Mäṣḥafä Milad*) and the *Epistle of Humanity* (*Ṭomarä təsbə'ət*).[44]

Some monastic communities, however, did not accept the monarchy's tight grip on the definition of Orthodoxy. These communities debated doctrinal issues such as the definition of the Trinity or the place of the Virgin. Among these communities were disciples of the monk Ǝsṭifanos, who was tortured at the court and died in exile in 1444. Designated as heretics by the king, these disciples, known as Stephanites, were harshly oppressed by the sovereign. Known for manuscripts produced in the community of Gundä Gunde, the monks authored texts to defend their theological stance but also to attack their chief antagonist, the king.[45] One of these texts tells the story of the death of Zär'a Ya'əqob. In this text, a literary declaration of autonomy, the king is described as "terrified and fearful" because he thought that he would be killed by supernatural means. For that reason, he "executed countless persons from the nobility, the clergy and the monks."[46] The image of the king here is the exact opposite of the one promoted in the kingdom by the court's ecclesiastics.

Manuscript production in the Christian kingdom of Ethiopia thus reflects the relationships between the monks and the monarchs. Royal patronage encouraged the building of churches and the donations of books and wealth to monastic institutions. In return, the monks participated in the life of the kingdom: the control of territory, evangelization, and the dissemination of the ideal of a united Christian kingdom under the authority of the ruler (*nəguś*). All this did not come without conflict, however, as attested by texts written by the Ethiopian monks.

Images of God

MARILYN E. HELDMAN

Emperor Zär'a Ya'əqob (r. 1434–68) wrote that while no one has seen God, his perfect and terrifying divinity is akin to that of human form.[1] Various icons from his reign portray God directly or through union whereby Father and Son embody one being. Painted icons and an incised ebony icon (figs. 2.9 a and b) show God as the Ancient of Days (Daniel 7:9). An icon attributed to the mid-fifteenth-century Ethiopian painter Frē Ṣəyon shows a baby Jesus, while the inscription on his robe, "King of Kings and Lord of Lords" (Revelation 19:16), indicates this icon represents the consubstantiality of God the Father with the Son (fig. E5.1).[2]

Representations of the Holy Trinity (the Triune God, or Father, Son, and Holy Spirit, in the form of three identical persons) did not become common in Ethiopian art until the late seventeenth century,[3] when Emperor Iyasu I (r. 1682–1706) built the church of Däbrä Bərhan Śəllase, dedicated to the Holy Trinity, on the outskirts of Gondär. Consecrated in January 1694, the church was struck by lightning and burned in 1707 and was then rebuilt, and rebuilt again in the early nineteenth century (fig. 6.3). Depictions of the Holy Trinity in the later churches were probably modeled on that pictured in Iyasu I's original structure (fig. E5.2).[4]

The combination of the Crucifixion (*Seqlat*) and the *Tanse'a* (literally "raising up"), picturing Christ raising Adam and Eve from their sarcophagi in the Underworld (fig. E5.3), first appeared in Ethiopian diptychs during the sixteenth century. By the early seventeenth century, this pair of images, signifying Christ's triumph over death, emerged as an auxiliary theme in many icons, often in the form of a triptych. This addition is especially appropriate for icons dedicated to Our Lady Mary, Mother of Christ the Savior (fig. E5.4).

Tanse'a may also be translated as "resurrection"—a somewhat misleading title because the composition does not portray Christ's rising from the tomb on the third day as in the Gospel accounts (Matthew 28:1–8, Mark 16:1–6, Luke 24:1–7, John 20: 1–14). Instead, it refers to Christ's descent to Sheol (the Underworld) while his body hung on the Cross. Fifteenth-century Ethiopian literature yields a handful of references to Christ in the Underworld. And the Anaphora of the Apostles, an ancient liturgy that Zär'a Ya'əqob recognized above all others, states, "Who was delivered to the passion that he might destroy death, broke the bonds of Satan, tread down to hell, and lead forth the saints."[5]

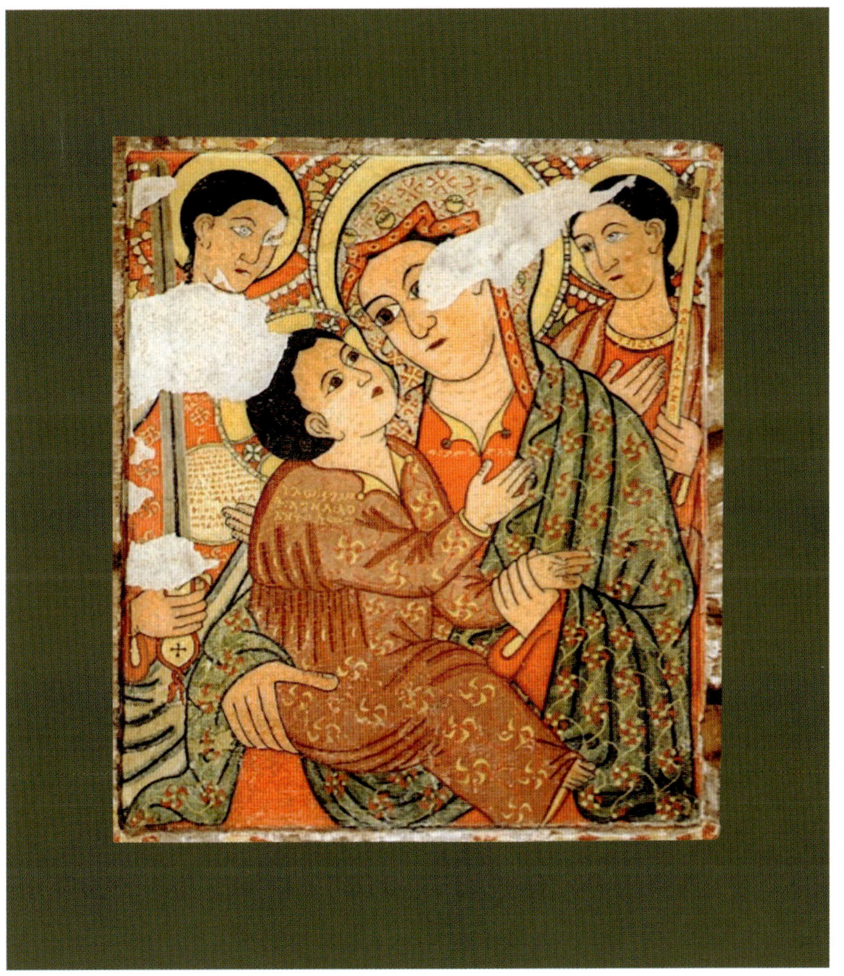

FIG E5.1

Frē Ṣəyon, Ethiopian, Spiritual Mirror (Illustration IV), Virgin and Christ, Saints Michael and Gabriel, 1445–80. Icon. Tempera on gesso-covered wood panel, 23 × 22 ¾ inches (58.4 × 57.8 cm). Private collection

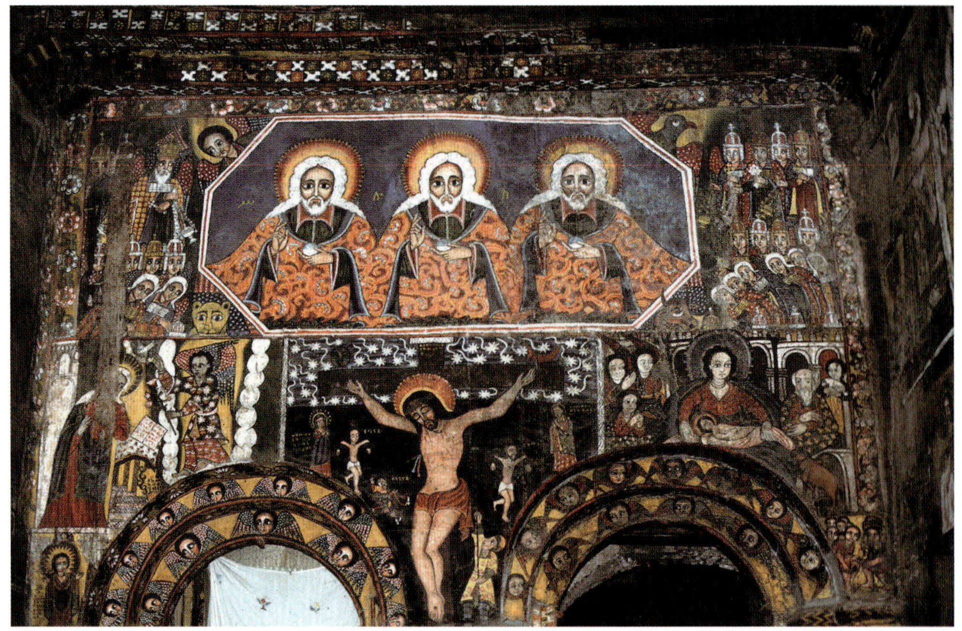

Zär'a Ya'əqob's embrace of this story led the Synaxary of the Ethiopian Orthodox Church to create an annual feast marking Christ's passage into the Underworld. Called *Tazkarä adhon* (Commemoration of the Savior), it takes place on 27 Maggabit. The Synaxary reading is brief, essentially stating that when Jesus Christ "was hung on the wood of the Cross, he descended into Hell in order to release those in bondage."[6] This commemoration of Christ may have prompted the creation of this visual epitome of Christ as Savior and the juxtaposition of the Crucifixion and the Raising of Adam and Eve.

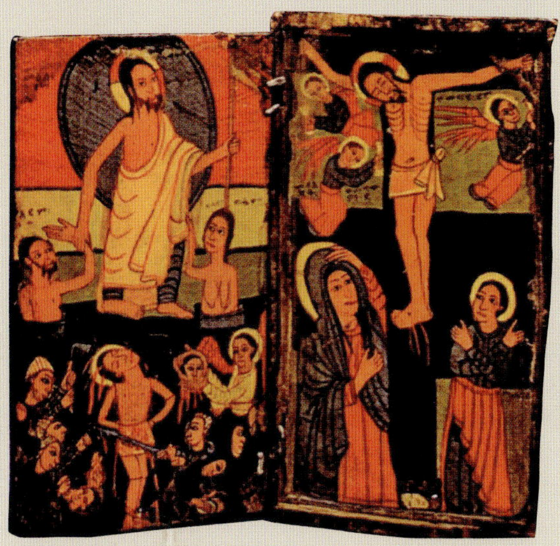

FIG E5.3

Ethiopian Orthodox, Crucifixion and Resurrection of Christ and the Martyrdom of Saint George, mid- to late 17th century. Tempera on gesso-covered wood panels, 10 ⅞ × 6 ⅛ × ⅝ inches (27.6 × 15.6 × 1.6 cm). Harn Museum, partial gift of Richard Faletti and museum purchase, funds provided by the Caroline Julier and James G. Richardson Acquisition Endowment, Michael A. Singer and the David A. Cofrin Art Acquisition Endowment

FIG E5.4

Ethiopian Orthodox, early 16th century. Distemper, gesso, and cloth on wood, 12 ¹³⁄₁₆ × 16 ⁵⁄₁₆ × ³⁄₁₆ inches (31 × 41.5 × 1.4 cm). National Museum of African Art, Smithsonian Institution, Gift of Ciro R. Taddeo in memory of Dr. Volker Stitz, Ph.D., 98-3-1

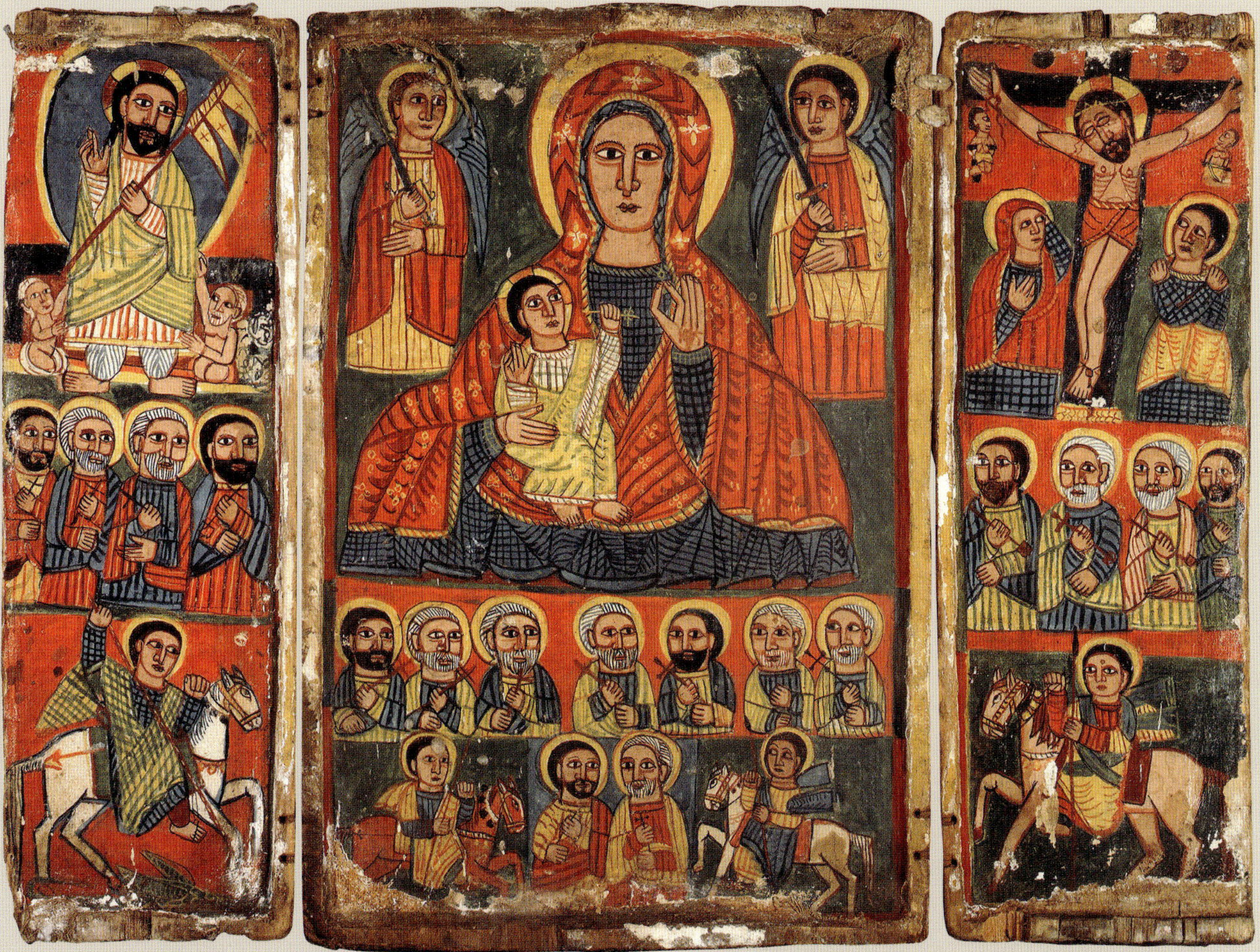

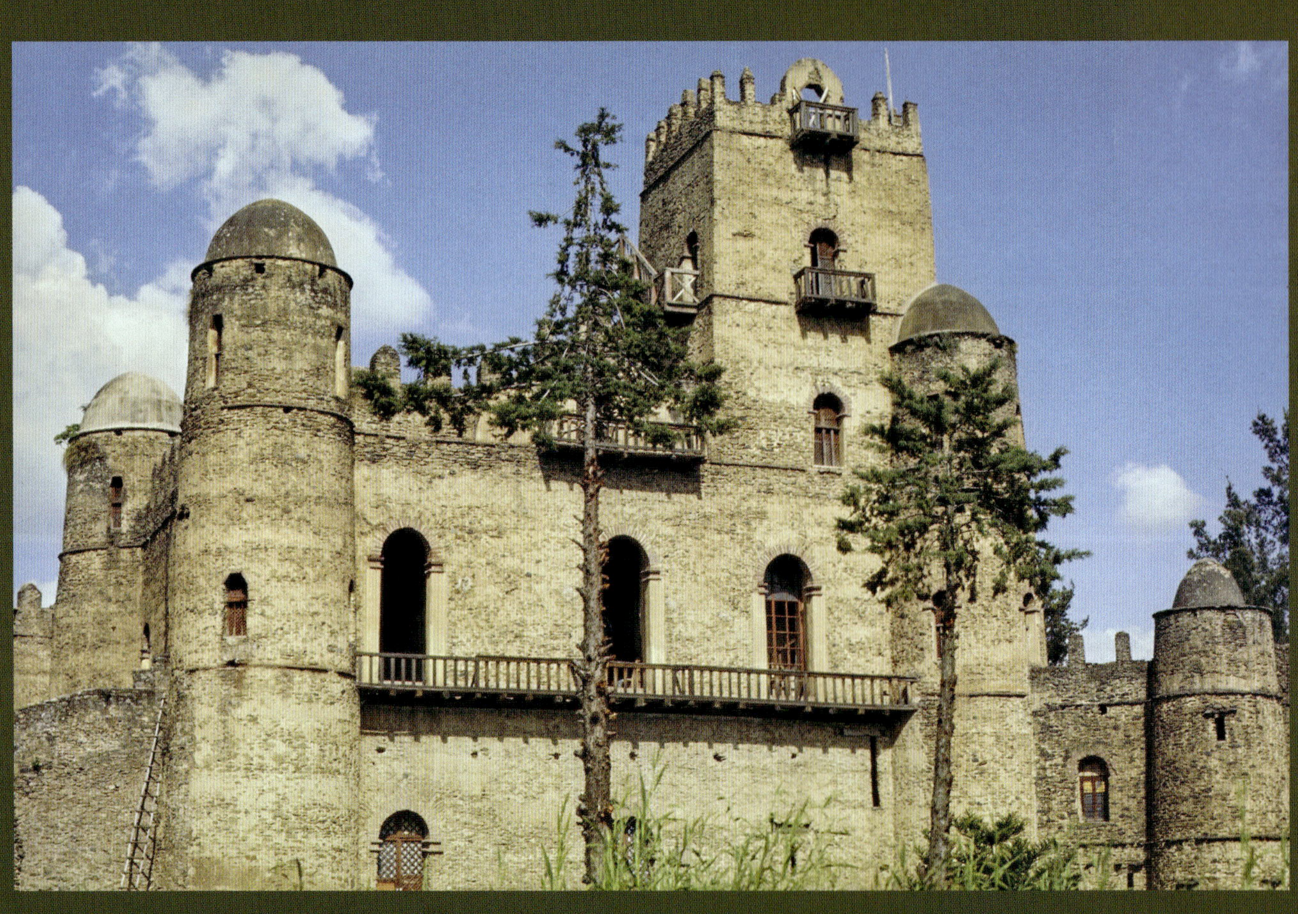

Chapter 6

*The Late Solomonic (Gondär) Period, the Mid-Sixteenth
to the Mid-Nineteenth Century*

LAVERLE BERRY

From the mid-sixteenth to the mid-nineteenth century, the Christian kingdom of Ethiopia faced threats to its very existence and identity as well as witnessed significant cultural achievements. Among the major threats were invasion, mass migration into the heartland of the kingdom, and religious strife. Once these challenges were overcome, an era of cultural flowering ensued that was especially notable in art and architecture. This flowering faded during the nineteenth century, but its influence is still in evidence today.

In the early sixteenth century, the kingdom and its society were very much as they had been during the reign of Emperor Yəkunno Amlak (r. 1270–85), the founder of the so-called Solomonic Dynasty in the late thirteenth century. The dynasty he established became known as "Solomonic" because he and his successors claimed descent from King Solomon and the Queen of Sheba (1 Kings 10:1–13) as a means of enhancing their legitimacy. As before, society was structured around the emperor and his court officials on the one hand, and the metropolitan (patriarch) of the Ethiopian Orthodox Church, known as the *abun*, together with the monks of the two or three dominant monasteries, on the other. Below them were the great nobles serving as governors in the provinces, the lesser nobility, clerics in local parishes, monks in monasteries, and, finally, the local population engaged in farming and/or herding. In addition, there were units of royal soldiers stationed at the kingdom's frontiers and a class of merchants and traders. Emperors were warrior-kings, military leadership being a primary function of the office. A succession of emperors had established military supremacy over their enemies, namely, the Muslim principalities along the kingdom's eastern frontier. The bond between church and state, established under Yəkunno Amlak, remained firm.

During the sixteenth century the kingdom confronted three major challenges to its security and identity, all of which had grave consequences for the future of the realm: an invasion by its Muslim neighbors from the east, the migration of the Oromo pastoralists from the south, and the introduction of Roman Catholicism by Jesuit priests.

In the late 1520s, the kingdom suffered military defeats in its southeast region that opened it up to invasion and occupation. Between 1529 and 1543, Muslim forces

Ethiopian Orthodox, Fasilädäs's castle within the royal enclosure of Fasil Ghebbi, Gondär, Ethiopia, 17th century. Photograph by Marilyn E. Heldman, ca. 1973. National Museum of African Art, Smithsonian Institution, Eliot Elisofon Photographic Archives, EEPA 2013-013-0111 from the kingdom of ʿAdal to the east-southeast of the kingdom under a remarkable leader, Aḥmad b. Ibrāhīm al-Gāzī—known to Ethiopians as Grañ, the "Left-Handed"—overran nearly the entirety of the kingdom. Their aim was to destroy the Ethiopian state and its Christian culture. In the process, Grañ's army destroyed much of the literary and artistic achievements of the early Solomonic period as they burned down churches, killed monks and nuns, destroyed records and works of art, and forced mass conversions to Islam. Emperor Ləbnä Dəngəl (r. 1508–40) was compelled to flee from pillar to post to escape Grañ's army. He sought extensive assistance from Portugal, whose envoys had visited Ethiopia in the 1520s and whose fleet was based at Goa in India. With the help of a Portuguese expeditionary force that arrived in 1541, Grañ was killed in 1543, and his forces thereafter driven back to their homeland.[1]

The war with Adäl, however, paved the way for the Oromo, a pastoral people to the south whose culture and language were only distantly related to those of the Christian highlanders, to migrate into the kingdom. The Oromo advanced relentlessly north and west into the heartland of the kingdom in a series of raids and warfare that lasted for more than a century. They displaced as well as settled among the local population, the beginning of a long process of acculturation in Christian Ethiopia. In frontier regions such as those along the Abbay (Blue Nile) River and in the central province of Wällo, they gradually assimilated into northern society and its Christian culture.[2] As for Roman Catholicism, Catholic prelates were present by midcentury but their presence was of limited consequence until the first decade of the seventeenth century.

Reconstructing the kingdom's administration and institutions in the aftermath of the Muslim invasion and the Oromo's ongoing incursions were the major tasks confronting Emperor Śärṣ́ä Dəngəl (r. 1563–97). He came to the throne at the age of thirteen and spent his first years struggling to secure his succession. He faced conspiracies and rebellions by the governors of the major provinces, who wished either to claim the throne for themselves or seat a candidate of their own choosing. Amid the wars against Grañ, provincial nobles and governors had recruited armies of their own and were now, in the mid-sixteenth century, far less reliant on the throne than previously in matters of defense and governance, and sometimes not even for their appointments. And while Śärṣ́ä Dəngəl and his successors continued to rule by right of Solomonic blood and to function in their role as warrior-kings, they were forced to ally themselves with groups of nobles and to rule with the support of factions that formed coalitions of these same provincial nobles.

In keeping with his royal forebears, Śärṣ́ä Dəngəl initially based himself in the province of Šäwa, the traditional heartland of the kingdom. From there he campaigned against the Oromo, who nonetheless continued to push north and northwest into what up till then had been the domain of Amhara and Ṭəgray farmers and herdsmen. In the mid-1570s, however, he moved his military headquarters from Šäwa to the district of Ǝnfraz on the northeast shore of Lake Ṭana in part to enforce payment of tribute from his governors, profit from commerce in the region, and perhaps also find a locale safely removed from Oromo raids. There, he built a stone castle and a church in the midst of monasteries and churches inhabited by monks and clerics of the Orthodox Church who had escaped the chaos and warfare of recent decades. Known as Guzara, the new military camp served as headquarters for annual military campaigns, for celebrations of Lent and Easter, and as the site to which Śärṣ´ä Dəngəl and his army returned to spend the rainy season year after year. Ǝnfraz also became a hub for the spiritual rejuvenation of Orthodoxy. In an effort to reverse mass conversions to Islam under Grañ, Ǝnfraz's clerics and monks copied Gospels, theological treatises, and the like, and distributed them throughout the northern highlands. They also produced a revised Synaxary of the Orthodox Church.[3]

After a short, troubled interregnum, the empire passed to Emperor Susǝnyos (r. 1605–32). He was the archetypal warrior-king; he fought for the throne and thereafter campaigned constantly against the Oromo, the Betä Ǝsra'el, and the Agäw, the Indigenous inhabitants of the northern highlands. As his reign progressed, Susǝnyos became increasingly intrigued by Roman Catholicism, thereby posing one of the most significant challenges ever to Ethiopian Orthodoxy and to his countrymen's national identity. From their inception, Solomonic monarchs were effectively the secular heads of the Orthodox Church; they were the chief protectors of the Church and the guarantors of its mission and well-being. It was this bond between church and state, forged by Yǝkunno Amlak and maintained by his successors, that Susǝnyos abandoned in his fascination with and later conversion to Roman Catholicism.

The conversion came at the hands of Jesuit missionaries, who initially entered the kingdom in part to attend to the spiritual needs of the remnants of the Portuguese military expedition of the early 1540s but also to attempt to Romanize the Orthodox Ethiopians. By the early seventeenth century they were present at the royal court, where they discussed matters of theology and ecclesiastical organization and practice with Susǝnyos, his courtiers, and Orthodox prelates. Susǝnyos showed increasing interest in Catholicism and also, it appears, in the technical skills the Jesuits and their laymen demonstrated in constructing European-style buildings. He publicly announced his conversion in 1622, which was followed by those of the royal family, his courtiers, and a segment of the nobility with their soldiers and kinsmen. By the late 1620s, the Jesuits claimed a large number of converts in the Lake Ṭana region, and Roman Catholicism had become the official state religion. The fathers were in regular attendance at Susǝnyos's capital, Dänqäz, where he built a castle and the Jesuits a church alongside it. They also established other centers, including a major complex at Azäzo, a short distance north of Lake Ṭana.[4]

The attempt to implant Roman Catholicism, however, provoked revulsion and rebellion among the staunchly Orthodox Ethiopians. Susǝnyos fell ill and died in 1632, still a Roman Catholic, but Fasilädäs (r. 1632–67), his son and successor and himself a former Roman Catholic, expelled the Jesuits and immediately reinstated Ortho- doxy. Nonetheless, the impact of the kingdom's encounter with the Jesuits and Roman Christianity continued to manifest itself in succeeding decades in art, theology, and statecraft.[5]

Fasilädäs abandoned Dänqäz and its association with the Jesuits and in 1636 established his court at Gondär, some thirty-five kilometers north of Lake Ṭana, which featured a way station for Muslim merchants. It was a well-watered site and easily defended, being surrounded by mountains on three sides and open on the south to Lake Ṭana, to long-distance commerce, and fertile agricultural lands. There, he built a castle (fig. 6.1) and founded seven churches, among them Mädḥane ʿAläm ("Savior of the World") and Gəmǧa Bet Maryam ("Mary of the Treasury"), which are still in existence today. Bridges and a large water basin used in annual Epiphany celebrations, known locally as "Fasil's Bath," are also attributed to him. Fasilädäs's son, Yoḥannəs I (r. 1667–82), and his grandson, Iyasu I (r. 1682–1706), chose to remain at Gondär, building their own castles and churches, so that by the late seventeenth century Gondär had become a permanent capital with artisans, clerics, merchants, nobles, and soldiers all gathered around the royal court in distinct quarters. This permanence was in contrast with earlier Solomonic practice, when rulers were based in Šäwa. There, emperors lived in mobile tent camps, moving constantly as they campaigned, as they sought sustenance for their courts, and as a way to assert royal power and authority. Although Gondär rulers maintained a permanent capital, they continued the practice of annual military campaigns during the dry season and residence in the royal camp, now Gondär, during the rainy season. The permanence gave rise to a new dynamic in artistic, political, religious, and social affairs.[6]

More than a search for security brought Fasilädäs to Gondär. The Lake Ṭana basin was the hub of a network of trade routes. The prospect of profiting from the commerce that flowed along these routes was a primary factor that drew Śärṣʾä Dəngəl to the Ṭana region and helps explain why his successors chose to remain there as well. A major trade route ran from the Red Sea at Məṣəwwaʾ across the province of Ṭəgray to Ṭana and from there farther south across the Abbay to rich agricultural lands in the kingdom's southern provinces. Subsidiary branches ran southeast to Šäwa, east to salt flats along the Red Sea, and west to gold lands in present-day Sudan. These routes all converged in or close to northern Lake Ṭana, where communities of Muslim merchants and traders were long established in places such as Ǝnfraz and Gondär. These merchants brought gold, coffee, civet, and even slaves from the south and west to Red Sea ports, where they exchanged them for cloth (primarily silk from India), clothing, carpets, glassware, and other luxury goods from the Middle East and India prized by the Ethiopian nobility and royal court. This flow of commerce constituted a source of wealth, and it was to protect, supervise, and levy tolls on it that Fasilädäs located his new camp alongside the merchants at Gondär.[7]

Other than court expenses and payments to soldiers, the newfound wealth was used for monumental construction and to patronize the arts, craftwork, and the production of manuscripts, both religious and historical, including royal chronicles, thereby continuing a tradition of records written in Gəʾəz, an indigenous script that was more than a thousand years old. Distinctive features of Gondär Period Ethiopia, as the era from the mid-seventeenth century to the later eighteenth century is known, were castles and churches constructed in a new architectural style unrelated to any prior buildings in the northern highlands. Churches were long-established features of the highland landscape; castles, however, were an innovation. A new style of architecture as well as new methods of construction were introduced into the kingdom in the mid-sixteenth century, most likely from the Red Sea region, and Emperor Śärṣ´ä Dəngəl employed them when he built the first castle at Ǝnfraz on the main north-south caravan route (fig. 6.2). Constructed of brown basalt, it was a two-story building with round, domed towers on the corners, arched doors and windows decorated with colored stone, and crowned with a battlemented terrace roof, features present in nearly all subsequent castles that define the new architecture, known as the Gondär Style. While clearly military in appearance, the castles were not meant for defense. Rather, they seem to have been intended to project—and perhaps help reconstitute—the power and image of Solomonic kingship as a military office, towering as they did over the humble dwellings of common folk.[8]

Churches, especially those commissioned by a succession of emperors, were also built in the Gondär Style, most notably in their surrounding walls with domed towers and entrance gates. Nonetheless, they always retained their traditional trifold division of interior sacred space. Several were built in Gondär in the royal compound and in the different quarters of the city. Among the best known is Däbrä Bərhan Śəllase ("Mount of the Light of the Trinity"), constructed by Iyasu I in the late 1690s as a church in the round but subsequently rebuilt in a smaller, rectangular design (fig. 6.3). Further afield, Fasilädäs rebuilt in Gondär Style architecture the ancient church of Maryam Ṣəyon ("Mary of Zion") at Aksum that had been destroyed in the Muslim wars with Grañ. Fasilädäs' son, Yoḥannəs I, commissioned Ǝgzi'abəher-Ab ("God the Father") at Ṭädda, twenty-five kilometers south of Gondär, in a similar architectural style. Churches continued to be built in and around Gondär not only by emperors but also by local notables such that by the later eighteenth century the greater Gondär region had become famous as the home of forty-four churches.[9]

These included Täklä Haymanot at Azäzo, which Fasilädäs constructed on land once allocated to the Jesuits. There, he settled the monks and abbot (*ačǯage*) of the monastery of Däbrä Libanos, who had lost their home after the Muslims and then the Oromo overran Šäwa. Other monastic houses also found homes in and around Gondär, such as at Waldəbba to the north, or those of Ewosṭatewos, who maintained a presence in Gondär but whose home base was in Goǧǧam, south of Lake Ṭana. Somewhat further removed were the much older churches and monasteries in Lake Ṭana, which were now connected to the kingdom's political center as never before.

This proximity was unlike the early Solomonic period, when the Church establishment was divided among several centers. One was the royal court, where the *abun* was always in residence. Others were major monastic enclaves such as Däbrä Libanos in Šäwa and Däbrä Ḥayq Ǝsṭifanos in Wällo. By contrast, Gondär became the ecclesiastical locus of the Church and the kingdom to a degree probably not seen since the days of ancient Aksum. The *abun* and the *ačǯage* resided in their own quarters of the city.

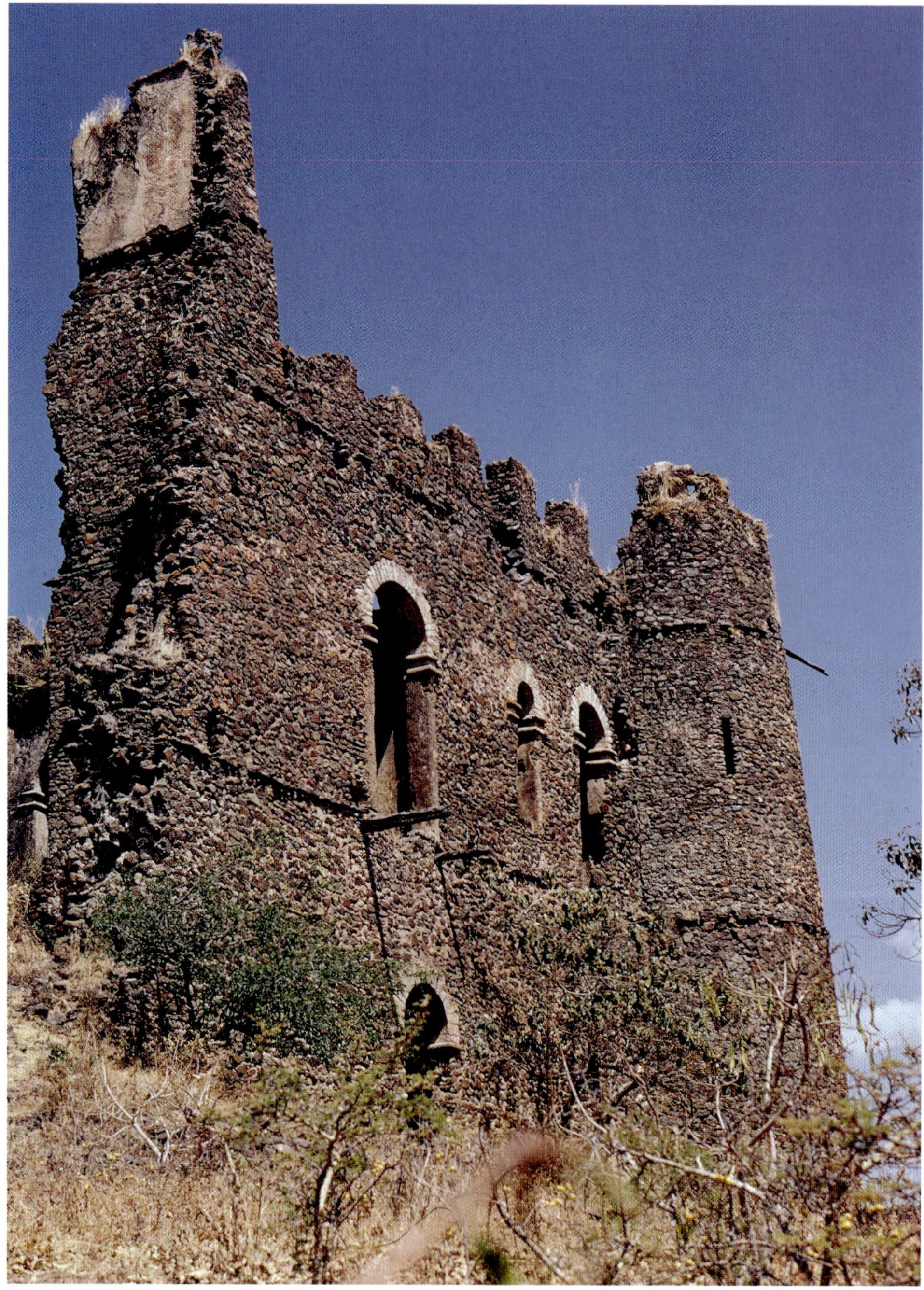

FIG 6.2

Ethiopian Orthodox, Śärśä Dəngəl's castle, Ǝnfraz, Ethiopia, ca. 1575. Photograph by Marilyn E. Heldman, ca. 1965. National Museum of African Art, Smithsonian Institution, Eliot Elisofon Photographic Archives, EEPA 2013-013-0216

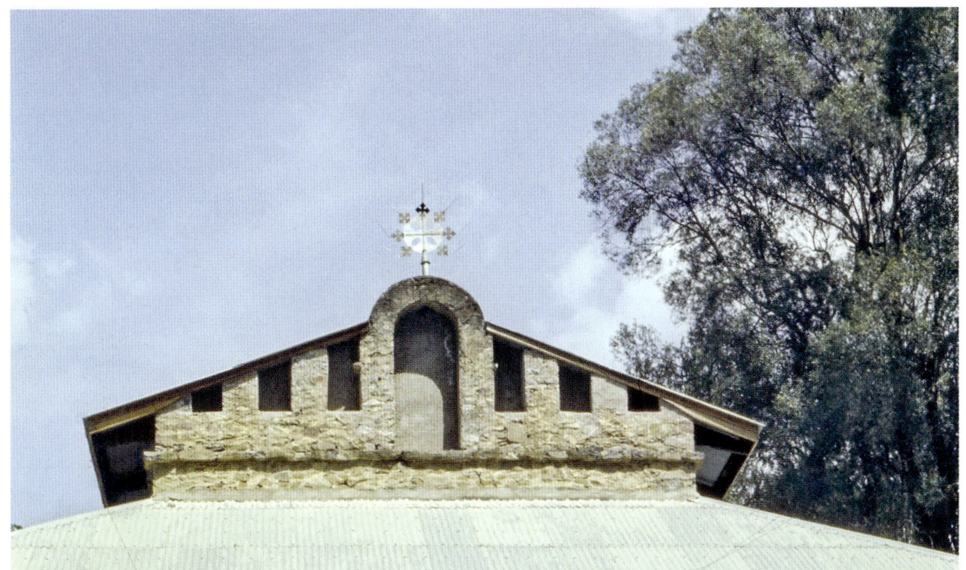
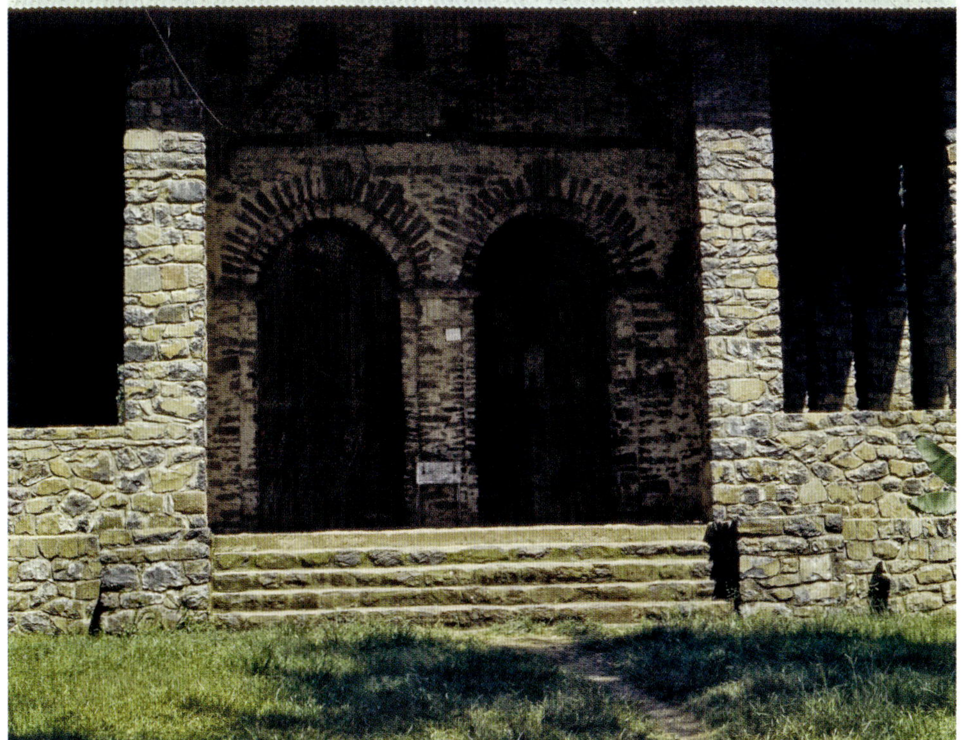

FIG 6.3
Ethiopian Orthodox, Däbrä Bərhan Śəllase, near Gondär, Ethiopia, 17th century. Photograph by Marilyn E. Heldman, 1965–96. National Museum of African Art, Smithsonian Institution, Marilyn E. Heldman Collection, Eliot Elisofon Photographic Archives, EEPA 2013-013-0101

In addition to the royal court, their presence attracted clerics and monks, who based themselves around churches in the various quarters of the capital. These communities of ecclesiastics turned Gondär into a hub of learning and literacy, filling the city not only with erudite clerics but also students from throughout the kingdom. The major monastic communities were evidently the scriptoria that produced the large volume of historical records and artistic creations that appeared during the Gondär Period. These included annals summarizing the history of the northern highlands since Aksumite times, detailed chronicles of individual reigns, illuminated manuscripts, theological treatises, and records of land grants to churches, along with items in demand by the court and nobility such as prayer books, amulets, and wood and metal crosses. Gondär also gave rise to a new style of painting named for the city.

As mentioned above, the Jesuits, with the support of Susənyos and a portion of the nobility, attempted to convert Ethiopian Orthodox Christians to Roman Catholicism. They ultimately failed, and Fasilädäs expelled them from the kingdom in 1634. Nevertheless, their teachings, writings, and debates with Orthodox clergy had revived older controversies and led to a new schism within the Ethiopian Church. The basis of the schism resided in opposing views on the nature of Christ, in particular, the manner in which his divinity was fused with his humanity. On one side were the unionists, who held that body and spirit were united at the time of Christ's birth; on the other were the unctionists, who believed that Christ became divine only through his anointing when he was baptized with the waters of the Jordan River by John the Baptist (John 1:19–33). The unionist (*Täwaḥədo*) dogma was identified with the monks of Däbrä Libanos, the unctionist (*Qəbat*) doctrine with the monks of Saint Ewosṭatewos.[10] Both schools were well represented in Gondär and in the farther reaches of the land. This theological controversy divided the Ethiopian clergy into two hostile camps, a situation that undermined the long-standing unity between church and state. It influenced political developments, as the clerics of each camp sought support from the nobles and commoners in the various provinces and locales in which they served.

The nobles themselves were divided by personal and regional rivalries. Throughout the seventeenth and eighteenth centuries, they formed factions that merged to become one of two coalitions competing for influence and power in the kingdom, with the throne being the ultimate prize. The coalitions engaged in a seesaw dynamic in which first one and then the other achieved dominance and succeeded in placing its candidate on the throne. The clerical division became an added element in this larger political contest. At assemblies before the court, rival clerics, backed by their allies among the nobility, argued their cases, hoping the throne would decree their views as state religious policy and condemn their opponents, as often happened. Resolution and reconciliation proved virtually impossible, leaving the kingdom divided into two antithetical camps, each composed of nobles and clergy.[11]

Clerical considerations aside, the potential consequences of the political give-and-take revealed themselves as the dynamic progressed in the later years of Iyasu I's reign. The quintessential warrior-king, Iyasu campaigned relentlessly against Oromo forces south of the Abbay or other peoples on the western edge of the kingdom. In ecclesiastical matters, he sought to establish peace between the antagonistic clerical camps, a goal that eluded him. He ascended to the throne with the support of unionist nobles and clerics, and for most of his reign he was partial to the unionist doctrine championed by the monks of Däbrä Libanos. It was, for example, apparently at their behest that Täklä Haymanot (figs. 4.5 and E4.4), patron saint of Däbrä Libanos, was elevated to the status of patron saint of the kingdom, a status enshrined in art and popular culture that endures to the present day. When, however, Iyasu appeared to shift political alliances and then in illness abdicated the throne, an act without precedent in the kingdom, a struggle ensued among the great nobles over a possible successor and the appointments, prerogatives, and prestige that would flow therefrom. It ultimately led to Iyasu's murder in 1706, a hitherto unthinkable act of regicide that became all too common in succeeding decades.[12]

At the same time that these ecclesiastical and political events were unfolding and a new style of monumental architecture emerged, Gondär Period Ethiopia witnessed significant developments in the artistic realm, especially painting. European paintings had appeared in the kingdom in prior centuries and made their presence felt in Ethiopian visual art. Now, new influences and models emerged, primarily by way of the Jesuits. They included the Arabic Gospel Book, a printed volume presented to King Susənyos featuring full-page illustrations composed of black linear designs printed on white paper (see example of similar Arabic Gospel Book, fig. 6.4). Ethiopian painters used some of these images as visual models, frequently painting works composed of linear designs (fig. 6.5).

The Jesuits also introduced printed visual images such as the Madonna of Santa Maria Maggiore (fig. 6.6). A half-length portrait of the Virgin Mary with the infant Jesus, the image is named for the Roman church where it occupied a special chapel and where it was venerated by the Jesuits.[13] The fathers disseminated copies of this portrait widely in their missionary work. It appeared in Ethiopia in the late sixteenth century and in time became perhaps the most widely reproduced of all sacred images of the Virgin and Child.

The fathers also evidently presented the royal court with a painting of Christ wearing a crown of thorns. Famous in European art as an early sixteenth-century Ibero-Flemish bust-length portrait of Christ crowned with thorns, the painting was inspired by the Passion of Christ, in particular his "crowning" by Roman soldiers before his Crucifixion (Matthew 27:27–30; Mark 15: 16–20). The image is known in Ethiopia as Kʷər'atä rə'əsu, whose literal translation is "The Striking of His Head": a phrase taken from Gospel accounts of Christ's humiliation at the hands of soldiers, who placed a crown of thorns on his head and struck him on the head with a reed. The earliest reference to it in Ethiopia appears in the mid-seventeenth century chronicle of Emperor Yoḥannəs. This icon of the crowned Christ (similar to that in fig. 6.7) was not only greatly revered by clergy and laity alike but it also became the royal palladium, a painting that signified royal authority. As such, it was honored and protected by

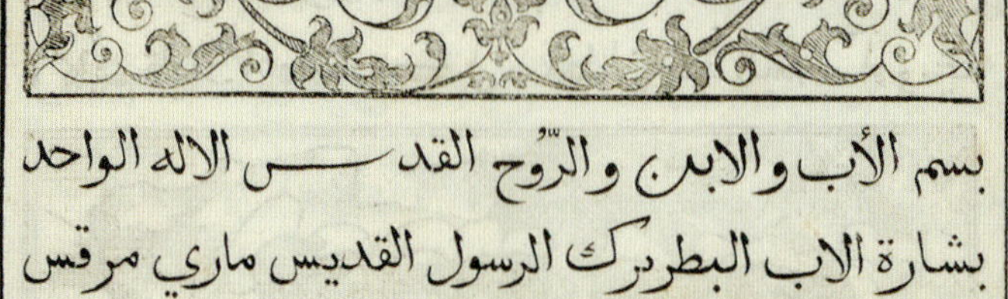

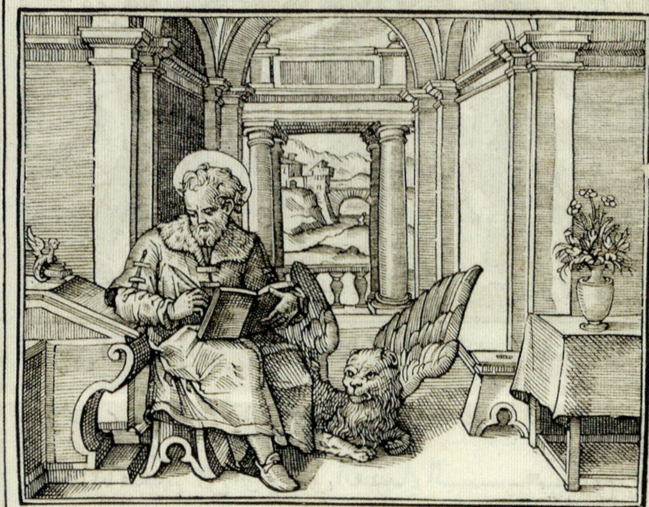

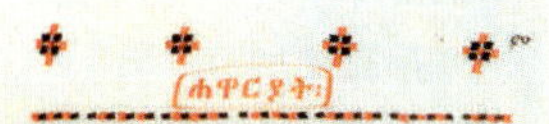
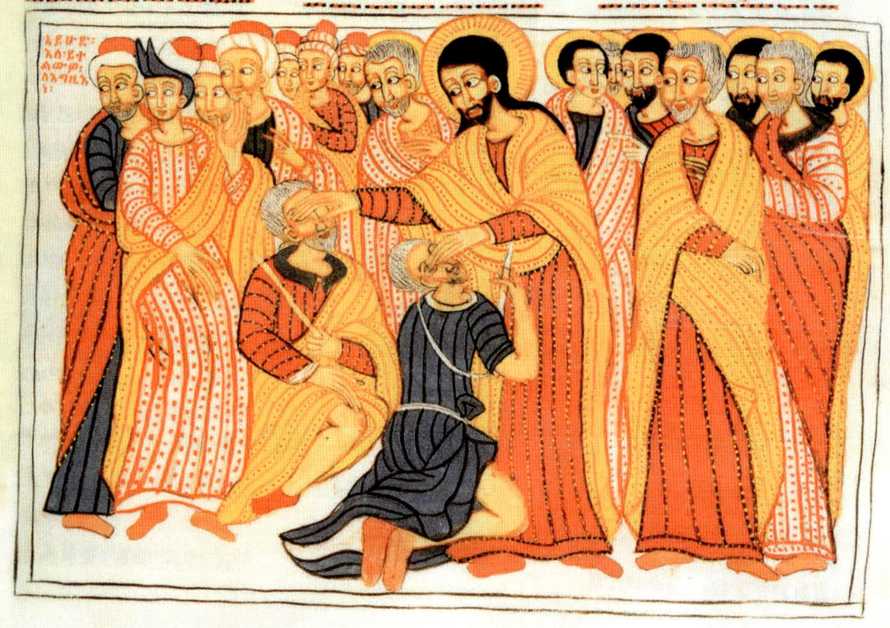
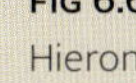
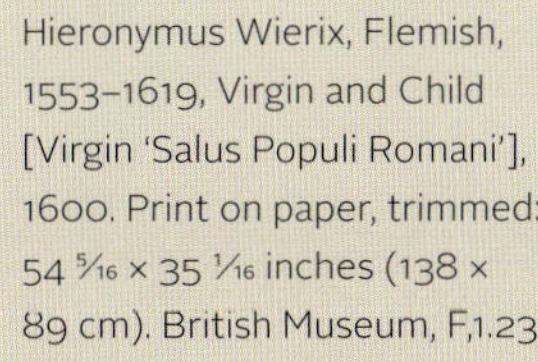

FIG 6.5

Ethiopian Orthodox, Four Gospels, Gondär, Ethiopia, 1664–65. Parchment, original stamped leather-covered endboards, and striped and flowered silk lining, 18 5/16 × 16 1/8 inches (46.5 × 41 cm). CPA Media Pte Ltd / Alamy Stock Photo

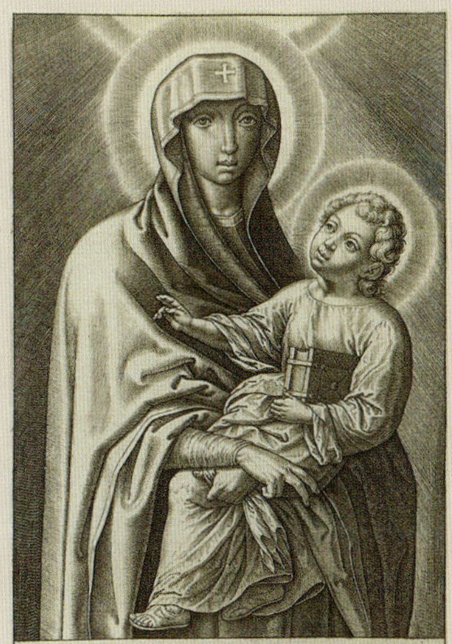

FIG 6.6

Hieronymus Wierix, Flemish, 1553–1619, Virgin and Child [Virgin 'Salus Populi Romani'], 1600. Print on paper, trimmed: 54 5/16 × 35 1/16 inches (138 × 89 cm). British Museum, F,1.23

FIG **6.7**

Ethiopian Orthodox, Kʷ ərʼatä
räʼəsu (Christ Crowned with
Thorns), after 1700. Icon.
Wood, paint, leather, and iron,
26 ⅜ × 31 ⅞ × 1 ⁵⁄₁₆ inches
(67 × 81 × 3.4 cm). National
Museum of African Art,
Smithsonian Institution, Gift
of Joseph and Patricia Brumit,
2004-7-3

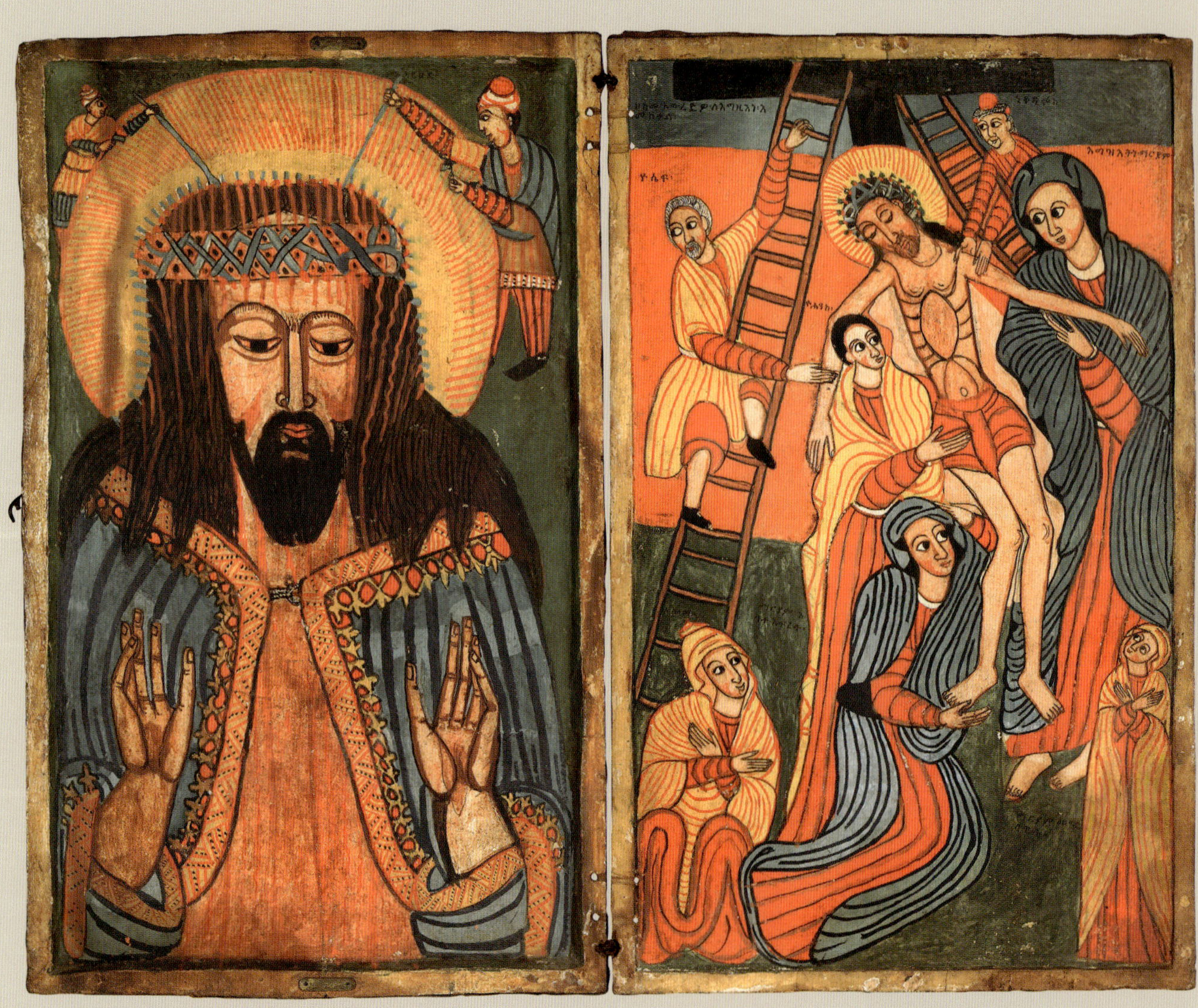

every Solomonic ruler. Oaths were sworn upon it, including by soldiers before military campaigns, and it was carried into battle along with altar tablets from the most prominent royal churches to inspire and rally the soldiers. So revered was the Kʷ ərʿatä rəʾəsu that when it and other holy relics were captured by Sudanese forces during a disastrous campaign under Iyasu II in 1744, they were ransomed back at great cost in gold.[14]

In response to these and perhaps other imports of European printed religious books, a new style of painting emerged in early seventeenth-century Gondär at scriptoria where monks were working for the royal court and elite society. Illuminated manuscripts were produced for emperors and wealthy patrons in what became the First Gondär Style. Representative are versions of Tä ʾammərä Maryam ("Miracles of Mary"), a collection of miraculous acts popularly attributed to the Virgin Mary (fig. 6.8). Editions that survive from the mid-seventeenth century are richly illustrated in a new idiom that had clearly evolved from earlier models. Another prominent manuscript with lavish illustrations in the First Gondär Style from later in the century is Dərsanä Mika ʾel, a cycle of annual liturgical observances in honor of the Archangel Michael.[15]

Art and craftsmanship further evolved during the eighteenth century. By that point, Gondär had become the artistic, commercial, political, and religious center of the kingdom. As such, it attracted numerous foreign visitors, several of whom left accounts of events that supplement Ethiopian records. Among these artisans, missionaries, and European visitors was the Scottish traveler James Bruce, in-country from 1769 to 1771, who recorded a wealth of information on events and personalities at midcentury.[16] This was an era of relative peace in the land and of flourishing in the arts. It is closely identified with the person of Bərhan Mogäsa, better known as Məntəwwab (whose name translates to "How Beautiful She Is!"), the consort of Emperor Bäkaffa (r. 1721–30).

Məntəwwab was without a doubt one of the dominant personalities of mid-eighteenth-century Ethiopia. Born in Qʷara, a province west of Gondär, she was present in the early 1720s at the court of Emperor Bäkaffa, by whom she had a son, the future Emperor Iyasu II (r. 1730–55). As Bruce reports, she was not only beautiful but also politically astute, traits she displayed throughout her remarkable life. She secured court appointments for her close relatives such that when Bäkaffa died, the Qʷarans quickly installed the young Iyasu as the next emperor, despite determined opposition. Thereafter, she and her brothers dominated the court and governed the kingdom during the nearly forty years she served as regent for Iyasu II and her grandson, Iyo ʾas (r. 1755–769). Aside from matters of state, the four decades of the Qʷaran regency mark the highest achievements in architecture, craftsmanship, and painting of the Gondär Period, a development largely due to her patronage (figs. 6.9 a and b).

Indeed, the long interregnum of the regency saw an outpouring of high-quality artistic production in the so-called Second Gondär Style. As with earlier artistic traditions, the Second Gondär Style of painting found expression in icons, church murals, illuminated manuscripts, and personal prayer books for wealthy patrons as well as in craftwork in metal and wood. Clothing designs were more fluid and brightly

FIG **6.8**
Ethiopian Orthodox, Tä 'ammərä
Maryam (Miracles of Mary),
ca. 1670–80. Parchment and
stamped, leather-covered wood
endboards, 18 ¼ × 15 ¹⁵⁄₁₆ inches
(46.3 × 40.5 cm). British Library,
Or. 635, f.63r

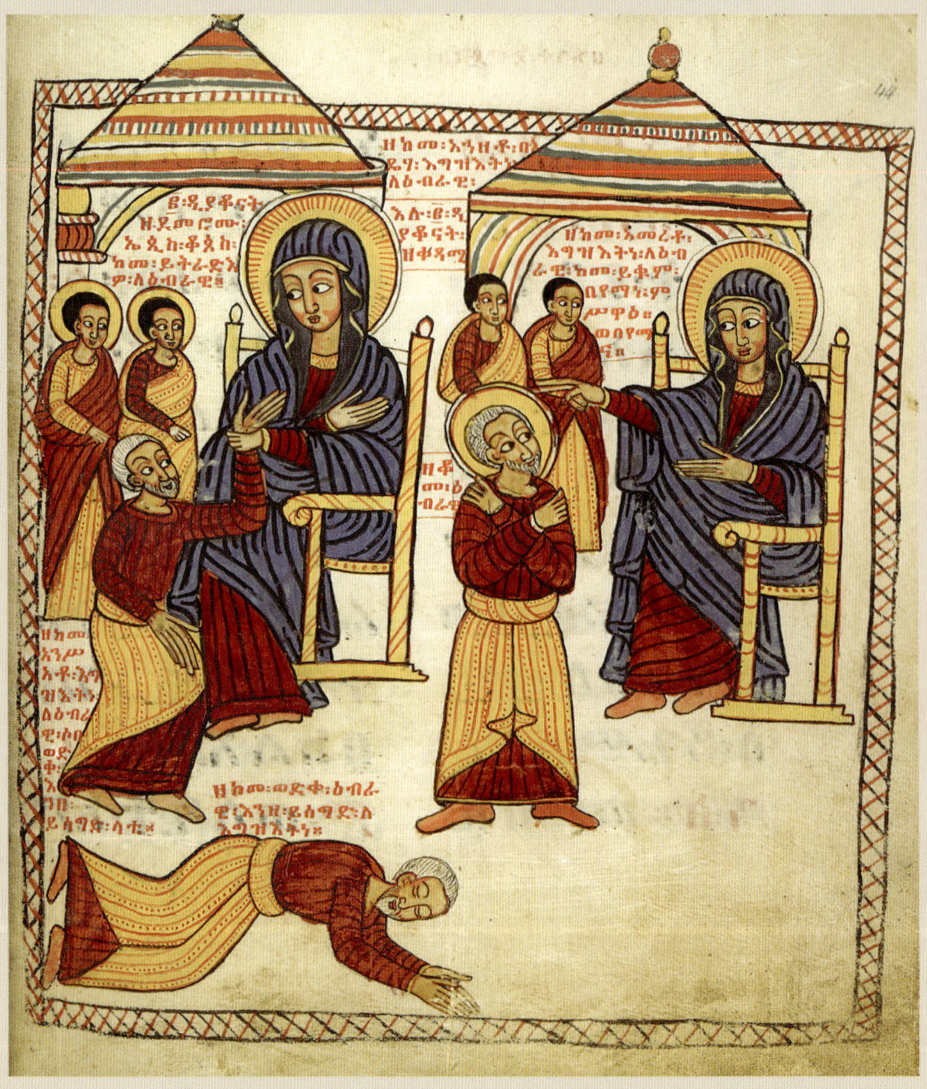

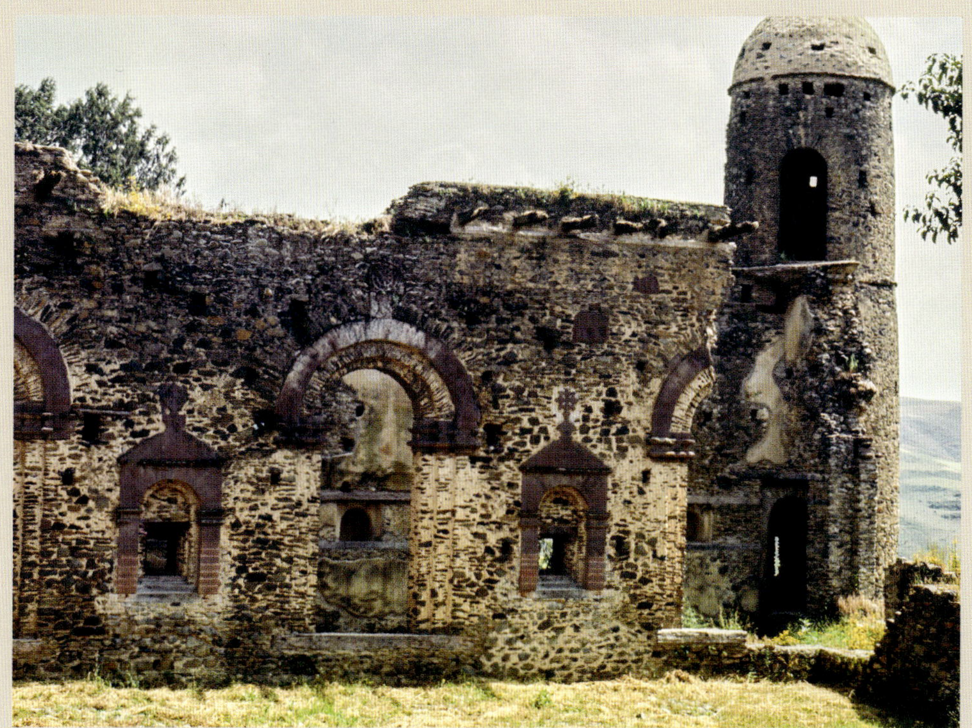

FIG 6.9 A AND B
Ethiopian Orthodox, Məntəwwab's palace, Qwesquam, Gondär, Ethiopia. Photographs by Marilyn E. Heldman, ca. 1974. National Museum of African Art, Smithsonian Institution, Eliot Elisofon Photographic Archives, EEPA 2013-013-0182, 0180

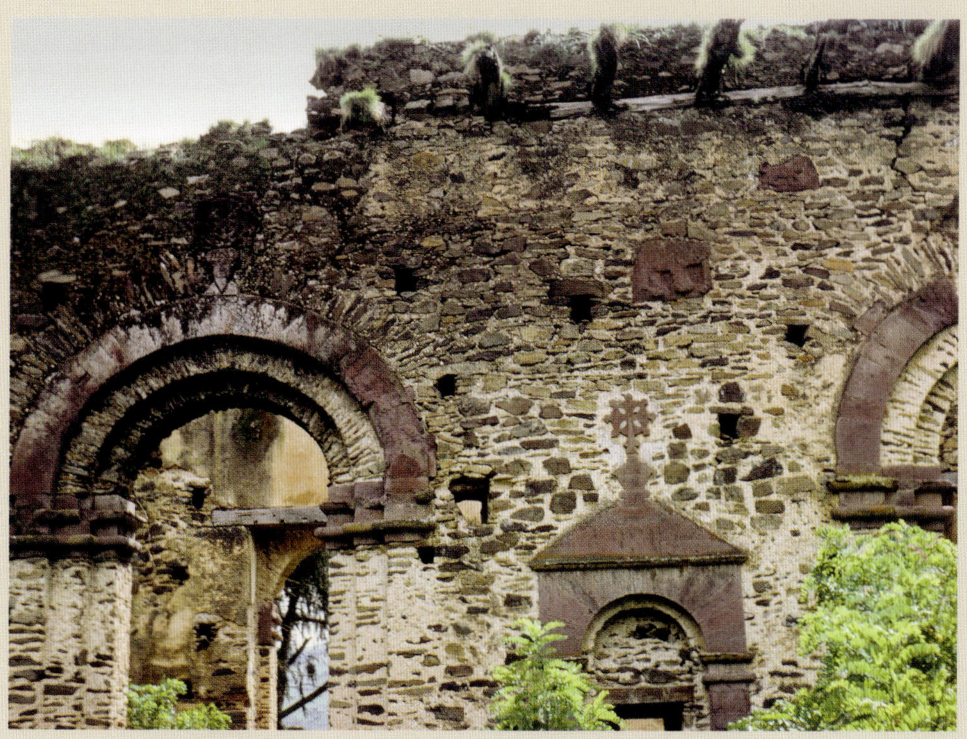

colored than before. Individuals were depicted in a more detailed fashion wearing garments of imported silk from India, Persia, and Turkey. Skilled craftsmen produced hand and processional crosses in gold and silver (see Essay 1) as well as other implements needed for Orthodox worship or desired by the court and nobility.[17]

In architecture, decorative refinements were added that softened the otherwise austere façades of Gondär Style buildings. They were incorporated into the small castle Məntəwwab and Iyasu constructed in Gondär and into the audience hall and residence of Məntəwwab's personal estate at Qʷəsqʷam, a few kilometers west of Gondär, embellishments that Məntəwwab surely inspired. Doors and windows were framed with red tuff, some frames appearing in the form of a stylized Orthodox church. Decorative plaques of the same material were set into the walls of the audience hall and perhaps other structures at Qʷəsqʷam as well.[18] Although somewhat weathered these artistic flourishes can still be seen on the walls of the audience hall and on those of Məntəwwab's and Iyasu's castle in Gondär.

Məntəwwab and Iyasu commissioned two major churches: Däbrä Ṣ̌ ähay Qʷəsqʷam ("Mount of Sunlight at Qʷəsqʷam") and Narga Śəllase ("Sweetness of the Trinity") in Lake Ṭana. Däbrä Ṣ̌ ähay was lavishly furnished with gold crosses, murals, hanging lamps, Turkish carpets, porcelain plaques, silk draperies, and clerical accoutrements, and it was endowed with abundant land to support the two hundred clerics assigned to it. Narga Śəllase was likewise richly appointed and endowed. While Məntəwwab was alive, Däbrä Ṣ̌ ähay eclipsed all other Gondär churches in prestige; additionally, its clerics were the foremost spokesmen for the *qəbat* (unctionist) doctrine favored by the Qʷarans.[19]

Däbrä Ṣ̌ ähay was destroyed in the late nineteenth century. It has undergone restoration along with Narga Śəllase, but only Narga Śəllase, protected and safe because of its location in Lake Ṭana, has survived with its original façade, part of its original murals, and its charm intact. Although damaged by moisture and the passage of time, many of the murals still retain their vibrant color as seen in images of the Virgin Mary, scenes from the life of Christ, angels, Ethiopian saints, and heroic figures. Məntəwwab herself appears at Mary's feet in a painting at the west (main) entrance.[20] Narga Śəllase's murals exemplify the imagery and quality of the wall paintings, now lost, that Məntəwwab commissioned at Däbrä Ṣ̌ ähay Qʷəsqʷam.

The Qʷaran regency collapsed in the late 1760s. It was followed by nearly a century in which royal power and prerogatives were usurped by a series of provincial and regional warlords who fought among themselves for control of their lands as well as of the kingdom. Emperors were elected and dethroned, sometimes in rapid succession, by first one and then another magnate, being reduced during the nineteenth century to impoverished figureheads living amid ruined castles in Gondär. These were decades of general cultural impoverishment compared with the prior two centuries. Although they continued the tradition of founding and endowing churches, virtually none of the warlords possessed the means to patronize the arts or commission monumental architecture in the manner of the Solomonic emperors.

This period of warring potentates, known in Ethiopia as the *Zämänä Mäsafənt* ("Era of the Princes"), continued until a member of the lesser nobility who claimed Solomonic blood ascended the throne as Emperor Tewodros (Theodore) II (r. 1855–68). Tewodros sought to revive the fortunes of the monarchy and to reestablish a unified state under his control, goals that he failed to achieve. He disliked Gondär, which to him symbolized imperial decline. Twice, he unleashed his army on the city and removed its treasures to a new capital and then to a mountain fortress in Wällo. Deprived of the royal court, Gondär declined further into a neglected and shrunken city composed of neighborhoods clustered around its once-prominent churches. Nonetheless, it remained the artistic and cultural capital of the kingdom and a major center of traditional education and ecclesiastical training.[21]

Tewodros's ambitions and methods of rule alienated many of his countrymen, who abandoned him in the face of a British military expedition that led to his defeat and death in 1868. Dispatched from India with orders to free the British consul and other Europeans whom Tewodros had detained, the expedition's soldiers carried off much of the treasure the emperor had accumulated. The treasure consisted of icons, crosses, implements used in Orthodox worship, illuminated manuscripts, prayer books, royal chronicles, and theological treatises, much if not most of it produced during the cultural flowering of the Gondär Period. These artifacts and literary compositions subsequently found their way into libraries, museums, and universities across Europe, where they formed the basis for the scholarly study of the history and culture of Ethiopia, an endeavor that continues to the present day.[22]

ESSAY 6

Protection

MARILYN E. HELDMAN

Devotional images of military saints of the Universal Church—including George, Theodore, Mercurius, Claudius, Victor, Fasilädäs, and Menas—are among the extant murals in ancient Ethiopian churches. Protective in nature, their images were painted on the walls of royal churches until the late nineteenth century. Emperor Zär'a Ya'əqob's cult of Our Lady Mary subsumed the cult of Saint George, Soldier of God.[1] Upon winning an important battle against the Muslim sultan of 'Adal on Christmas Day in 1445, the emperor attributed his victory to the intercession of Saint George and Our Lady Mary. Henceforth, beginning with the icons produced at the emperor's court by Frē Ṣəyon,[2] Saint George is usually depicted riding a white horse opposite a portrait of Our Lady Mary (fig. E6.1).

Pocket-size illuminated manuscripts and scrolls (figs. E6.2 a and b) also offer protection. Adorned with numerous pictures, *eqabanni* (literally, "help me") are accompanied by prayers to be recited while gazing at the images. *Sensuls* ("chain of paintings")—long, narrow, accordion-like strips of parchment—with scenes of the life of Saint Mary or portraits of saints (figs. E6.3, E6.4, and E6.5 a, b, and c) afford protection while carried in a pocket during the day and when suspended over one's bed at night. All equestrian saints of the Ethiopian Universal Church are known to have apotropaic power, which provides divine protection. Portraits of the archangels are frequently painted on or beside doors that they then have the power to protect.[3] Certain icons of Our Lady Mary attributed to the hand of Saint Luke the Evangelist are traditionally held to be sacred.[4] Copies of Saint Luke icons carry some of this sanctity, although they are not deemed as powerful.

During the reign of Yohannes (r. 1667–82), a bust-length European painting of Christ crowned with thorns was adopted as the palladium of Ethiopia's monarchs. A special chapel in honor of this icon, named *Kʷ ər'atä rə'əsu* (literally, "Striking of His Head"), was built within the palace compound at Gondär. Gondärine monarchs carried the royal palladium, while other military leaders carried copies of this icon into battle to ensure victory (fig. 6.7).

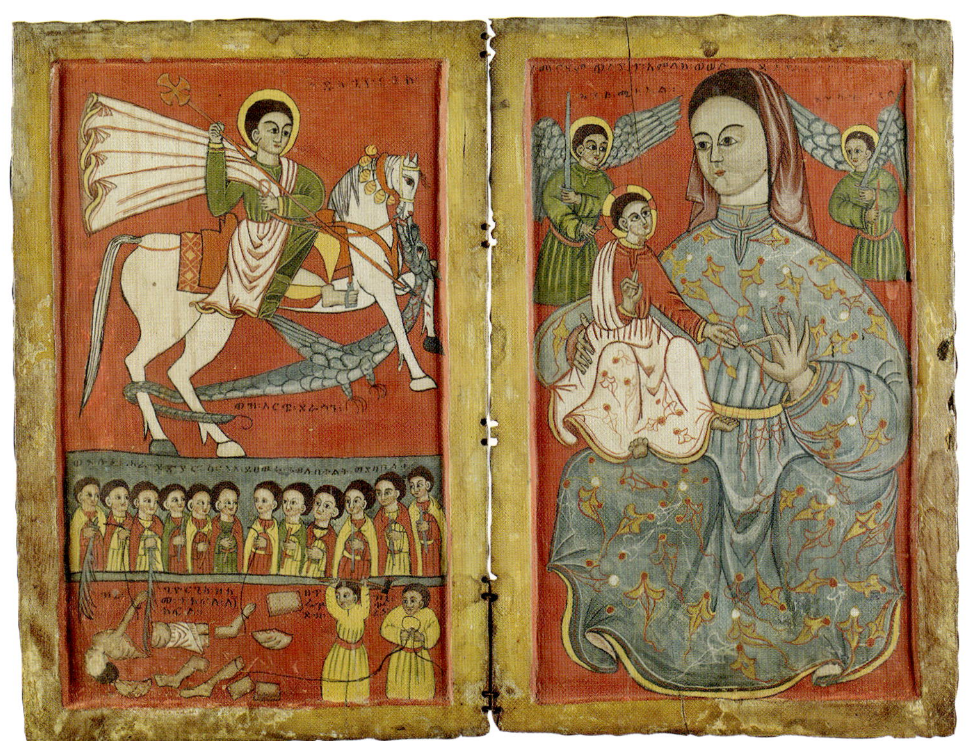

FIG E6.1
Ethiopian Orthodox, Saint
George; Virgin and Child, Saints
Michael and Gabriel, 15th to
16th century. Icon. Wood, gesso,
and paint, 20 ½ × 26 ⁵⁄₁₆ × 1 ³⁄₁₆
inches (52 × 66.8 × 3 cm).
National Museum of African Art,
Smithsonian Institution, Gift
of Joseph and Patricia Brumit,
2004-7-2

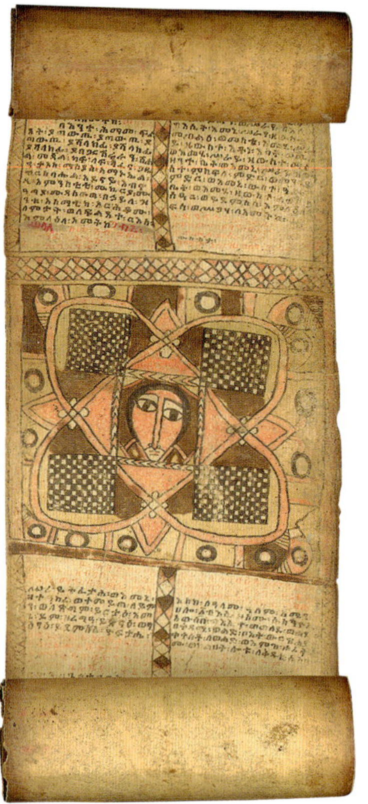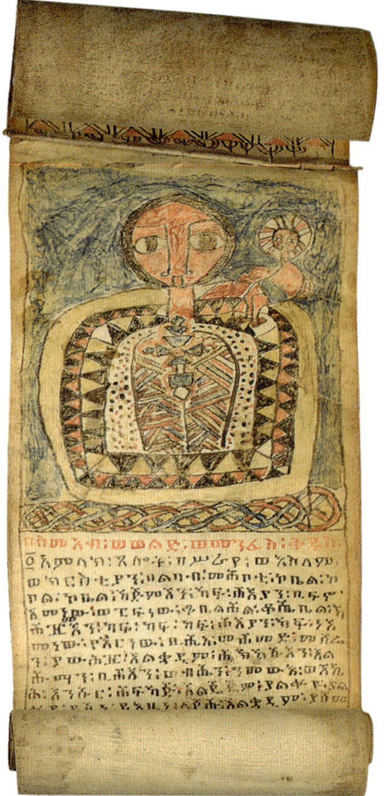

FIG E6.2 A AND B

Ethiopian Orthodox, healing scrolls (magic scrolls), 19th century. Parchment and ink, 8 ⅝ × 76 inches (21.9 × 193 cm). National Museum of African Art, Smithsonian Institution, Gift of Franklin H. Williams, 73-19-63

FIG E6.3

Ethiopian Orthodox, *Sensul*, Gondär, Ethiopia, late 17th century. Hide and parchment, unfolded: 3 × 23 inches (7.6 × 58.4 cm); each panel: 3 ⅝ × 3 ⅛ inches (9.2 × 9 cm). Walters Art Museum, museum purchase with funds provided by the W. Alton Jones Foundation Acquisition Fund, 1996, 36.10

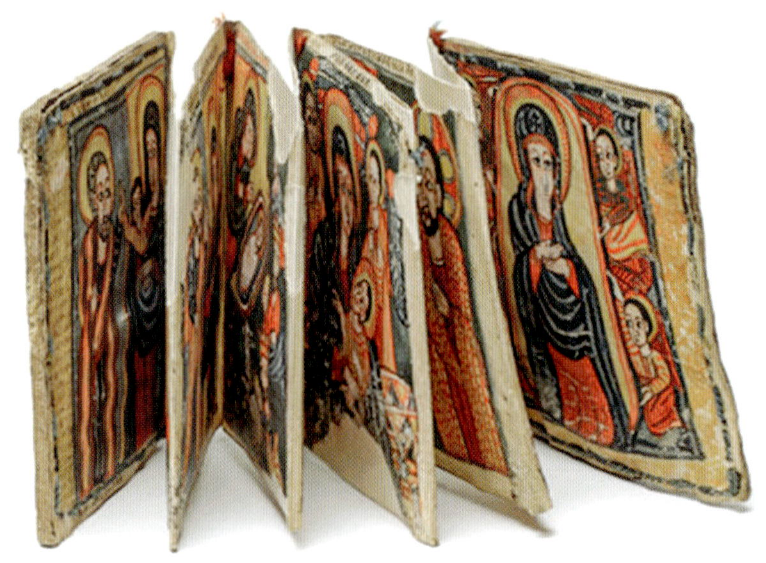

ETHIOPIAN DEVOTIONS

FIG E6.4
Ethiopian Orthodox, Saint
George Slaying the Dragon;
Virgin and Child, Michael &
Gabriel, *Sensul*, Gondär, Ethiopia,
late 17th century. Hide and
parchment, unfolded: 3 × 23
inches (7.6 × 58.4 cm); each
panel: 3 ⅝ × 3 ⅛ inches (9.2 ×
9 cm). Walters Art Museum,
museum purchase with funds
provided by the W. Alton Jones
Foundation Acquisition Fund,
1996, 36.10

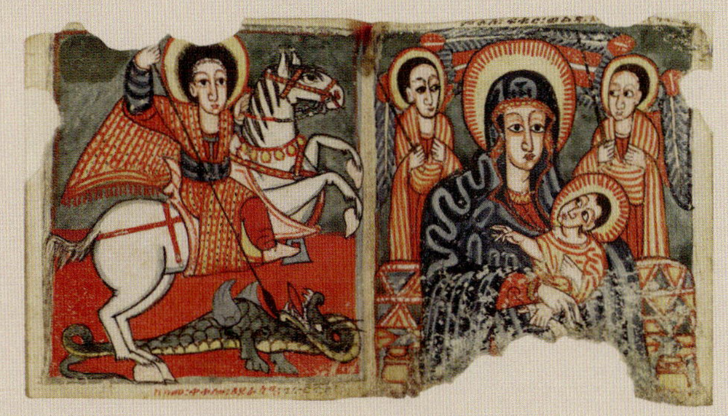

FIG E6.5 A, B, AND C
Ethiopian Orthodox, (a)
Annunciation; Adoration of
the Magi, (b) Flight into Egypt;
Convent of Mercy, (c) Dormition;
Assumption of Mary, *Sensul*,
Gondär, Ethiopia, late 17th
century. Hide and parchment,
unfolded: 3 × 23 inches (7.62 ×
58.4 cm); each panel: 3 ⅝ × 3 ⅛
inches (9.2 × 9 cm). Walters Art
Museum, museum purchase with
funds provided by the W. Alton
Jones Foundation Acquisition
Fund, 1996, 36.10

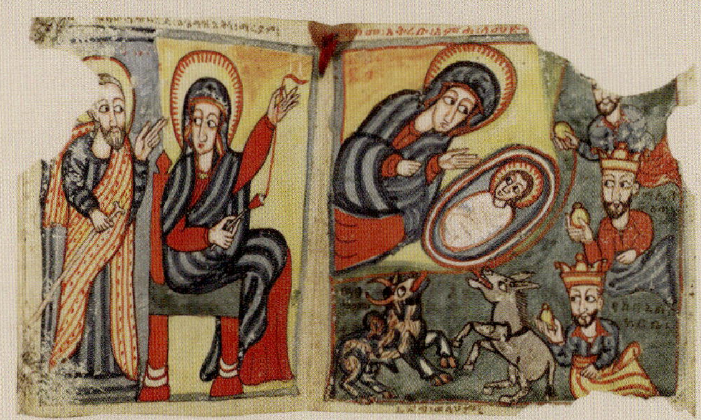

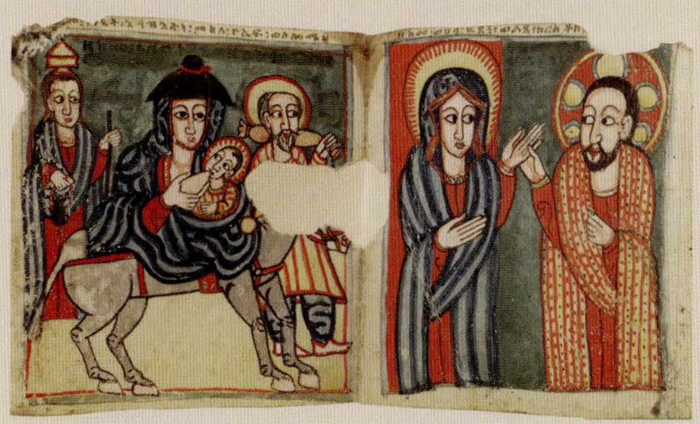

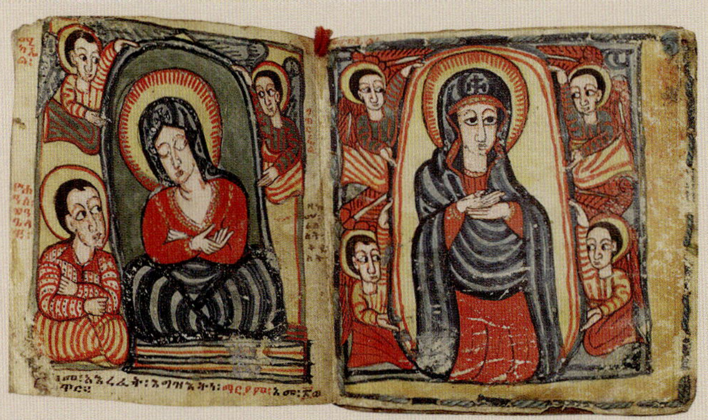

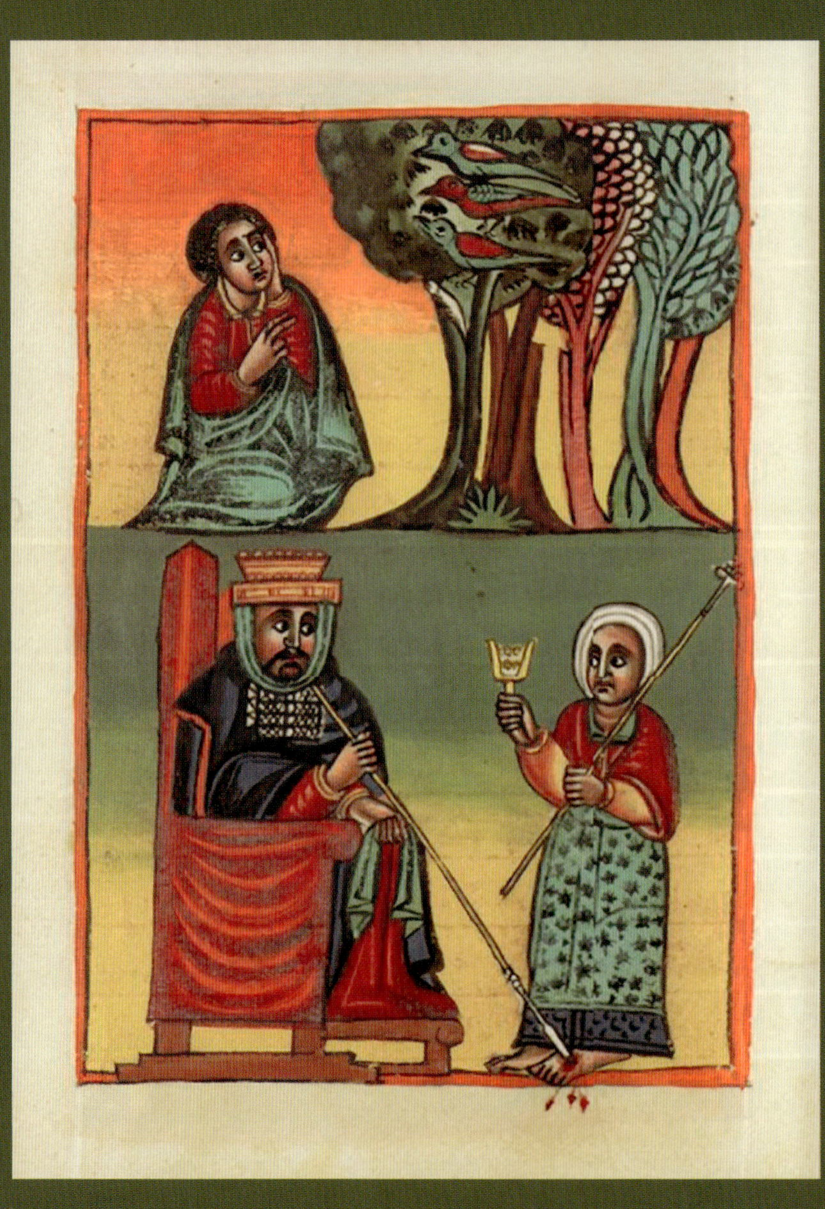

Chapter 7

An Image of Performance, an Emblem of Power:
Saint Yared and Liturgical Music of the Ethiopian Orthodox Church

KAY KAUFMAN SHELEMAY

A miniature in an illuminated manuscript of biblical canticles created for Queen Məntəwwab in the mid-eighteenth century (fig. 7.1) invites the viewer to enter the realm of musical performance in the religious tradition of the Ethiopian Orthodox Church. Along with the memory of their founder, the musical events depicted have inspired Ethiopian Christians from early times until the present.

The subject of the miniature is Saint Yared, who, according to tradition, lived in the sixth century and established the large body of chants that form the core of Ethiopian Orthodox ritual and worship.[1] The miniature shows two defining moments from the Life of Saint Yared. The upper register shows Yared with three birds from the Garden of Eden, on whose wings he will be lifted up to Heavenly Jerusalem; there, he learns the chants of the twenty-four Priests of Heaven who sing before the throne of God (Rev. 4:10). After this mystical experience, Saint Yared is returned to Aksum, where he is said to have established the musical liturgy of the Ethiopian Orthodox Church at the First Church of Aksum, the capital and religious center in that period.

The lower register of the miniature signifies Saint Yared's generative musical role in the Ethiopian Church. Sistrum and prayer staff in hand, Yared is seen performing chants before the Ethiopian king Gäbrä Mäsqäl, who is believed to have been a contemporary of Yared who recognized and supported his musical gifts. As Saint Yared performs, he is so transported by the chant he is unaware that the king's spear has accidentally pierced his foot. Distressed at the sight of Yared's bleeding foot, the king offers the musician anything he desires in compensation for the injury. Yared responds that he would like to go into isolation as a monk, a request the king reluctantly grants. The musician withdraws to an unknown location and spends the rest of his life in solitude and meditation. Thus, these two scenes present a narrative that unites two pivotal moments: the point at which Saint Yared's heavenly musical inspiration begins and the final moment of his musical career at the cathedral of Aksum.

The commemoration of Yared on 11 Gənbot was introduced to the revised Ethiopian Orthodox Synaxary, dated 1581 CE (EMML No. 2054). This reading for 11 Gənbot represents the earliest extant source on the life of Saint Yared.[2] The Synaxary is essentially a church calendar of the fixed festivals that includes appropriate readings for each day as well as brief life stories of the saints and martyrs of the Ethiopian Church.

Ethiopian Orthodox, Life of Saint Yared, from an illuminated manuscript created for Queen Məntəwwab, 18th century. Vellum, tempera, and leather binding, 12 ⅝ × 8 ¹¹⁄₁₆ × 2 ⅜ inches (32 × 22 × 6 cm). Princeton University of Art Museum, Gift of Frank Jewett Mather, Jr., y1951-28

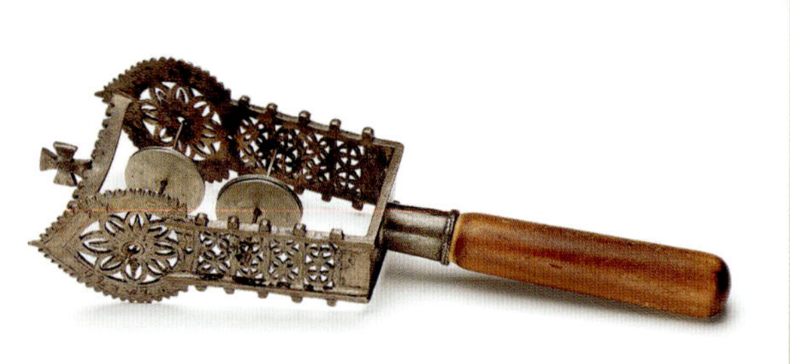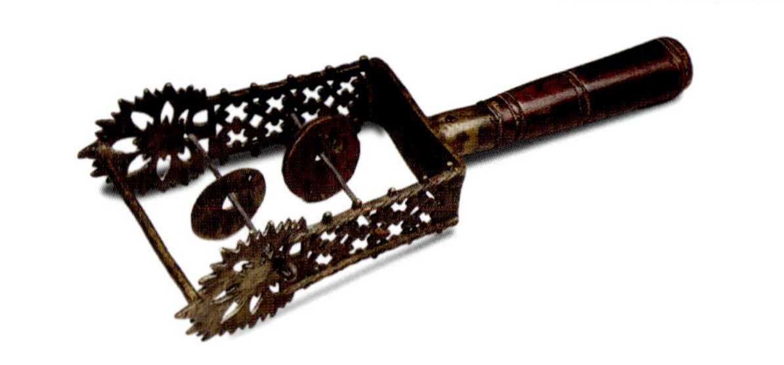

FIG 7.2 A

Ethiopian Orthodox, sistrum, mid-20th century. Wood and white metal, 9 7/16 × 3 1/4 × 2 1/16 inches (24 × 8.3 × 5.2 cm). National Museum of African Art, Smithsonian Institution, Gift of Joseph and Patricia Brumit, 2004-7-21

FIG 7.2 B

Ethiopian Orthodox, sistrum, early 20th century. Wood, copper alloy, and iron, 8 1/16 × 3 1/8 × 1 3/4 inches (20.5 × 8 × 4.4 cm). National Museum of African Art, Smithsonian Institution, Gift of an anonymous donor in memory of Louis Gilden, 2011-2-1

FIG 7.2 C

Pilgrims praying and playing sistrum *s'enas'els*, Betä Mädḫane Aläm, Lalibäla, Ethiopia. Photograph by Michael Doochin, 2010. National Museum of African Art, Smithsonian Institution, Michael and Linda Doochin Collection, Eliot Elisofon Photographic Archives, EEPA 2020-001-2465

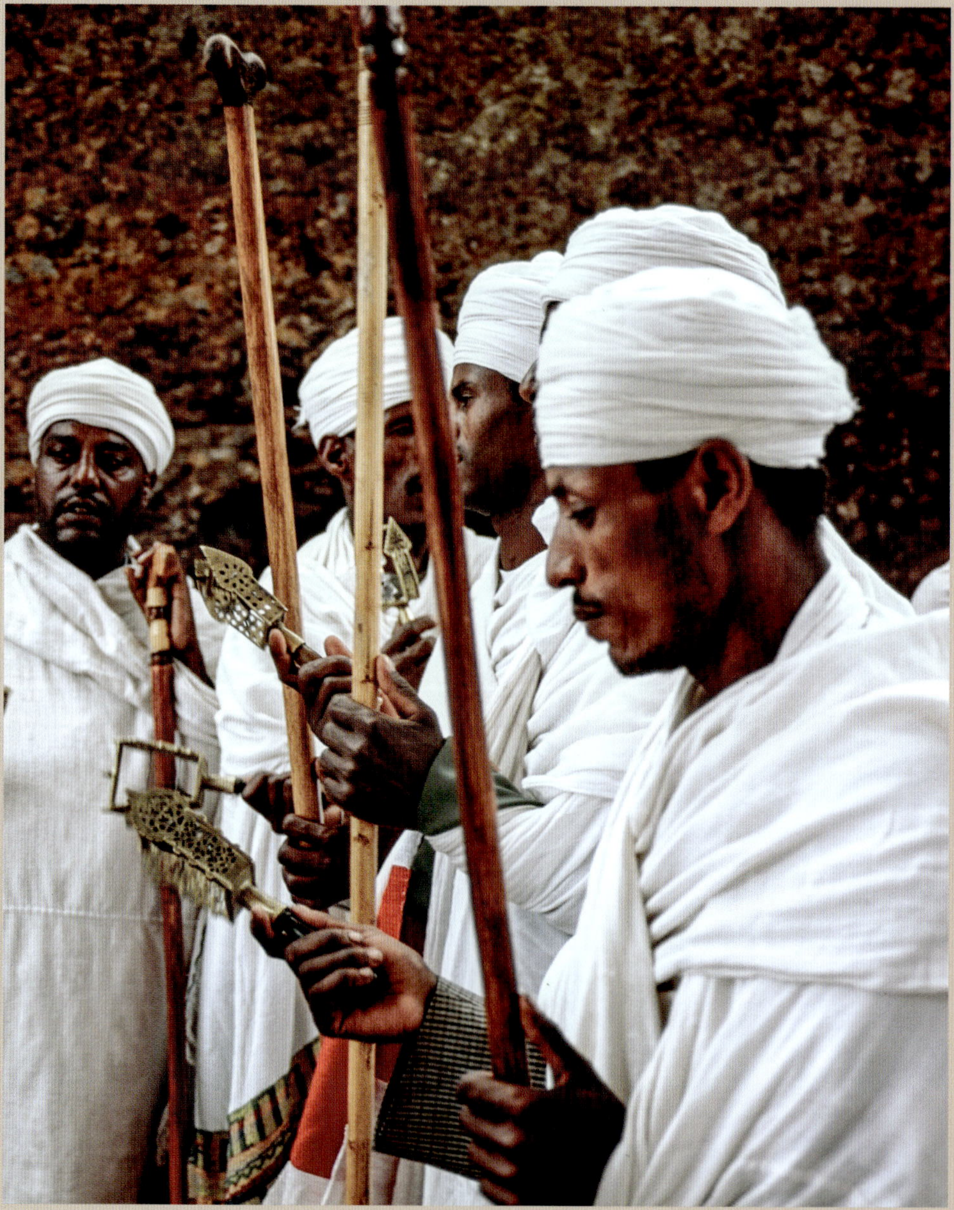

These narratives also survive in various oral and written traditions sustained for centuries by generations of musicians. Many church musicians (*däbtära*) recorded these and other stories of Saint Yared's life and music that they, in turn, passed down to their students.[3] To be a musician in the Ethiopian Orthodox Church is to be an heir to Yared's legacy, to transmit faithfully tales of his life story and to sustain for posterity the musical and textual content of his chants.

The two scenes in the miniature provide considerable insights into the practices of this venerable church-music tradition in the mid-eighteenth century. For instance, the image in the lower register shows Yared wearing a turban, called a *t'ät'ämiya*. Traditionally, all *däbtära* wear this garment, "a long cloth of cotton or of linen wound tight around the head."[4] Saint Yared holds in his right hand a sistrum (*s'enas'el*), a small rattle used to accompany Ethiopian chants (figs. 7.2 a, b, and c). The instrument in the miniature is made of gold, as became customary for royal regalia; in contrast, instruments for the nobility would be crafted out of silver, and those for use in a regular church would be fashioned in bronze. In his left hand, Saint Yared grasps a prayer staff (*mäqwammiya*), which marks chant rhythms and reinforces accents by being pounded on the floor.

Images of Saint Yared hint at the centrality of the musician and music in Ethiopian Orthodox religious life, providing tantalizing clues as to its deep significance and connection to the divine. The lower scene also intimates that music may have the power to transcend and alleviate pain. Both scenes provide a window on the continuing impact of Saint Yared and the chant tradition. For instance, musicians still use the prayer staff (figs. 7.3 a and b), which continues to carry its own historical associations: the rod represents the cross of the Crucifixion, while the armrest at the top signifies the head of a lamb, a reference to Saint John the Baptist's pronouncement "Behold the Lamb of God who takes away the sin of the world" (John 1:29).[5]

Written descriptions that predate the miniature in Queen Məntəwwab's mid-eighteenth-century book of canticles, such as one of the earliest surviving descriptions of Ethiopian Christian life and rituals, from 1545–80, provide further insight into these two images. These eyewitness accounts were written down and later sent to Rome by two Jesuits serving their order in Ethiopia. Their observations, which were subsequently edited and published in 1615,[6] include a brief description of an Ethiopian church ritual, which begins:

They perform nothing from writing, but everything from memory. When they say Matins, apart from the usual torches before the altar, in which grease burns instead of oil, there is no other light in the church, nor in the choir. They chant the psalm-verses, not alternately, but each one altogether ... no one recites seated; the older men are allowed to lean on wooden props when they are tired.

This passage sheds light not only on some details regarding musical practices, to which we will return below, but also on the practical function of the prayer staff: it serves

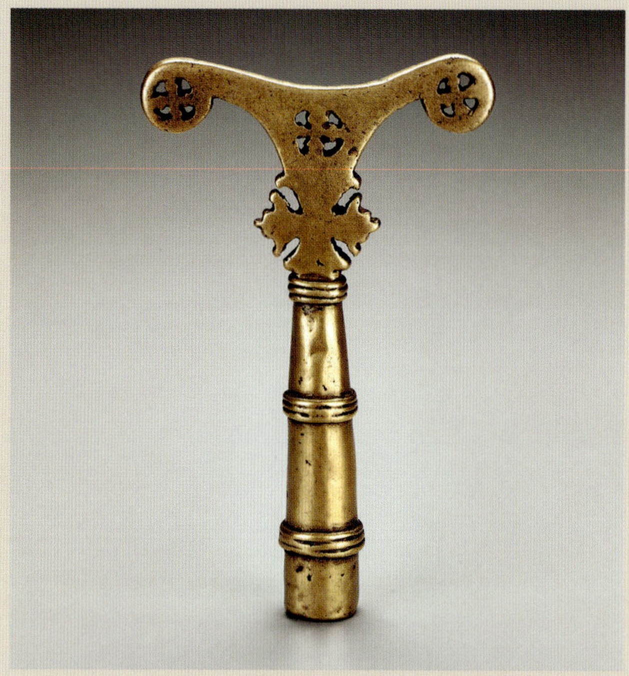

FIG 7.3 A

Ethiopian Orthodox, prayer staff finial, 17th century. Copper alloy, 6 ⅛ × 3 ¹³⁄₁₆ × 1 inches (15.6 × 9.7 × 2.5 cm). National Museum of African Art, Smithsonian Institution, museum purchase, 97-19-4

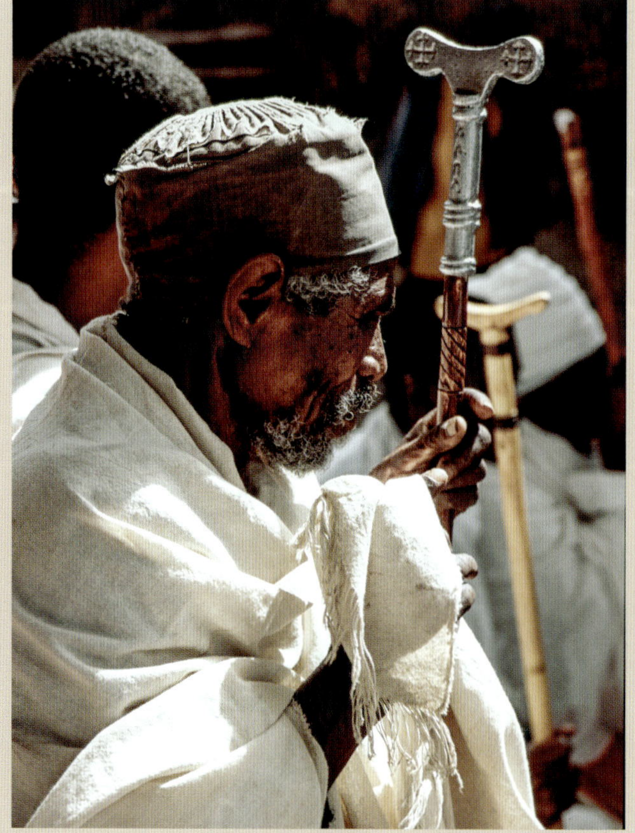

FIG 7.3 B

Pilgrim in prayer, Lalibäla, Ethiopia. Photograph by Michael Doochin, 2010. National Museum of African Art, Smithsonian Institution, Michael and Linda Doochin Collection, Eliot Elisofon Photographic Archives, EEPA 2020-001-2465 as a support on which the musician can lean for the lengthy, often hours-long rituals. The following passage offers more colorful details of holiday instrumental use and holiday processions:

There are many occasions set apart for thanksgiving and festivals. After each of their services the worshippers proceed about the building, the more often as the festival celebrated is important. It can happen that in one celebration the church is encircled thirty and more times. In these celebrations they carry four or five silver crosses like scepters in their right hands, and as many thuribles [metal censers] in their left; and many rattles join with the sung psalms and hymns.[7]

The sixteenth-century use of processional crosses and sistra in processions closely corresponds to twenty-first-century Ethiopian Christian practices, attesting to continuity in the liturgical tradition over the course of centuries. Figure 7.4 illustrates one portion of the liturgical celebration of Christ's Baptism, T'emqät (Epiphany), on 11 Tərr at Debre Selam Kidist Maryam (St. Mary's) Ethiopian Orthodox church in Washington, DC, in 2007. The ceremony there greatly resembled the sixteenth-century account. The three priests have just stepped from behind the green silk curtains of the Holy of Holies, each supporting on his head a *tabot* wrapped in gold-embroidered silk to shield it from the gaze of the laity. The *tabot* is a sacred altar tablet used in every Ethiopian Orthodox church for the celebration of the Eucharist in the Holy of Holies. Made of wood or stone, it is engraved with the name of the saint to whom the altar is dedicated. It is an embodiment of the saint and is also seen as a replica of the Tablets of the Law. The gold-embroidered red-silk covering of the altar tablets drapes over the shoulders of each priest's silk vestments. Turbaned church musicians (*däbtära*) in white robes stand several steps below the three priests, facing one another in two lines. They are singing the traditional chant while swaying to the resonant beats of the *kebaro*, the large kettledrum, as seen in figure 7.5. Each musician shakes his sistrum with his right hand, while his left anchors a prayer staff extending back over his left shoulder. The musicians are led by Liqä Mäzemrat (Master of Liturgical Chant) Moges Seyoum, who stands second from rear in the right-hand line of musicians, with a microphone instead of a prayer staff in his left hand. Behind the musicians, both to the right and the left of the *tabot* display, one can see priests or deacons holding up large processional crosses.

The *tabot* procession will head down from the altar and be followed by deacons, not visible in this photograph except for the tops of the large ritual umbrella that, when unfurled, will function as a portable honorific dome over the altar tablets. The deacons will swing censers as they proceed down the center aisle of the sanctuary and then around the circumference of the hall. The musicians will follow, trailed by members of the congregation who sing, dance, and ululate. When the procession ends, the priests will return the *tabot* to the altar cabinet located behind the curtains in the Holy of Holies.

Celebration of Christ's Baptism, T'emqät (Epiphany), Debre Selam Kidist Maryam (St. Mary's), Washington, DC. Photograph by Kay Kaufman Shelemay, 2007

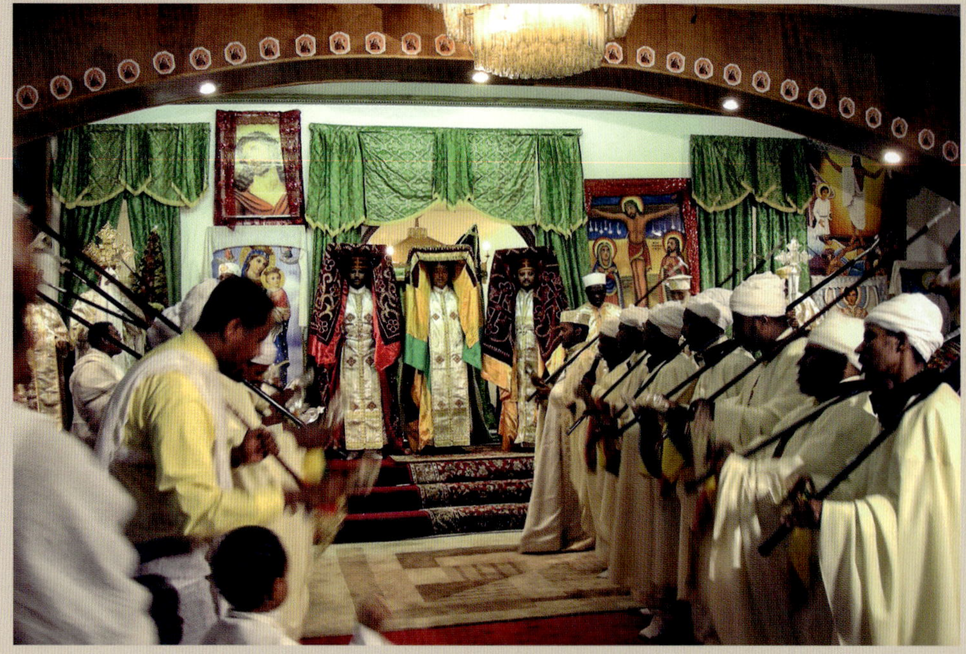

Drummer accompanying Ethiopian liturgical dance, Washington, DC. Photograph by Kay Kaufman Shelemay, 2007

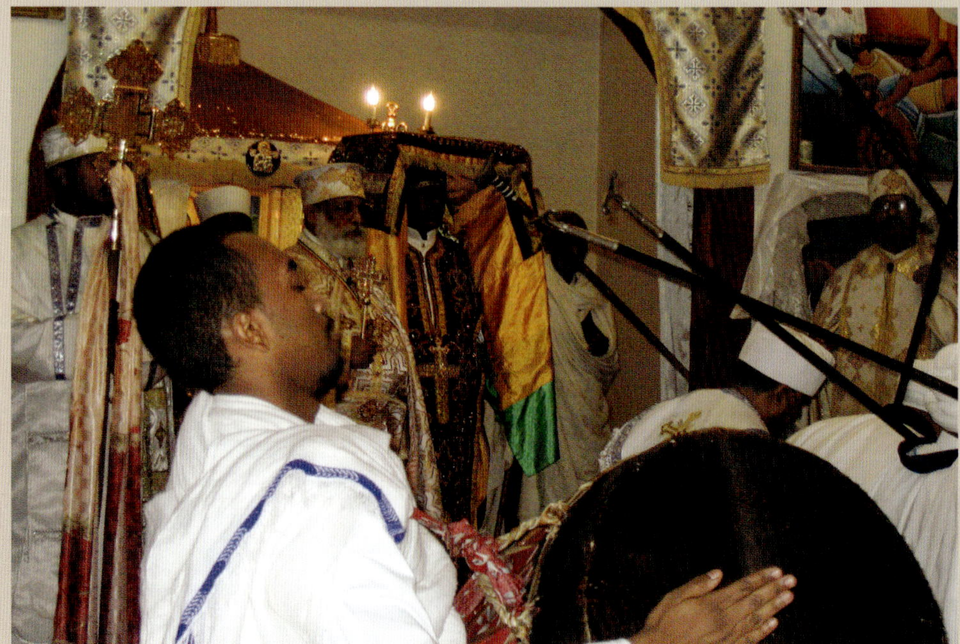

   ETHIOPIAN DEVOTIONS

Throughout this colorful ritual, the sung melodies play an important role. First and foremost, they convey esoteric liturgical texts within the ritual settings, enabling the musicians to perform orders of the hours-long service by memory. Thus, the performance of chant melodies carries with it great responsibility as well as a spiritual connection with Saint Yared's creative power.

This Ethiopian Orthodox Christian ritual heritage is dependent on the extensive training these musicians must undergo to master complex liturgical materials. The education of an Ethiopian *däbtära* begins no later than age five at a local church school. Many young boys who embark on this educational regimen are the children of local *däbtäras* and priests. Their elementary training involves learning to read the Ethiopic (Gə'əz) syllabary;[8] memorizing and reciting Gospel texts and different recitation styles; studying penmanship; and memorizing the complete Dawit, the biblical book of Psalms attributed to King David (fig. 7.6), and the Wəddase Maryam (Praise of Mary).[9] Once the student musician masters all 150 psalms, he can graduate from the church school and move on to advanced studies at another church or monastery. There, the student attends *zema* (chant) school for at least four years and masters all the melodies and different types of chants of the Hymnary (Dəggwa). Each student must copy his own Hymnary manuscript, replete with signs of the indigenous system of musical notation.[10] After completing *zema* school, some musicians decide to specialize in more esoteric aspects of church-music performance at yet more specialized schools and monasteries, focusing on *aqqwaqwam* (dance and instrumental usage), *qene* (improvised liturgical poetry), or one of the special liturgical books associated with Saint Yared used only for certain holidays and at funerals.

Beyond music's role in carrying forward the liturgical text and ensuring that it remains embedded in memory, the melodies have their own clear associations with the sacred. There are three categories of melody (*zema* or *səlt*) in the Ethiopian Church music system, all of which are attributed to the inspiration of Saint Yared. The first is the *gə'əz zema*, which is described as being "strong" and "dry," and is heard most frequently throughout the liturgy. The second *zema*, *araray*, is described as the "daily *zema*" and is characterized as "strong, light, and pleasurable." *Araray* can be sung for any occasion, sometimes in alternation with *gə'əz zema*, but is especially prominent in holiday vespers rituals. In terms of its sound, *araray zema* is often characterized by a higher vocal range, while *gə'əez zema* has frequent distinctive vocal slides (*rekrek*). The third category, *'əzl zema*, which translates as "to separate, isolate, or set aside" or "to retire, withdraw from," is heard less frequently within the liturgy; *'əzl* is mainly associated with some annual holidays and Holy Week. Musicians further acknowledge another level of sacred association for each of the three categories of melody: *gə'əz zema* is associated with God, the Father; *'əzl zema* with Christ, the Son; and *araray zema* with the Holy Spirit.[11]

The chant is first sung in unison by the musicians, or sometimes in alternation between the "two sides" on which the musicians stand. Next, entire chants or sections thereof are repeated with different instrumental accompaniment. Initially, the chant is

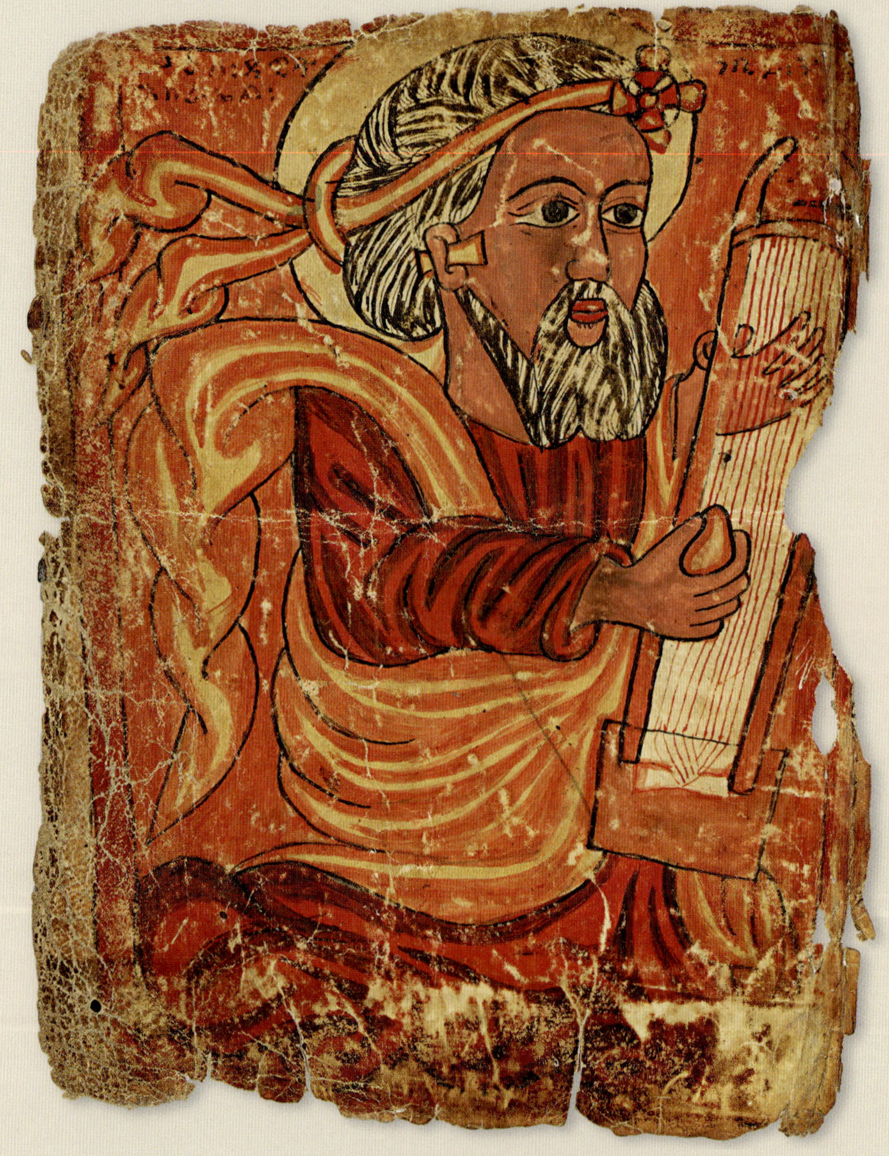

ETHIOPIAN DEVOTIONS

sung slowly by the entire group, accompanied by graceful motions of the prayer staff, called *zemmame*. The patterns traced by the prayer staff can be quite complex, ranging from holding the staff and tossing it in the air to moving it from side to side, sometimes hitting the bottom of the staff on the floor to emphasize a particular beat. The *zemmame* is followed by a multipart section of the ritual known as *märägd*, in which the chant is accompanied by sistra and drums. The tempo changes several times during repetitions within this section, with different sistra and drum patterns interacting. And then the musicians begin the final section with drumming and dance, with the prayer staff carried on the left shoulder. The concluding section of the dance is performed at double speed, with the drummers "moving rapidly, jumping and circling around. This is likened to the flapping of the wings of the bird."[12] One can only wonder whether the comparison of dance to the flapping of wings relates to the birds said to have lifted Saint Yared up to heaven.

These melodies, instrumental parts, and the dance can inspire the congregations of the faithful. Their power to elicit an emotional response rests in part on how the chant reflects the meaning of the words, as well as how a *däbtära* inflects and ornaments the melody. But beyond the virtuosity of the performance at hand, the legend of Saint Yared brings to the chant the power of its connection with both nature and God:

The legend on Yared's life holds that he was transported to Heaven in a Spiritual trance where he heard the angels, the Seraphim and the Cherubim, sing "Holy! Holy! Holy!" The legend further maintains that he was led to the Garden of Eden by three angels in the guise of three white birds, and there mastered the sounds of the animals and the beasts. Yared, the polyglot of nature's varied sounds, incorporated in his hymns, reflections and observations of nature and its kaleidoscopic phenomena, all to the glory of the Creator. Thus, his compositions reflect the periodicity of the seasons, and of the agricultural cycle.[13]

Portuguese Jesuits noted in detail the deep emotional content of Ethiopian liturgical performance and commented on its impact on both the musicians and their congregations:

Whatever they say, they accompany with suitable movements of face and body. Thus they speak weeping the words of tears; laughing those of laughter; leaping those of leaping; loudly those of clamour; softly those of silence; in short, whatever they utter, they show with such bodily gesture as to be understood no less through the speaker's signs than through his voice. ...They carry out the divine offices with so much piety and inward feeling that those who are present can hardly restrain their tears.[14]

There are other factors that shape the power of the *däbtära*, both within and outside the liturgical setting. As noted above, there are clear indications that Ethiopian chants have since early times induced states of intense joy or sadness on the part of their performers and listeners. We have also seen that Saint Yared is portrayed as being in

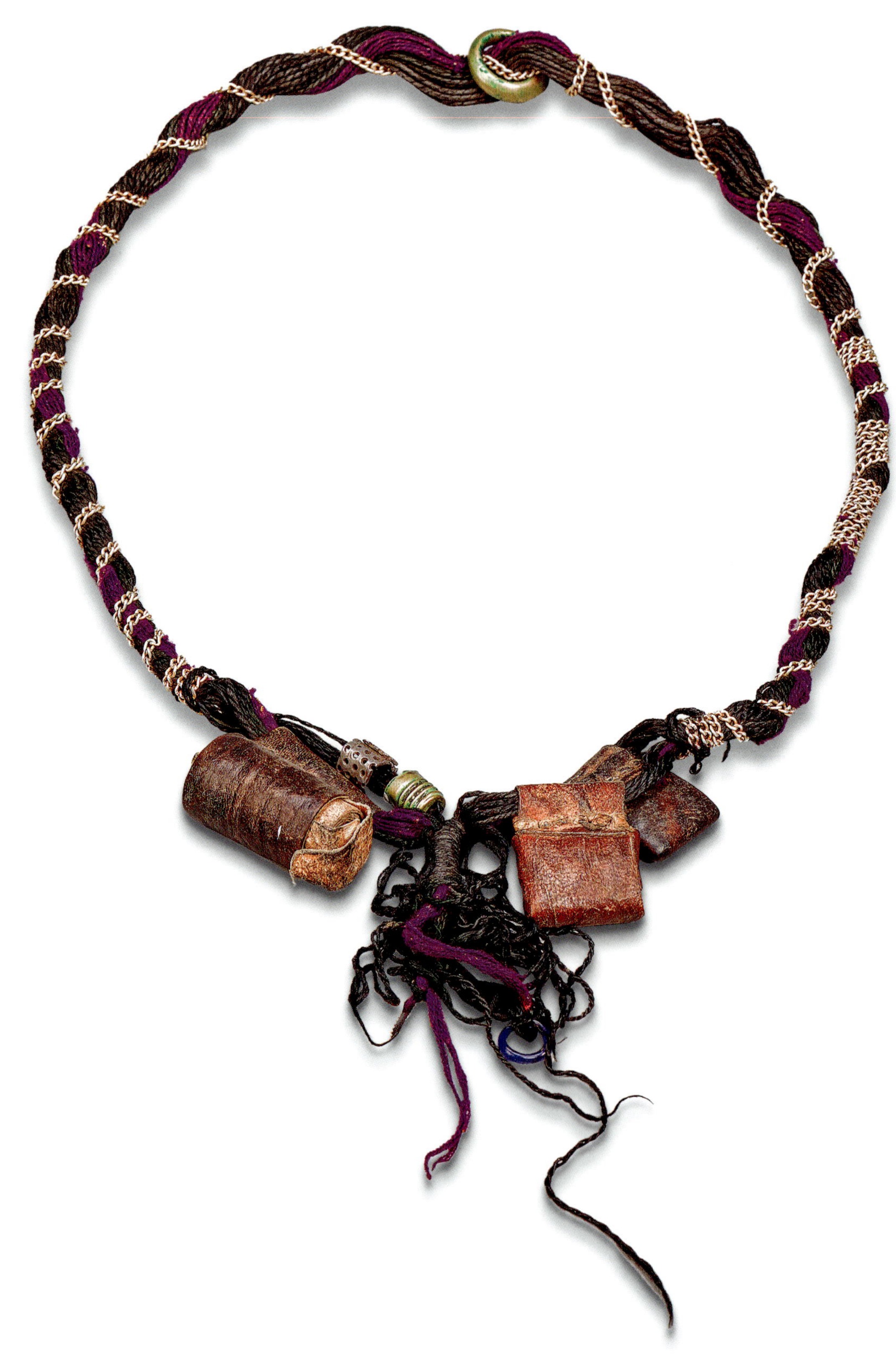

what resembles an altered state during his chant performance before the king, to the extent that he did not experience pain when the king's spear entered his foot.[15] While it is well known that Ethiopian *däbtäras* sometimes work as healers, a great deal of secrecy surrounds healing practices, and these activities are rarely discussed.[16] Largely due to their literacy and expertise with the written and verbal arts, some young *däbtäras* became masters at *abennät*, performing an array of therapies including preparing herbal remedies, writing magic scrolls worn as amulets, and reading divinatory texts. While there are other secular healers in Ethiopia who make use of herbal therapies, only the *däbtära* can prepare therapies or charms based on sacred texts. These charms, called *dägam*, can be recited orally or written down and sewn into an amulet (fig. 7.7); in either written or oral form, these charms invoke sacred church texts to identify and defeat supernatural elements that are causing illness or misfortune among the faithful. In the case of Ethiopian *däbtäras*, their association with healing has led to ambivalence as to their status within the Ethiopian Orthodox Church hierarchy, enhancing their prestige but at the same time linking them to the supernatural.

Familiarity with the legend of Saint Yared and the liturgy with which he is associated provides a rich context for understanding the relationship of music and musicians to the closely related domains of Ethiopian art and manuscript illumination. Together, they reveal a world of religious practice that interacts with musical instruments and other sacred objects believed by the faithful to descend from Yared's time and practice. In the realms of Ethiopian Orthodox Christian belief, liturgical performance enacts the story of Saint Yared and brings it to life for the congregation as much more than myth.

Ethiopian Orthodox, *Dagm* (amulets) necklace. Fiber, metal, shell, animal skin, and plastic, diameter: 18 inches (45.7 cm). National Museum of African Art, Smithsonian Institution, Gift of Franklin H. Williams, 73-19-75

Acknowledgments

This book is dedicated to Marilyn E. Heldman, in recognition of her life and work in defining the field of Ethiopian Church art history and continuing to contribute to it for more than five decades.

Dr. Heldman, along with members of the staff of the National Museum of African Art, began work on *Ethiopian Devotions* in 2009. Unfortunately, the progress on the book proved more complex than anticipated and, for a time, other projects demanded the Museum's attention, delaying publication.

The National Museum of African Art is profoundly grateful to the family of Dr. Heldman, her stepdaughter, Nina Gilden Seavey, filmmaker and film professor, George Washington University, and to each of the distinguished scholars who contributed to this publication: Dr. LaVerle Berry, Library of Congress (now retired); Prof. Marie-Laure Derat, National Center for Scientific Research (CNRS); Prof. Getachew Haile, Hill Museum and Manuscripts Library (posthumously); Dr. Denis Nosnitsin, Universität Hamburg, Hiob Ludolf Centre for Ethiopian and Eritrean Studies; and Prof. Kay Kaufman Shelemay, G. Gordon Watts Research Professor of Music and of African and African American Studies, Harvard University. Their unwavering dedication to honor Dr. Heldman and her scholarship throughout this publication served as an inspiration to all of us.

With Dr. Heldman's passing in 2019, we turned to her network of friends and colleagues engaged in similar research to maintain the depth and breadth of her signature high-quality scholarship. We acknowledge with deep gratitude Prof. Finbar Barry Flood, William R. Kenan Jr. Professor of Humanities, Institute of Fine Arts and Department of Art History, New York University; Prof. Michael Gervers, professor of art history, University of Toronto; Dr. Jacopo Gnisci, lecturer & exams chair, Department of History of Art, University College London, and visiting academic in the Department of Africa, Oceania and the Americas, The British Museum; and Carolin Schäfer, PhD candidate in the Department of Art History, University of Toronto.

Individuals and institutions supported our efforts to gather materials and images. We thank Tezera Belheu, who hand delivered a lithograph print from Dire Dawa; Mario Di Salvo, architect and architectural historian, who loaned us use of his plans for Ethiopia's basilica churches; and Dr. Rebecca Nagy, director emeritus of the

Harn Museum of Art, who aligned connections for quick response to an image request. Drs. Takele Merid and Yohannes Adigeh, the former and current directors of the Institute of Ethiopian Studies, Addis Ababa University, respectively, as well as Messay Yohannes, head of audiovisual, were incredibly responsive and generous with their time and expertise. Prof. Masresha Fetene was a true partner in facilitating and co-ordinating activities in Addis Ababa to help us meet our tight editing and publishing timelines.

The Lilly Foundation Inc. provided the financial support needed to make possible the publication of this stunning volume.

Finally, Dr. Heran Sereke-Brhan, deputy director of the National Museum of African Art, led the *Ethiopian Devotions* staff team that included Migs Grove, now-retired senior editor; Jarrett Smith, head of projects; Brad Simpson, photographer; Haley Steinhilber, archivist; and Henry W. Niepoetter from the Museum's Warren M. Robbins Library.

Our hope is that the publication of *Ethiopian Devotions* will serve as a fitting capstone to Dr. Heldman's groundbreaking career.

John K. Lapiana | Director, National Museum of African Art

Notes

PREFACE

1. I thank Nina Gilden Seavey, director, Documentary Center in the School of Media and Public Affairs, George Washington University, and Almaz Baraki, Kotebe University College, Addis Ababa, for their invaluable assistance in writing this preface. Jan Ziolkowski, Arthur Kingsley Porter Professor of Medieval Literature at Harvard University and the director of Dumbarton Oaks Research Library and Collection, graciously provided details of Marilyn Heldman's work as a Dumbarton Oaks Fellow during 2005–6. Getatchew Haile offered additional valuable suggestions on a draft of this text. We are all deeply indebted to Fentahun Tiruneh, senior reference librarian (Ethiopian Languages Collection), African and Middle Eastern Reading Room of the Library of Congress, for his devoted efforts to archive Marilyn Heldman's research materials, personal papers, and photographs.

2. "Early Byzantine Miniatures Revealed. Marilyn E. Heldman, University of Missouri, St. Louis, Fellow 2005–2006, Fall," *Oaks News* (Dumbarton Oaks, Research Library and Collection) (Fall 2005).

FOREWORD

1. Heran Sereke-Brhan, ed., "Festschrift in Honor of Richard and Rita Pankhurst," special issue, *Journal of Ethiopian Studies* 40, nos. 1–2 (2007).

2. Several obituary essays commemorating Marilyn's life and contributions helped inform this essay. See Kay Kaufman, "Personalia—In Memoriam Marilyn E. Heldman (1935–2019)," *Aethiopica: International Journal of Ethiopian and Eritrean Studies* 22 (2019): 253–61; and Jacopo Gnisci, "Marilyn Heldman, 1935–2019," *Rassegna di Studi Etiopici*, 3a serie, vol. 4, no. 51 (2020): 233–34.

INTRODUCTION
THE ABRAHAMIC TRADITION IN THE HORN OF AFRICA
MARILYN E. HELDMAN

1. See BL MS Oriental No. 821.

CHAPTER 1

THE CHURCH OF GÄNNÄTÄ MARYAM

MARILYN E. HELDMAN

1.   Monti della Corte, *Lalibelà*, 104–6; Buxton, *Christian Antiquities of Northern Ethiopia*, 31–32, pl. X; Sauter, "Où en est notre connaissance des églises rupestres," 270; Gerster, *Churches in Rock*, 115–18, pls. 130–43; Lepage, "L'art du Xe au XVe siècle," 59–63, figs. 1–18. The road from Lalibäla runs through Gännätä Maryam and Kulmesk before reaching Woldiya.

2.   The ceremonial center built by the Zag^{w}e kings, today known as Lalibäla but originally named Roha, with its "ten churches carved from a single rock," was created as a replica of the Holy Land and continues to be an important pilgrimage center for Ethiopia's Christians. Adafa, the political half of the bifurcated Zag^{w}e capital, is no longer extant. For Lalibäla, see Perruchon, *Vie de Lalibala*, 126; Haile, "Forty-Nine Hour Sabbath," 6:10, 15. For a summary of the history of the Zag^{w}e dynasty and its documentation, see Tamrat, *Church and State in Ethiopia*, 53–68; for plans and photographs of the churches of Lalibäla, see Bianchi Barriviera, *Le chiese in roccia di Lalibelá*; Gerster, *Churches in Rock*, pls. 89–90; for an analysis of the cult of King Lalibäla at the site, see Heldman, "Legends of Lālibalā."

3.   On foot, Gännätä Maryam is about four hours from Lalibäla.

4.   Michael, Chojnacki, and Pankhurst, eds., *Dictionary of Ethiopian Biography*, vol. 1, with earlier bibliography; Heldman and Haile, "Who Is Who in Ethiopia's Past."

5.   *Äbba* ("Father") is an honorific title applied to religious leaders, including monks. Äbba Mätta' is commemorated on the third day of the month Tərr in the Ethiopian calendar. Haile, "Homily of Abba Eləyas," and *The Beauty of Creation*.

6.   Conti Rossini, "L'Evangelo d'oro di Dabra Libanos." See also Bausi and Lusini, "Appunti in margine."

7.   Heldman and Haile, "Who Is Who in Ethiopia's Past," 3–4. I wish to acknowledge my gratitude to Getatchew Haile for the many authoritative translations of Gə'əz he provided for my studies over the years.

8.   Perruchon, *Vie de Lalibala*, 124.

9.   Conti Rossini, "L'Evangelo d'oro di Dabra Libanos"; Schneider, "L'évangéliaire de Dabra Libanos," 2: 163; Bausi and Lusini, "Appunti in margine."

10.   Translation by Getatchew Haile.

11.   Their martyrdom is commemorated on 15 Tərr: Budge, *History of Ethiopia, Nubia & Abyssinia*, 2: 497–500; Colin, *Le synaxaire éthiopien: Mois de Tərr*, 1990.

12.   Mary of Egypt is commemorated on 6 Miyazya: Budge, *History of Ethiopia, Nubia & Abyssinia*, 3: 784–87; Colin, *Le synaxaire éthiopien: Mois de Miazya*. Her feast is celebrated on the same day in the calendars of the Egyptian and Greek Churches, i.e., 6 Barmudah and 1 April; and also in the Greek Church on the fifth Sunday of Lent (*The Lenten Triodion*, 447–62).

13.   An Ethiopic Miracle of Mary composed in the fifteenth century relates how Our Lady Mary appeared in the company of female saints and matriarchs including Sophia, Barbara, Juliana, Anba Marina, and Sarah. See Haile, "Identity of Silondis." According to the text, the bodies of Barbara and Juliana were located in a church in Cairo.

14.   Saint Anba Marina is commemorated on 15 Nahase along with Saints Christina and Lawrence: Budge, *History of Ethiopia, Nubia & Abyssinia*, 4:1217ff; Guidi, *Le synaxaire éthiopien: Mois de Nahasê et de Paguemên*. She is celebrated on the same day (21 August) in the Egyptian Church (Meinardus, *Monks and Monasteries of the Egyptian Deserts*, 152). L. Clugnet's monograph on the subject, *Vie et office de sainte Marine* (Paris, 1905), was unavailable to me.

15.   Budge, *History of Ethiopia, Nubia & Abyssinia*, 2: 564–66.

ESSAY 1
HOLY SANCTUARY

1.   Heldman, "Church Buildings," 737–40.

2.   Heldman, "Creating Sacred Space," 285–302.

3.   Budge, *History of Ethiopia, Nubia & Abyssinia*, 1: 27–75.

CHAPTER 2
EMPEROR ZÄRʾA YAʿƏQOB AND THE CULT OF OUR LADY MARY
MARILYN E. HELDMAN

1.   Heldman, *Marian Icons*, 75.

2.   The Book of Saints (Synaxary) of the Ethiopian Orthodox Church defines Our Lady Mary's intercessional role: Our Lady Mary "intercedes with her Beloved Son on behalf of the children of men and makes Him to forgive the sins of those who call upon her name."

3.   In present-day Ethiopia, it is important to give one's child a meaningful name, and that was evidently the case in the fifteenth century at the time of the emperor's birth.

4.   Chojnacki, *Ethiopian Icons*, 416.

5.   Wishing to avoid a schism in the Ethiopian Orthodox Church, Zär'a Ya'əqob decreed that both the Sunday Sabbath and the Saturday Sabbath be celebrated. This decree is symbolized by the dual portraits of Saint Ewosṭatewos and Saint Täklä Haymanot that then appeared in Marian devotional images usually at Our Lady Mary's left (viewer's right). Images of the two wearing the fluffy monastic *qob* (hat) are depicted side by side in Ethiopian Marian icons. As the elder, Saint Täklä Haymanot has white hair, and Saint Ewosṭatewos has black hair. They symbolize the unity of the Ethiopian Orthodox Church. Sometimes, they are accompanied by the monastic Saint Gäbrä Mänfäs Qəddus, who is depicted with holy hair.

ESSAY 2
OUR LADY MARY

1.   See Haile, *The Mariology of Emperor Zär'a Ya'əqob*.

CHAPTER 3

THE BLESSED VIRGIN: INSPIRATION FOR ETHIOPIAN ARTISTS
GETATCHEW HAILE

1. *Dərsanä Kidanä Məhrät*, EMML 1860, ff. 34v–38r; Haile, *Catalogue* 4: 370.

2. Matthew 12:42; Luke 11:31.

3. There are Ethiopian women named "Azeb," as there are those who are named "Ethiopia."

4. Cf. 1 Cor 2:9; and the *Mystagogia*, which is part of the *Testament of Our Lord*; Hammerschmidt, *Äthiopische liturgische Texte*, 40–42.

5. Haile, *Mariology*, 6

6. Clergy who have no priestly ordination. They perform the different services in the Church that do not require priestly authority, such as the rituals. The Ethiopian Orthodox Church is indebted to the *däbtära* for most of its locally composed religious literature.

7. They are called *Bartos* and *Säne Golgota*, respectively.

8. Several versions of the text exist. This one is a translation from EMML 5996, ff. 14r–15v. For the edited text, see Euringer, "Die Binde."

9. Budge, *Miracles*, 94–97.

10. Arras, *Patericon*, 180–81.

11. The teachers have not yet caught the mistake of misreading of *Əmənnä Ṣəyon* ("from Zion") as *Əmmənä Ṣəyon* ("our mother [is] Zion").

12. It was presumably composed by Emperor Zär'a Ya'əqob as a counterpart of the Arabic *Al-Fatḥah*, sura 1 of the Qur'an.

13. Perruchon, *Chroniques*, 6.

14. Haile. *Mariology*, 143.

15. Heldman, *Marian Icons*.

16. Walters Museum of Art, Baltimore, MS W. 850, fol. 207v.

17. See Heldman, "Style." See also the Gundä Gunde illuminated manuscripts in this volume.

18. An altar tablet of wood or stone represents the stone tablets received by Moses. This holy tablet functions as a table for the fraction of the Eucharistic bread, and it is revered and feared as much as the Ark of the Covenant as recounted in the Old Testament. Haile, "Forty-Nine Hour Sabbath," 13–14.

19. Arras, *Collectio*, 17–18.

20. Conti Rossini, *Historia*, 73. The Oromo fortune teller looks at the fat covering the heart of the cow they slaughter and reads from it what will occur in the near future.

21. E.g., Budge, *Miracles*, 6–7.

22. Budge, *Miracles*, 48, 55.

23. Cf. Psalms 113/114:4 and 6.

24. Psalms 132/133:1.

25. In the *Tä'ammərä Maryam*, published in Addis Ababa in 1961 Ethiopian Calendar (1968/9 Gregorian Calendar), there is a Miracle about an Ethiopian pilgrim's failed attempt to take to his country the icon that he brought from Jerusalem for Märina/Martha of Saidnaya (43–48). This is based on the

Synaxary reading for the tenth day of Mäskäräm (Budge, *History of Ethiopia, Nubia & Abyssinia*, 1: 34–36). The commemoration was added to the revised Synaxary of 1581 AD (EMML 2054).

26. EMML 6835, fol. 131v–132r. This manuscript is not yet catalogued, but it is described in detail in Haile, *Homily*, 6–8.

27. Spencer, "Icons," 67–93; Spencer, "Travels," 201–20; Spencer, *Woman from Tedbab*, 201. See also Heldman, "St. Luke," 125–48.

28. Cf. *Ḥamärä Noḫ*, "Ark of Noah."

29. The story appears in many copies of the Miracles of Mary. This one is a translation of the text in EMML 5988, fols. 39v–40r.

30. Kidane, "Hymns," 817–19. Authors of religious texts prefer to remain anonymous by virtue of their modesty.

31. The Anaphora that is widely used is ascribed to the Egyptian bishop Cyriacus; the second and the third are ascribed to an individual known only as Gregory and the fourth to the Apostle Nathaniel. See Hammerschmidt, *Studies*, 16, 25, 26, and 33, respectively.

ESSAY 3
HOLY MANUSCRIPTS

1. Bausi, *Languages and Cultures*, 130.

2. Heldman, *Marian Icons*, 65–67

3. *Actes de Marḥa Krǝstos*, 92.

4. Budge, *History of Ethiopia, Nubia & Abyssinia*, 746.

CHAPTER 4
ETHIOPIC HAGIOGRAPHY: HISTORY, SAINTS, AND TEXTS
DENIS NOSNITSIN

1. The present study was begun as part of the project Ethio-SPaRe: Cultural Heritage of Christian Ethiopia—Salvation, Presrvation, and Research, headed by myself and funded by the European Research Council under the seventh Research Framework Programme IDEAS (Independent Researcher Starting Grant 240720, December 2009–May 2015), https://www.aai.uni-hamburg.de/en/ethiostudies/research/ethiospare.html. It was completed with the support of the long-term project Beta Maṣāḥǝft: Manuscripts of Ethiopia and Eritrea, funded by the Academy of Sciences and Humanities in Hamburg, based at the Hiob Ludolf Center for Ethiopian and Eritrean Studies, https://www.betamasaheft.uni-hamburg.de/. Many phenomena described in the essay continue today in the Orthodox culture of the neighboring state of Eritrea. Keeping this in mind, I will refrain from systematic reference to Eritrea for the sake of simplicity, unless indispensable.

2. See Tamrat, "Hagiographies," 12. Zelleke, "Bibliography," lists 201 Ethiopian saints, most of them with their Acts; Cañellas, Virgulin, and Guaita, *Enciclopedia*, includes articles on approximately 260 saints. There are also higher estimations; cf. Alehegne, "Regularity," 145. An updated register of all Ethiopian Christian saints and hagiographic works is a desideratum.

3.   In quantitative terms of manuscript production, a study of some ninety ecclesiastic libraries in Ṭəgray (northern Ethiopia) carried out by Ethio-SPaRe (see Nosnitsin, *Churches*) showed that manuscripts with major hagiographic works comprise 20 percent of approximately 2,000 recorded manuscripts. The number of hagiographic manuscripts in the microfilm collection in the Hill Monastic Microfilm Library totals 1,213, out of 8,000 manuscripts microfilmed (the calculation of Adam C. McCollum, see https://hmmlorientalia.wordpress.com/2013/07/01/hagiography-among-the-emml-manuscripts/).

4.   Presenting an in-depth discussion accompanied by a comprehensive bibliography on the subject is not the aim of this essay. Mostly the edited Acts of the saints will be referred to. For more information and relevant bibliography on the saints, texts and editions, place names, and other aspects of the Acts discussed, the reader is advised to consult such works as *Encyclopaedia Aethiopica*, featuring informative articles on Ethiopic hagiography and on nearly all saints whose Acts have been edited; Zelleke, "Bibliography"; Cañellas, Virgulin, and Guaita, *Enciclopedia*; Brita, *Racconti*; see also surveys of the history of Ethiopic literature. Some seminal contributions and basic bibliography are gathered in Bausi, *Languages and Cultures*; Brita, "Genres," has an updated bibliography.

5.   The transmission of the hagiographic works and text-critical studies of Ethiopic hagiography, as a separate topic, are not addressed here. The survey is arranged in four parts according to the purported origin of the hagiographic works (which in most cases corresponds to the saint's primary veneration center or "sanctuary") to provide a cognitive aid for those not acquainted with the Ethiopic material. A number of hagiographic works became popular across wider areas; for many others, we cannot be sure about their place of creation.

6.   By the fourteenth century at the latest, Gə'əz was no longer a spoken language but endured as the literary and liturgical language of the Ethiopian Orthodox Church.

7.   This was a group of monk-missionaries from the Middle East, traditionally credited with introducing monasticism to Ethiopia; see Brita, *Racconti*; "Nine Saints," and other relevant articles in *Encyclopaedia Aethiopica*.

8.   The saint is also known as Äbba Sälama Käsate Bərhan (Sälama "Revealer of Light").

9.   These ancient manuscripts are scattered in different parts of the country, MSS EMML no. 1763, dating to 1336/37 or 1339/40, Däbrä Ḥayq Əsṭifanos (Haile, *Catalogue*, 5: 218–31; various homilies from this manuscript have been edited by Getatchew Haile); EMML no. 7602 (uncatalogued), possibly dating to the late thirteenth or fourteenth century, also known as the Homiliary of Tulluu Guddoo (an island in Lake Zʷay where the manuscript has been preserved; see Meyer, "Tulluu Guddoo," 2010); EMML no. 8509 (Ṭana Qirqos; uncatalogued), eleventh or twelfth century; London, British Library Or. 8192, a fourteenth-century homiliary from Gʷənagʷəna, today in Eritrea (Strelcyn, *Catalogue*, 89–92), its early fourteenth-century "twin homiliary" was found in the church of 'Ura Qirqos, Ṭəgray (photographed by Ethio-SPaRe).

10.   See Nosnitsin, "Ancient Chants," with the edition and analysis of the ancient chants for Yoḥanni of Däbrä Sina.

11.   On Saint Yared, see, most recently, Heldman and Shelemay, "Concerning Saint Yared," 70–74. See Shelemay's essay in this volume.

12.   Cf. Bausi, *Versione etiopica*.

13.   See Bausi, "Ethiopic Literary Production," and Bausi, "Translations."

14. See Bausi, "Massacre." A number of other Ethiopic "hagiographical cycles" are noted in Cerulli, *Letteratura etiopica*.

15. Cf. Bausi, "Osservazioni"; Pisani, "Apocryphal Acts."

16. On the translated literature and the oldest layer of Ethiopic literary tradition, see Bausi, "Translations."

17. On the forms of Byzantine hagiography, see Kazhdan and Talbot, "Hagiography"; for Coptic hagiography, see Orlandi, "Hagiography."

18. The author of the Acts of Gärima, probably representing a kind of transition, describes them as *dərsan*, and the Acts of Yared as *gädl wä-dərsan*, "acts and homily."

19. But cf. the case described in Nosnitsin, "Ethiopic Synaxarion."

20. Each strophe begins with words *Sälam la-* … , or "Salutation to (your). … "

21. See Chaîne, "Répertoire"; Haile, "Builders of Churches."

22. For the *Dəggʷa*, the main antiphonary of the Ethiopian Orthodox Church, see Jeffery, "Liturgical Year"; on other chant collections, see Velat, "Le mawāše'et" and relevant articles in *Encyclopaedia Aethiopica*.

23. The process is aptly described in Tamrat, *Church and State*, 156–205. See also Kaplan, *Monastic Holy Man*; Derat, *Le domaine des rois*.

24. Possibly fourteenth century; see Brita, *Racconti*, 145–87; and Brita, "Ṗänṭälewon."

25. In 1450 CE, King Zär'a Ya'əqob formally approved the observance of the Saturday Sabbath as well as the Sunday Sabbath at the Council of Däbrä Məṭmaq, thereby ending the controversy; see Tamrat, *Church and State*, 229–30.

26. See Lusini, *Studi*, 35–67.

27. See Bausi and Lusini, "Philological Study."

28. Its sophisticated captions are interpreted in Fiaccadori, "Ewosṭateans," 465 (figure).

29. The unique illuminated manuscript with these two Acts originating from the monastery of Gundä Gunde is located in the New York Public Library, Spencer Collection, Ethiopic Ms 7. See Heldman, *African Zion*, 190.

30. See Nosnitsin, "New Branches."

31. This is the only known Ethiopic literary work to have been translated into Arabic during the reign of King Gälawdewos (r. 1540–59); see Nosnitsin, "Täklä Haymanot"; Wadi, "Arabic Lives."

32. See Heldman, *Marian Icons*, 52–54, 81, 83.

33. On the Ethiopian female saints and their Acts, see Belcher, "Life and Visions."

34. Cf. Derat, *L'enigme*.

35. For the *tabot*, the so-called altar tablet of Ethiopian churches, see Heldman, "Tabot."

36. There is an essential difference between the hundreds of saints who are known and venerated in Ethiopia (e.g., many foreign saints from the Synaxarion and the Acts of the Martyrs) and a smaller group of saints for whom a full-scale liturgical veneration has been established. For the latter, at least one *tabot* was consecrated and placed in a church or monastery; see Brita, "Agiografia"; Nosnitsin, "Introduction." An institution was considered to be dedicated to the saint if his or her *tabot* was elevated to the position of the "principal *tabot*." The feast of the saint was then celebrated as the church's main annual feast.

37.   Frequently, the saint's burial was also located at that institution, the destination of pilgrimage and the site where believers expect the saint's miraculous powers to be the strongest.

38.   The chronological and geographical scope of the saint's cult (primarily the death and burial days) form the system of the so-called "hagiographic coordinates" of scholarly hagiographic studies.

39.   The time span between the death of the saint and the composition of their Acts could vary significantly; cf. Kaplan, "Hagiographies," 108–9; Conti Rossini, *Ethiopian Hagiography*, 330–33.

40.   Cf. Tamrat, "Hagiographies," 15; Kaplan, "Hagiographies," 110–15.

41.   Here I follow the definition of the hagiographic topos as explained in Von der Nahmer, *Die lateinische Heiligenvita*, 155–56; see also Brita, *Racconti*, 239–55; Brita, "Agiografia."

42.   The depiction of saints' childhoods in Ethiopic hagiography has been addressed in numerous studies; see, for instance, Kaplan, "Hagiographies"; Kaplan, *Holy Man*; Marrassini, "Infanzia"; Kaplan, "Seen but Not Heard"; Brita, "Agiografia"; Alehegne, "Regularity."

43.   In Gə'əz, it is called *kidan* (covenant); it is often regarded as a distinctive feature of Ethiopic hagiography; cf. Tamrat, "Hagiographies," 16; Kur and Nosnitsin, "Iyäsus Mo'a," but also Conti Rossini, *Ethiopian Hagiography*, 330; Bumazhnov, "Ascetic Suicides," 8.

44.   Cf. Brita, *Racconti*.

45.   The mechanisms of the reuse of literary material in Ethiopic hagiography (today falling within the broader notion of intertextuality) are studied and discussed in Nosnitsin, "Vite"; Brita, *Racconti*, 252–55; Marrassini, "Text," 390–91.

46.   Ultimately, the aims of medieval Ethiopian hagiographers and historiographers were not so different. Both dealt with the study and interpretation of the past, but from different perspectives and for different purposes. Some scholars (e.g., Marrassini, "Text") have noticed the subtle connection between Ethiopic hagiography and historiography and the absence of a clear boundary between the two.

47.   The Acts of Äbba Yoḥanni of Däbrä 'Aśa; see Basset, "Vie de Abbâ Yohanni."

48.   As was anticipated more than once; see Kaplan, "Hagiographies," 115.

ESSAY 4
NARRATIVE IMAGERY

1.   Di Salvo, *Churches of Ethiopia*, 198–208.

CHAPTER 5
THE ETHIOPIAN STATE AND THE RELIGIOUS CENTERS FROM THE THIRTEENTH TO THE SIXTEENTH CENTURY
MARIE-LAURE DERAT

1.   See the two classical syntheses on this issue, Tamrat, *Church and State*, and Kaplan, *Holy Man*, as well as Derat, "Modèles," and the most recent survey of medieval Ethiopian history, Kelly, ed., *Companion to Medieval Ethiopia and Eritrea*.

2.   Gerster, *Kirchen im Fels*, 116; Heldman, "Architectural Symbolism," 230–32.

3.   Heldman and Haile, "Who Is Who," 4.

4.	Mercier, "Peintures," 144–45. See also the recent study of this cave church by Derat et al., "The Rock-Cut Churches."

5.	Dillmann, *Über die Regierung*, 18–20; Leslau, *Comparative Dictionary of Ge'ez*, 401. See also Matthew 26:6–13 and Mark 14:3.

6.	For the paintings in the narthex of Gännätä Maryam, see Heldman, "Wise Virgins," 6–9, and Heldman, "Metropolitan Bishops," 87–95; for the names Kʷäläṣewon and Täḥräyännä Maryam, see Balicka-Witakoswka, "Liturgical Fan," 28–29. For a recent discussion of this topic, see Derat, "L'enigme."

7.	Nosnitsin, "Wäwähabo qob'a wä'askema," 230.

8.	Haile and Macomber, *Catalogue*, 294–301; Bosc-Tiessé, *Spirit*.

9.	Hable-Sellassie, "Monastic Library," 246–47.

10.	Hable-Sellassie, "Monastic Library," 254.

11.	Bosc-Tiessé, *Spirit*, 202–3.

12.	Bosc-Tiessé, *Spirit*, 223.

13.	Kropp, "Welt," 307–11; Kropp, "Die dritte Würde," 192, 197–98.

14.	Kropp, "Die dritte Würde," 194.

15.	Derat, "Modèles," 94–95

16.	Derat 2006: 73. This correspondence was copied in the Gospel of the Church of Däbrä Kärbe. The letter reads: "I, 'aqqabe *sä'at* Amḥa Lä Ṣäyon, greet you. Peace be with you all the community of holy monks who are living in Däbrä Kärbe. May the peace of the Father, the Son and the Holy Spirit be with you, each day and at all times."

The Lord has appointed you to travel on the way of the Gospel, the road of life. He turns you away from the path of sin, that leads to the fires of hell, and Jesus, the great High Priest, will lead you into His kingdom of Heaven, for ever and ever, Amen.

I have heard that some of you do not follow the monastic rule. Instead you are calling yourselves my children, you are living in the (secular) world, building houses near the residence of the women. Then you return to the monastery of monks, and again you go back into the (secular) world. He who behaves like this, may he renounce this bad habit, may he repent of his previous sin with great penitence and may he do as the priest ordered. If he does not renounce this habit, may he ever return to the monastery.

"May this message be written in the Gospel, so that it will be a testimony before God, between me and you. And all of you, monks who love the Lord and who go on His way, He will bless you and will let you enter into His kingdom, forever, Amen."

17.	For the various recensions of the Life of Täklä Haymanot, see Nosnitsin, "Täklä Haymanot."

18.	This episode has been studied by many scholars: Cerulli, *Ethiopie*, vi–x; Tamrat, *Church and State*, 161–68; Kaplan, "Iyäsus Mo'a"; Derat, *Le domaine des rois*, 103–5; Nosnitsin, "Wäwähabo qob'a wä'askema."

19.	Cerulli, "Gli abbati," 284.

20. Tamrat, *Church in Ethiopia*, 95–96.

21. See the account of the victories of King Amdä Ṣəyon against the Ifat sultanate in the Italian translation (Marrassini, *Lo scettro e la croce*) or in the German translation (Kropp, *Der siegreiche Feldzug*).

22. Haile, "Religious Controversies."

23. Derat, "Modèles," 189–96.

24. Turaev, ed., *Vitae*, 220.

25. *Actes de Marḥa Krestos*, 89–90. One manuscript from the early the sixteenth century, now in the Schøyen collection (MS 2258), preserves the Life of Märḥa Krəstos copied after the Life of Täklä Haymanot, the Life of Filəṗṗos, and the Miracles of Täklä Haymanot.

26. *Actes de Marḥa Krestos*, 92.

27. Marilyn Heldman, in *Marian Icons*, was the first to highlight these specific institutions founded by the kings through her study of the artistic production of Fəre Ṣəyon.

28. Derat, *Le domaine des rois*, 259–313.

29. *Actes de Marḥa Krestos*, 59.

30. On this church, its Gospel, and the donations recorded in it, see Derat and Ayenachew, "Les sites," 25–37.

31. Perruchon, *Chronique*, 72–79.

32. For Francisco Alvares's account of being present at the translation of the body of King Na'od (r. 1494–1508) in the royal church of Mäkanä Śəllase in the 1520s, see Beckingham and Huntingford, *Prester John*, 338.

33. The Ethiopian *Book of the Miracles of Mary* has been studied and partly translated by Cerulli (*Il libro etiopico dei Miracoli di Maria e le sue fonti nelle letterature del medio evo latino*) and Colin (*Le livre éthiopien des miracles de Marie*).

34. Haile, " Religious Controversies."

35. Many of these homilies were edited and translated, including the *Book of the Light* (Zare'a Ya'eqob, *Il libro del luce*); the *Homily in Honor of Saint John the Evangelist* (Haile, "Anqäṣä Haymanot"); the *Epistle of Humanity* (Haile, *Epistle*); the *Homily in Honor of Archangel Gabriel* and the *Revelation of the Miracles of Mary* (Haile, *Mariology*).

36. Haile, *Beauty of the Creation*, 54–63; Derat, "Questions," 214–23.

37. Perruchon, *Chronique*, 5.

38. As demonstrated by Getatchew Haile (*Catalogue*, 1:599–603), EMML 1480 preserves a homily in honor of Saint Gabriel, a history of the patriarchs of the Old Testament, the Acts of Saint Yosṭinos, the *Epistle of Humanity* (Ṭomarä təsbə'ət), the *Homily in Honor of Saturday*, the *Handling of the Eucharist with Care* (Tä'aqəbo məsṭir), the *Book of Pearl* (Mäṣḥafä baḥrəy), and the *Introduction to the Miracles of Mary* (Ra'əy ta'ammər).

39. Lusini, *Studi*, vi.

40. Haile, "On the Identity of Silondis."

41. Derat, "Gomit."

42. Derat, "Royal Correspondence," 65.

43. Cerulli, "L'Etiopia del secolo XV," 80–99.

44. Derat and Aynachew, "Sites," 37–38.

45.   Ǝsṭifanos and his followers (known as the Stephanites) have received recent attention from scholars. See in particular Haile, *Ge'ez Acts*; Haile, *A History of the First Ǝsṭifanosite Monks*; Nosnitsin, *Ecclesiastic Landscape*. On the Stephanites' scriptorium, see in particular Heldman, "An Ēwosṭāthian Style."

46.   Haile, "Strict Observance," 227; Tesfaye, "Inscriptions," 126.

ESSAY 5
IMAGES OF GOD

1.   Haile, "On the Identity of Silondis," 59.

2.   Heldman, *Marian Icons*, 194–96.

3.   Heldman, "Trinity," 994–96.

4.   Haile, "Builders of Churches," 370; Haile to the author, September 21, 1988.

5.   *Liturgy of the Ethiopian Church*, 59.

6.   Colin, *Le synaxaire éthiopien: Mois de maggābit*, 426–27.

CHAPTER 6
THE LATE SOLOMONIC (GONDÄR) PERIOD, THE MID-SIXTEENTH TO THE MID-NINETEENTH CENTURY
LAVERLE BERRY

1.   Basset, *Histoire de la conquête de l'Abyssinie*, 2:246–310; Trimingham, *Islam in Ethiopia*, 84–94; Muth, "Aḥmad Grañ," 155–57

2.   Gebissa, "Oromo History," 61–62

3.   Conti Rossini, *Historia Regis Sarsa Dengel*, 50–51, 95, 133; Pankhurst, *History (Middle Ages)*, 94–100.

4.   Basset, *Études*, 131–32; Beguinot, *Cronaca*, 45–48; Beccari, *Rerum*, 7:179–89.

5.   Beshah and Wolde Aregay, *Union*, 79–97; Martínez d'Alòs-Moner, *Envoys*, 83–134.

6.   Basset *Études*, 132; Beguinot, *Cronaca*, 48; Berry, "Gondär-Style Architecture," 838.

7.   Wolde Aregay, "Gondar and Adwa," 57–61.

8.   Berry, "Architecture and Kingship."

9.   Crummey, *Land and Society*, 77, 82; Berry, "Architecture and Kingship."

10.   Guidi, *La chiesa*, 123–28, 186–90, 252–56.

11.   Guidi, *Annales (Iohannis)*, 23–24, 39–43; Guidi, *Annales (Iysu)*, 108–11; Crummey, *Land and Society*, 82–85.

12.   Basset, *Études*, 167–71; Beguinot, *Cronaca*, 82–86; Guidi, *Annales (Iohannis)*, 61–62, 80–83, 90–98.

13.   Heldman, "Madonna," 527–28.

14.   Bruce, *Travels*, 2:635–42; Guidi, *Annales (Iysu)*, 122–26; Balicka-Witakowska, *Steh auf*, 465–66.

15.   Heldman, *African Zion*, 195; Mercier, "Art History," 57–61, 64.

16.   Bruce, *Travels*, 2:599.

17.   Heldman, *African Zion*, 195–238; Di Salvo, *Churches of Ethiopia*, 11–31; Mercier, "Art History," 61–68.

18. Heldman, *African Zion*, 195–97; Ofcansky and Berry, *Ethiopia*, 318–20.

19. Guidi, *Annales (Iysu)*, 52–54, 95–114; Di Salvo, *Churches of Ethiopia*, 97–191; Crummey, *Land and Society*, 103–10.

20. Di Salvo, *Churches of Ethiopia*, 25, 160, 97–191.

21. Rubenson, *King of Kings*, 67–72; Pankhurst, *History (Mid-Nineteenth Century)*, 41–50; Berry, "Gondä Style Architecture," 841.

22. Rubenson, *King of Kings*, 85–89.

ESSAY 6
PROTECTION

1. Heldman, *Marian Icons*, 175–78.

2. Heldman, *Marian Icons*, 35–38, fig. 8.

3. Heldman, *Marian Icons*.

4. Heldman, "St. Luke as Painter," 125–48.

CHAPTER 7
AN IMAGE OF PERFORMANCE, AN EMBLEM OF POWER: SAINT YARED AND LITURGICAL MUSIC OF THE ETHIOPIAN ORTHODOX CHURCH
KAY KAUFMAN SHELEMAY

1. See Heldman and Shelemay, "Concerning Saint Yared," for details on the written sources and a new perspective on the dating of this tradition.

2. Budge, *History of Ethiopia, Nubia & Abyssinia*, 3: 875–77; Colin, *Le synaxaire éthiopien: Taḥśaś*.

3. See, for example, Giyorgis, *Tintawi Serate Mahelet ZeAbuna Yared*, 1997. This unusually long and detailed commemoration of Saint Yared and his musical system includes an English introduction by Hailu Habtu, xiii–xxxiv. A shorter volume, in English, was published in 1999: Abraham Habte-Sellassie, *St. Yared and Ethiopian Ecclesiastical Music*.

4. Habte-Sellassie, *St. Yared*, 37.

5. Hailu Habtu, "Introduction," xxviii.

6. Godinho, *De Abassinorum rebus*, 1:xxii.

7. Ethiopic is an ancient Semitic language with twenty-six consonants, each of which occurs in seven different forms modified to accommodate the seven vowels.

8. The *Wǝddase Maryam* is a famous office of the Ethiopian Orthodox Church containing blessings and praise of the Virgin Mary, a section of which is sung each day of the week. Weninger, "Sounds of Gǝʿǝz."

10. See Shelemay, "The Musician and Transmission of Religious Tradition," for additional details on these extended studies. The Ethiopian Christian notational system, which church musicians innovated in the sixteenth century, uses interlinear signs consisting of one or more characters from the Ethiopic syllabary. Each sign (*mǝlǝkkǝt*) is an abbreviated form of a word or phrase from the text of a well-known liturgical passage and cues the melody associated with that source text. The notation cannot be read without full knowledge of the oral tradition and is not used during ritual performance; see Shelemay and Jeffery, *Ethiopian Christian Chant*.

11. Shelemay and Jeffery, *Ethiopian Christian Chant*, 1:7.

12. Habtu, "Introduction," xxxii.

13.	Habtu, "Introduction," xxii.

14.	Godinho, *De Abassinorum rebus*.

15.	Many cultures past and present acknowledge the powerful role musicians play in altering states and relieving pain, with music serving as a common channel through which the experience of and response to pain is managed and mediated. Music's transformative role is more often than not a subject of marked ambivalence, and musicians engaged in healing practices have often been subjected to discrimination and derision. However, activities associated with healing are formally banned by the Ethiopian Orthodox Church, which considers the practices to be "outside approved disciplines." See Imbakom, *Traditional Ethiopian Church Education*, 2. See also Shelemay, "The Musician and Transmission of Religious Tradition."

16.	Many young *däbtära* in the past found it necessary to become mendicants, merchants, or healers in order to defray their expenses during the extraordinarily long period of traditional schooling. For further discussion of the economic aspects of these professions and *däbtäras'* activities as healers, see Shelemay, "The Musician and Transmission of Religious Tradition," 249–52.

Bibliography

Actes de Marḥa Krestos. Trans. Stanislas Kur. Louvain: Secrétariat du Corpus SCO, 1972.

Alehegne, Mersha Mengistie. "Regularity and Uniformity in the Ethiopian Hagiographical Tradition: A Particular Focus on Narrating the Childhood of Saints." *Aethiopica* 18 (2015): 145–62.

Arras, Victor. *Collectio monastica: Ethiopic Text*. Louvain: Secrétariat du Corpus SCO, 1963.

———. *Patericon aethiopice*. Louvain: Secrétariat du Corpus SCO, 1967.

Balicka-Witakowska, Ewa. "The Liturgical Fan and Some Recently Discovered Ethiopian Examples." *Rocznik Orientalistyczny* 17, no. 2 (2004): 19–46.

———. *Steh auf und geh nach Süden: 2000 Jahre Christentum in Äthiopien*. Frankfurt: Legat Verlag, 2007.

Basset, René. *Études sur l'histoire d'Éthiopie*. Paris: Imprimerie Nationale, 1882.

———. *Histoire de la conquête de l'Abyssinie par Chihab Eddin 'Ahmed ben 'Abd el Qâder*. 2 vols. Paris: Ernest Leroux, 1897.

Basset, René, ed. and trans. "Vie de Abbâ Yohanni: Texte éthiopien, traduction française avec une introduction." *Bulletin de correspondance africaine* 3 (1884): 433–53.

Bausi, Alessandro. "Alcuni osservazioni sul Gadla ḥawāryāt." *Annali dell'Istituto Orientale del Napoli* 60–61 (2000–2001): 77–114.

———. "Appunti sul Gadla Libānos." *Warszawskie Studia Teologiczne* 12, no. 2 (2000): 11–30.

———. "Ethiopic Literary Production Related to the Christian Egyptian Culture." In *Coptic Society, Literature and Religion from Late Antiquity to Modern Times: Proceedings of the Tenth International Congress of Coptic Studies, Rome, September 17th–22nd, 2012, and Plenary Reports of the Ninth International Congress of Coptic Studies, Cairo, September 15th–19th, 2008*, ed. P. Buzi, A. Camplani, and F. Contardi, 1:503–71. Leuven: E. Peeters, 2016.

———. "The Massacre of Najrān. The Ethiopic Sources," in *Juifs et chrétiens en Arabie aux Ve et VIe siècles*. Regards croisés sur les sources, eds. J. Beaucamp, F. Briquel-Chatonnet, and Ch. J. Robin, 241–54. Paris: Association des amis du Centre d'histoire et civilisation de Byzance, 2010.

———. "Translations in Late Antique Ethiopia." In *Egitto crocevia di traduzioni*, ed. F. Crevatin, 67–97. Trieste: EUT Edizioni dell'Università di Trieste, 2018.

Bausi, Alessandro, ed. *Languages and Cultures of Eastern Christianity: Ethiopian*. Burlington, VT: Ashgate 2012.

________ . *La versione etiopica degli Acta Phileae nel Gadla samā'tāt.* Naples: Istituto Universitario
Orientale, 2002.

Bausi, Alessandro, and Gianfrancesco Lusini. "Appunti in margine a una nuova ricerca sui conventi
eritrei." *Rassegna di Studi Etiopici* 36 (1992): 5–35.

________ ."The Philological Study of the Eritrean Manuscripts in Gǝ'ǝz: Methods and Practices."
In *International Conference on Eritrean Studies 20–22 July 2016*, vol. 1, *Literature, Linguistics,
Philology, History, Discourse Analysis, Education, Sociocultural Issues, Gender, Law, Regional
Dynamics, and Tigrinya Literature*, ed. Zemenfes Tsige et al. 125–41. Asmara: National Higher
Education and Research Institute 2016.

Beccari, Camillo, ed. *Rerum aethiopicarum scriptores occidentales inediti a saeculo XVI ad XIX.* 7 vols.
Rome: De Luigi, 1903.

Beckingham, C. F., and G. W. B. Huntingford. *The Prester John of The Indies: A True Relation of the Lands
of the Prester John; Being the Narrative of the Portuguese Embassy to Ethiopia in 1520, Written
by Father Francisco Alvarez.* Cambridge: Hakluyt Society, 1961.

Beguinot, Francesco. *La cronaca abbreviata d'Abissinia: Nuova versione dall'Etiopico e commento.*
Rome: Pronava, 1901.

Belcher, Wendy. "The Life and Visions of Krǝstos Śämra, a Fifteenth-Century Ethiopian Woman Saint."
In *African Christian Biography: Narratives, Beliefs, and Boundaries*, ed. Dana L. Robert, 80–100.
Pietermaritzburg, South Africa: Cluster Publications, 2018.

Berry, LaVerle L. "Architecture and Kingship: The Significance of Gondar-Style Architecture."
Northeast African Studies 2, no. 3 (1995): 7–19.

________ ."Gondär-Style Architecture." In Uhlig, ed., *Encyclopedia Aethiopica*, 2: 843–45. Wiesbaden:
Harrassowitz, 2005.

Beshah, Girma, and Merid Wolde Aregay. *The Question of the Union of the Churches in Luso-Ethiopian
Relations.* Lisbon: Centro de Estudos Historicos Ultramarinos, 1964.

Bianchi Barriviera, Lino. *Le chiese in roccia di Lalibelá e di altri luoghi del Lasta.* Rome: Istituto
per l'Oriente, 1963.

Bosc-Tiessé, Claire. *Spirit and Materials of Ethiopian Icons.* Addis Ababa: Institute of Ethiopian Studies,
Haile Sellassie I University, 2010.

Brita, Antonella. "Agiografia e liturgia nella tradizione della chiesa etiopica." In *Popoli religioni e chiese lungo il corso del Nilo: Dal faraone cristiano al Leone di Giuda*, ed. C. Alzate and L. Vaccaro, 515–39. Vatican City: Libreria Editrice Vaticana, 2015.

———. "Genres of Ethiopian-Eritrean Christian Literature with a Focus on Hagiography." In *A Companion to Medieval Ethiopia and Eritrea*, ed. Samantha Kelly, 252–81. Leiden: Brill, 2020.

———. *I racconti tradizionali sulla "Seconda Cristianizzazione" dell'Etiopia: Il ciclo agiografico dei Nove Santi*. Naples: Università degli Studi di Napoli "L'Orientale," 2010.

———. "Pänṭälewon." In Uhlig and Bausi, eds., *Encyclopaedia Aethiopica*, 4: 111a–113a.

———. "Nine Saints." In Uhlig and Bausi, eds., *Encyclopaedia Aethiopica*, 4: 1188b–1191a.

Bruce, James. *Travels to Discover the Source of the Nile, in the Years 1768, 1769, 1770, 1771, 1772, and 1773*. Edinburgh: J. Ruthven, 1790.

Budge, E. Wallis. *History of Ethiopia, Nubia & Abyssinia*. 4 vols. London: Methuen, 1928.

———. *One Hundred and Ten Miracles of Our Lady Mary*. London: Medici Society, 1923.

Bumazhnov, Dmitrij. "Ascetic Suicides in the Vita of St Paul of Tamma: An Egyptian Drama and Its Ethiopian Continuation." In *Veneration of Saints in Christian Ethiopia: Proceedings of the International Workshop "Saints in Christian Ethiopia: Literary Sources and Veneration," Hamburg, April 28–29, 2012*, ed. D. Nosnitsin, 1–13. Wiesbaden: Harrassowitz, 2015.

Buxton, D. R. *The Christian Antiquities of Northern Ethiopia*. London: Society of Antiquaries of London, 1947.

Cañellas, Juan Nadal, Stefano Virgulin, and Giovanni Guaita, eds. *Enciclopedia dei santi: Le chiese orientali*, vols. 1–2. Rome: Città Nuova, 1998–1999.

Cerulli, Enrico. *Éthiopie et Érythrée*. Brussels: Éditions de l'Institut de Sociologie, Université Libre de Bruxelles, 1965.

———. "Gli abbati di Dabra Libanos, capi del monachismo etiopico, secondo la lista rimata." *Orientalia* 12 (1943): 229–93.

———. *Il libro etiopico dei Miracoli di Maria e le sue fonti nelle letterature del medio evo latino*. Rome: G. Bardi, 1943.

———. *La letteratura etiopica: L'oriente cristiano nell'unità delle sue tradizioni*. Florence: Sansoni, 1968.

———. "L'Etiopia del secolo XV in nuovi documenti storici." *Africa italiana* 2 (1933): 57–112.

———. *Storia della letteratura etiopica: L'oriente cristiano nell'unità delle sue tradizioni*. Florence: Sansoni, 1968.

Chaîne, Marius. "Répertoire des Salam et Malke'e contenus dans les manuscrits éthiopiens des bibliothèques d'Europe." *Revue de l'Orient chrétien* 2ème sér. 8, no. 18 (1913): 183–203, 337–57.

Chojnacki, Stanislaw. *Ethiopian Icons: Catalogue of the Collection of the Institute of Ethiopian Studies, Addis Ababa University*. Milan: Skira, 2000.

Colin, Gérard. *Le livre éthiopien des miracles de Marie*. Paris: Gallimard, 2004.

———. *Le synaxaire éthiopien: Le mois de Maggābit*. Turnhout: Brepols, 1994.

———. *Le synaxaire éthiopien: Le mois de Miazya*. Turnhout: Brepols, 1995.

———. *Le synaxaire éthiopien: Le mois de Taḥśaś (fin)*. Turnhout: Brepols, 1997.

———. *Le synaxaire éthiopien: Le mois de Tərr*. Turnhout: Brepols, 1990.

Conti Rossini, Carlo. "Ethiopian Hagiography and the Acts of Saint Yāfqeranna-Egzi' (14th Century)." In Bausi, ed., *Languages and Cultures of Eastern Christianity: Ethiopian,* 329–54 [English translation of C. Conti Rossini, "L'agiografia etiopica e gli Atti del santo Yâfqeranna Egzí (Secolo XIV)," *Atti del Reale Istituto di Scienze, Lettere ed Arti* 96-2 (1937), 403–33].

———. *Historia Regis Sarsa Dengel (Malak Sagad).* Paris: E Typographeo Reipublicae, 1907.

———."L'evangelo d'oro di Dabra Libanos." *Rendiconti della Reale Accademia dei Lincei: Classe di scienze morali, storiche e filologiche* 5 (1901): 177–219.

Crummey, Donald. *Land and Society in the Christian Kingdom of Ethiopia: From the Thirteenth to the Twentieth Century.* Urbana: University of Illinois Press, 2000.

Derat, Marie-Laure. "'Do not search for another king, one whom God has not given you': Questions on the Elevation of Zär'ä Ya'eqob (1434–1468)." *Journal of Early Modern History* 8, nos. 3–4 (2004): 210–28.

———."Elaboration et diffusion du récit d'une victoire militaire: La bataille de Gomit, décembre 1445." *Oriens Christianus* 86 (2002): 87–102.

———. *Le domaine des rois éthiopiens (1270–1527): Espace, pouvoir et monachisme.* Paris: Éditions de la Sorbonne, 2003.

———. *L'énigme d'une dynastie sainte et usurpatrice dans le royaume chrétien d'Éthiopie du XIe au XIIIe siècle.* Turnhout: Brepols, 2018.

———."Modèles de sainteté et idéologie monastique à Dabra Libanos (XVe–XVIe siècles)." In *Saints, biographies et histoire en Afrique*, ed. Bertrand Hirsch and Manfred Kropp, 127–47. Frankfurt: Peter Lang, 2003.

———."A Royal Correspondence in the XVth and XVIth Centuries: The Documents of the Gospel of Däbrä Kärbe (Zana)." *Aethiopica* 9 (2006): 64–79.

Derat, Marie-Laure, and Woldetsadik Deresse Ayenachew. "Les sites de Meshalä Maryam et de Gebriel d'attente pour l'histoire du Mänz." In *Gebriel: Une eglise médiéval d'Ethiopie*, ed. M-L. Derat and A-M. Jouquand, 25–63. Paris: Annales d'Ethiopie, 2012.

Derat, Marie-Laure, Claire Bosc-Tiessé, Antoine Garric, Romain Mensan, François-Xavier Fauvelle, Yves Gleize, and Anne-Lise Goujon. "The Rock-Cut Churches of Lalibela and the Cave Church of Washa Mika'el: Troglodytism and the Christianisation of the Ethiopian Highlands." *Antiquity* 95, no. 380 (2021): 467–86.

Derat, Marie-Laure, Emmanuel Fritsch, Claire Bosc-Tiessé, Antoine Garric, Romain Mensan, et al. "Māryām Nāzrēt (Ethiopia): The Twelfth-Century Transformations of an Aksumite Site in Connection with an Egyptian Christian Community." *Cahiers d'études africaines* 239 (2020): 473–507.

Di Salvo, Mario. *Churches of Ethiopia: The Monastery of Nārgā Śellāsē.* Milan: Skira, 1999.

Dillman, August. *Über die Regierung, insbesondere die Kirchenordnung des Königs Zar'a-Jacob.* Berlin: Königliche Akademie der Wissenschaften, 1884.

Euringer, Sebastian. "Die Binde der Rechtfertigung." *Orientalia* 11 (1940): 76–99, 244–59.

Fiaccadori, Gianfranco. "Ewosṭateans." In Uhlig, ed., *Encyclopaedia Aethiopica*, 2:464–69.

Gebissa, Ezekiel. "Oromo History." In Uhlig and Bausi, eds., *Encyclopaedia Aethiopica*, 4:61–62.

Gerster, Georg. *Churches in Rock: Early Christian Art in Ethiopia*. London: Phaidon, 1970.

———. *Kirchen im Fels: Entdeckungen in Äthiopien*. Stuttgart: Kohlhammer, 1968.

Godinho, Nicolao. *De Abassinorum rebus, déque Aethiopiae patriarchis Ioanne Nonio Barreto, & Andrea Ouiedo, libri tres P. Nicolao Godigno Societatis Iesu auctore*. Rome, 1615.

Guidi, Ignazio. *Annales Iohannis I, Iyāsu I, Bakāffā*. Paris: E Typographeo Reipublicae, 1903.

———. *Annales regum Iyāsu II et Iyoʾas*. Paris: E Typographeo Reipublicae, 1910–12.

———. *La chiesa abissina*. Rome: Istituto per l'Oriente, 1922.

———. *Le synaxaire éthiopien: Mois de Nahasê et de Paguemên*. Turnhout: Brepols, 1981.

Gyorgis, Gabra (Lisane Worq). *Tintawi Serate Mahelet ZeAbuna Yared (The Ancient Order of Singing of Our Father Yared, the Master)*. Addis Ababa: Maison des Études Éthiopiennes, 1997.

Hable-Selassie, Sergew. "The Monastic Library of Däbrä Hayq." In *Orbis Aethiopicus: Studia in Honorem Stanislaus Chojnacki Natali Septuagesimo Quinto Dicata, Septuagesimo Septimo Oblata*, ed. Piotr O. Scholz, 1: 243–58. 2 vols. Albstadt: Schuler, 1992.

Habte-Sellassie, Abraham. *St. Yared and Ethiopian Ecclesiastical Music*. Washington, DC: Debre Selam Kidist Mariam Church, 1999.

Haile, Getatchew. "Anqäṣä Haymanot (or the Gate of Faith)." *Northeast African Studies* 5, no. 1 (1983): 29–37.

———. *Beauty of the Creation (Śǝnä Fǝṭrät)*. Manchester: Victoria University of Manchester, 1991.

———. "Builders of Churches and Authors of Hymns: Makers of History in the Ethiopian Church." In *Études éthiopiennes: Actes de la Xe conférence internationale des études éthiopiennes, Paris, 24–28 août 1988,* ed. Claude Lepage and É. Delage, 1:369–75. Paris: Société Française pour les Études Éthiopiennes, 1994.

———. *A Catalogue of Ethiopian Manuscripts Microfilmed for the Ethiopian Manuscript Microfilm Library, Addis Ababa, and for the Hill Monastic Manuscript Library, Collegeville*. 9 vols. Collegeville, MN: Hill Monastic Manuscript Library, St. Johns Abbey and University, 1979–87.

———. *A Catalogue of Ethiopian Manuscripts Microfilmed for the Ethiopian Manuscript Microfilm Library, Addis Ababa and for the Hill Monastic Manuscript Library, Collegeville*, vol. 5: *Project Numbers 1501–2000*. Collegeville, MN: Hill Monastic Manuscript Library, St. Johns Abbey and University, 1981.

———. *The Epistle of Humanity of Emperor Zärʾa Yaʾǝqob (Ṭomarä Tǝsbǝʾt)*. Louvain: Peeters, 1991.

———. "The Forty-Nine Hour Sabbath of the Ethiopian Church." *Journal of Semitic Studies* 33, no. 2 (1988): 233–54.

———. *The Geʿez Acts of Abba Estifanos of Gwendagwende*. Leuven: Peeters, 2006.

———. *A History of the First Ǝsṭifanosite Monks*, Ed. By Getatchew Haile. Louvain: Peeters, 2011.

———. *A History of the First Ǝsṭifanosite Monks*. Translated from the Ethiopian by Getatchew Haile. *A History of the First EsṭIfanosite Monks*. Louvain: Peeters, 2011.

———. "The Homily of Abba Elǝyas, Bishop of Aksum, on Mäṭṭa." *Analecta Bollandiana* 108, nos. 1–2 (1990): 29–47.

———. *The Homily of Zärʾa Yaʾǝqob's Mashafa Barhan on the Rite of Baptism and Religious Instruction*. Leuven: Peeters, 2013.

———. *The Mariology of Emperor Zär'a Ya'əqob of Ethiopia*. Rome: Orientalia Christiana Analecta, 1992.

———."The Monastic Genealogy of the Line of Täklä Haymanot of Shoa." *Rassegna di Studi Etiopici* 29 (1982): 7–38.

———."On the Identity of Silondis and the Composition of the Anaphora of Mary Ascribed to Hereyaqos of Behensa." *Orientalia Christiana Periodica* 49, no. 2 (1983): 366–89.

———."Religious Controversies and the Growth of Ethiopic Literature in the Fourteenth and Fifteenth Centuries." *Oriens Christianus* 65 (1981): 102–36.

Hammerschmidt, Ernst, ed. *Äthiopische liturgische Texte der Bodleian Library in Oxford*. Berlin: Akademie-Verlag, 1960.

———. *Studies in the Ethiopic Anaphoras*. Leiden: De Gruyter, 1987.

Heldman, Marilyn E. "Architectural Symbolism, Sacred Geography and the Ethiopian Church." *Journal of Religion in Africa* 22, no. 3 (1992): 222–41.

———."Church Buildings." In Uhlig, ed., *Encyclopaedia Aethiopica*, 1:737a–40a.

———."Creating Sacred Space: Orthodox Churches of the Ethiopian American Diaspora." *Diaspora* 15, nos. 2–3 (2006): 285–302.

———."An Ēwosṭāthian Style and the Gundā Gundē Style in Fifteenth-Century Ethiopian Manuscript Illumination." In *Proceedings of the First International Conference on the History of Ethiopian Art, Held at the Warburg Institute of the University of London, October 21 and 22, 1986*, ed. R. Parkhurst, 5–14, 135–39. London: Pindar Press, 1989.

———."From Strict Observance to Royal Endowment: The Case of the Monastery of Däbrä Halle Luya, EMML. 6343, ff. 117-118." *Muséon (Le) Louvain* 93, nos. 1–2 (1980): 163–72.

———."Legends of Lālibalā: The Development of an Ethiopian Pilgrimage Site." *RES: Anthropology and Aesthetics* 27 (1995): 25–38.

———. *The Marian Icons of the Painter Frē Ṣeyon: A Study in Fifteenth-Century Ethiopian Art, Patronage, and Spirituality*. Wiesbaden: Harrassowitz, 1994.

———."Metropolitan Bishops as Agents of Artistic Interaction Between Egypt and Ethiopia during the Thirteenth and Fourteenth Centuries." In *Interactions: Artistic Interchange Between the Eastern and Western Worlds in the Medieval Period*, ed. C. Hourihane, 84–105. University Park: Penn State University Press, 2007.

———."Santa Maria Maggiore, Madonna of." In Uhlig and Bausi, eds., *Encyclopaedia Aethiopica*, 4: 527a–28b.

———."St. Luke as Painter: Post-Byzantine Icons in Early Sixteenth-Century Ethiopia." *Gesta* 44, no. 2 (2005): 125–48.

———."Tabot." In Uhlig and Bausi, eds., *Encyclopaedia Aethiopica*, 4:802–4.

———."Trinity: Trinity in Art." In Uhlig and Bausi, eds., *Encyclopaedia Aethiopica*, 4: 994a–996a.

———."Wise Virgins in the Kingdom of Heaven: A Gathering of Saints in a Medieval Ethiopian Church." *Source* 19, no. 2 (2000): 6–12.

Heldman, Marilyn E., and Getatchew Haile. "Who Is Who in Ethiopia's Past, Part III: Founders of Ethiopia's Solomonic Dynasty." *Northeast African Studies* 9, no. 1 (1987): 1–11.

Heldman, Marilyn E., Stuart Munro-Hay, and Roderick Grierson, eds. *African Zion: The Sacred Art of Ethiopia*. New Haven, CT: Yale University Press, 1993.

Heldman, Marilyn E., and Kay Kaufman Shelemay. "Concerning Saint Yared." In *Studies in Ethiopian Languages, Literature, and History: Festschrift for Getatchew Haile Presented by His Friends and Colleagues*, ed. Adam Carter McCollum, 65–93. Wiesbaden: Harrassowitz, 2017.

Imbakom, Kalewold. *Traditional Ethiopian Church Education*. New York: Teachers College Press, 1970.

Jeffery, P. "The Liturgical Year in the Ethiopian Deggʷā (Chantbook)." In *Eulogēma: Studies in Honour of Robert Taft, S.J.*, ed. E. Carr, 199–234. Rome: Pontificia Ateneo S. Anselmo, 1993.

Kaplan, Steven. "Hagiographies and the History of Medieval Ethiopia." *History in Africa* 8 (1981): 107–23.

———. "Iyäsus Moʾa and Täklä Haymanot: Note on a Hagiographic Controversy." *Journal of Semitic Studies* 31, no. 1 (1986): 47–56.

———. *The Monastic Holy Man and the Christianization of Early Solomonic Ethiopia*. Wiesbaden: Steiner, 1984.

———. "Seen but Not Heard: Children and Childhood in Medieval Ethiopian Hagiographies." *International Journal of African Historical Studies* 30, no. 3 (1997): 539–53.

Kazhdan, A. P., and Alice-Mary Maffry Talbot. "Hagiography." In *The Oxford Dictionary of Byzantium*, ed. Kazhdan, A. P., Alice-Mary Maffry Talbot, Anthony Cutler, and Timothy E. Gregory, 2: 897–99. New York: Oxford University Press, 1991.

Kelly, Samantha, ed. *A Companion to Medieval Ethiopia and Eritrea*. Leiden: Brill, 2020.

Kidane, Habtemichael. "Dəggʷa." In Uhlig, ed., *Encyclopaedia Aethiopica*, 2: 123–24.

———. "Hymns to the Virgin Mary." In Uhlig, ed., *Encyclopedia Aethiopica*, 3: 817–19.

Kropp, Manfred. *Der siegreiche Feldzug des Königs ʿĀmda-Ṣeyon gegen die Muslime in Adal*. Leuven: Peeters, 1994.

———. "ʿ…der Welt gestorben': Ein Vertrag zwischen dem äthiopischen Heiligen Iyyäsus-Moʾa und König Yakunno-Amlak über 'Memoriae' im Kloster Hayq." *Analecta Bollandiana* 116, no. 1 (1998): 303–30.

———. "Die dritte Würde oder ein Drittel des Reiches." In *Saints, Biographies and History in Africa*, ed. Bertrand Hirsch and Manfred Kropp, 191–205. Frankfurt: Peter Lang, 2003.

Kur, Stanislas, and Denis Nosnitsin. "Iyäsus Moʾa." In Uhlig, ed., *Encyclopaedia Aethiopica*, 3: 257a–59a.

Lepage, Claude. "L'art du Xe au XVe siècle, des 'siècles obscures' aux 'siècles des lumieres.'" In *Étiopie millenaire: Prehistoire et art religieux*. Paris: Musée de Petit Palais, 1975.

The Lenten Triodion. Trans. Mother Mary and Kallistos Ware. London: Faber & Faber, 1977.

Leslau, Wolf. *Comparative Dictionary of Geʿez (Classical Ethiopic)*. Wiesbaden: Harrassowitz, 1987.

Liturgy of the Ethiopian Church. Trans. Marcos Daoud and Marsie Hazen. Addis Ababa: Ethiopian Orthodox Church, 1946.

Lusini, G. *Studi sul monachesimo eustaziano (secoli XIV–XV)*. Naples: Istituto Universitario Orientale, 1993.

Marrassini, Paolo. "A Hagiographic Text: The Royal Chronicle." In Bausi, ed., *Languages and Cultures of Eastern Christianity: Ethiopian*, 389–98.

_______ ."L'infanzia del santo nel cristianesimo orientale: Il caso dell'Etiopia." In *Bambini santi: Rappresentazioni dell'infaniza a modelli agiografici*, ed. Anna Benvenuti Papi and Elena Giannarelli, 147–81. Turin: Rosenberg & Sellier, 1991.

_______ . *Lo scettro e la croce: La campagna di ʿAmda Ṣeyon I contro l'Ifāt (1332)*. Naples: Istituto Universitario Orientale, 1993.

Martínez d'Alòs-Moner, Andreu. *Envoys of a Human God: The Jesuit Mission to Christian Ethiopia, 1557–1632*. Leiden: Brill, 2015.

Meinardus, Otto Friedrich August. *Monks and Monasteries of the Egyptian Deserts*. Cairo: American University of Cairo Press, 1961.

Mercier, Jacques. "Ethiopian Art History." In *Ethiopian Art: The Walters Art Museum*, 45–73. Lingfield: Third Millennium, 2001.

_______ ."Peintures du XIIIe siècle dans une église de l'Angot (Ethiopie)." *Annales d'Éthiopie* 18 (2002): 143–48.

Meyer, R. "Tulluu Guddoo." In Uhlig and Bausi, eds., *Encyclopaedia Aethiopica*, 4: 1000–1001.

Michael, Belaynesh, S. Chojnacki, and Richard Pankhurst, eds. *The Dictionary of Ethiopian Biography*, vol. 1, *From Early Times to the End of the Zagwé Dynasty, c. 1270 A.D.* Addis Ababa: Institute of Ethiopian Studies, 1975.

Monti della Corta, Alessandro Agosto. *Lalibelà: Le chiese ipogee e monolitiche e gli altri monumenti medievali del Lasta*. Rome: Società Italiana Arti Grafiche, 1940.

Muth, Franz-Christoph. "Aḥmad Grañ." In Uhlig, ed., *Encyclopaedia Aethiopica*, 1: 155–58.

Nosnitsin, Denis. "Ancient Chants for 'Abba Yoḥanni: Text Variance and Lost Identity." In *Written Sources About Africa and Their Study*, ed. V. Brugnatelli and M. Lafkioui, 287–311. Milan: Bulzoni, 2018.

_______ . *Churches and Monasteries of Təgray: A Survey of Manuscript Collections*. Wiesbaden: Harrassowitz, 2013.

_______ . *Ecclesiastic Landscape of North Ethiopia: Remarks on Methodologies and Types of Approach*. Wiesbaden: Harrassowitz, 2013.

_______ ."The Ethiopic Synaxarion: Text-Critical Observations on Täklä Haymanot's Commemoration (24 Nähase)." *Orientalia Christiana Periodica* 73, no. 1 (2007): 141–83.

_______ ."Introduction." In *Veneration of Saints in Christian Ethiopia: Proceedings of the International Workshop Saints in Christian Ethiopia: Literary Sources and Veneration, Hamburg, April 28–29, 2012*, ed. Denis Nosnitsin, xxiii–xxxix. Wiesbaden: Harrassowitz, 2015.

_______ ."New Branches of the Stephanite Monastic Network? Cases of Some Under-Explored Sites in East Təgray." In *Ecclesiastic Landscape of North Ethiopia: Proceedings of the International Workshop "Ecclesiastic Landscape of North Ethiopia: History, Change and Cultural Heritage," Hamburg, July 15–16, 2011*, ed. Denis Nosnitsin. Wiesbaden: Harrassowitz, 2013.

_______ ."Täklä Haymanot." In Uhlig and Bausi, eds., *Encyclopaedia Aethiopica*, 4: 831–34.

_______ ."Vite di santi etiopici: Ripetizione e diversità di un genere letterario." In *Nigra sum sed Formosa: Sacro e bellezza dell'Etiopia cristiana*, ed. G. Fiaccadori, G. Barbieri, and M. Di Salvo, 73–83. Vicenza: Terra Ferma, 2009.

______ ."'Wäwähabo qob'a wä'askema': Reflections on an Episode from the History of the Ethiopian Monastic Movement." In *Varia Aethiopica: In Memory of Sevir B. Chernetsov (1943–2005)*, ed. D. Nosnitsin, S. Frantousoff, L. Kogan, and B. Lourié, 197–247. Saint Petersburg: Byzantinorossica, 2005.

Ofcansky, Thomas P., and LaVerle Berry. *Ethiopia: A Country Study*. Washington, DC: Library of Congress, 2010.

Orlandi, Tito. "The Corpus dei Manoscritti Copti Letterari." *Computers and the Humanities* 24, nos. 5–6 (December 1990): 397–405.

______ ."Hagiography, Coptic." In *The Coptic Encyclopedia*, ed. Aziz S. Atiya, 4: 1191–97. New York: Macmillan, 1991.

Pankhurst, Richard. *History of Ethiopian Towns from the Middle Ages to the Early Nineteenth Century*. Ann Arbor: University of Michigan Press, 1982.

______ . *History of Ethiopian Towns from the Mid-Nineteenth Century to 1935*. Wiesbaden: Franz Steiner Verlag, 1985.

Perruchon, Jules. *Les chroniques de Zär'a Ya'əqob et de Ba'eda Maryam de 1434–1478*. Paris: Ernest Leroux, 1893.

Perruchon, Jules, ed. *Vie de Lalibala, roi d'Éthiopie*. Paris: Ernest Leroux, 1892.

Pisani, Vitagrazia. "The Apocryphal Acts of the Apostles: Unknown Witnesses from East Tegray." In *Essays in Ethiopian Manuscript Studies: Proceedings of the International Conference Manuscripts and Texts, Languages and Contexts: the Transmission of Knowledge in the Horn of Africa. Hamburg, 17–19 July 2014*, ed. A. Bausi, A. Gori, D. Nosnitsin, and E. Sokolinski, 75–94. Wiesbaden: Harrassowitz, 2015.

Rubenson, Sven. *King of Kings: Tewodros of Ethiopia*. Addis Ababa: Haile Sellassie I University, 1966.

Sauter, Roger. "Où en est notre connaissance des églises rupestres d'Éthiopie." *Annales d'Éthiopie* 5 (1963): 235–92.

Schneider, Roger. "L'évangéliaire de Dabra Libanos de Ham." In *Proceedings of the Eighth International Conference of Ethiopian Studies, University of Addis Ababa, 1984, II*. Addis Ababa: Institute of Ethiopian Studies, 1989.

Shelemay, Kay Kaufman. "The Musician and Transmission of Religious Tradition: The Multiple Roles of the Ethiopian Dabtara." *Journal of Religion in Africa* 22, no. 3 (1992): 242–60.

Shelemay, Kay Kaufman, and Peter Jeffery, eds. *Ethiopian Christian Chant: An Anthology*. CD, 3 vols. Madison, WI: A–R Editions, 1993–1997.

Shelemay, Kay Kaufman, Peter Jeffery, and Ingrid Monson. "Oral and Written Transmission in Ethiopian Christian Chant." *Early Music History* 12 (January 1993): 55–117.

Spencer, Diana. "In Search of St. Luke Icons in Ethiopia." *Journal of Ethiopian Studies* 10, no. 2 (1972): 67–93.

______ ."Travels in Gojjam: St Luke Ikons and Brancaleon Re-discovered." *Journal of Ethiopian Studies* 12, no. 2 (1974): 201–20.

______ . *The Woman from Tedbab*. London: Elizabeth Horne, 2003.

Strelcyn, Stefan. *Catalogue of Ethiopian Manuscripts in the British Library Acquired Since the Year 1877.* London: British Museum, 1978.

Tamrat, Taddesse. *Church and State in Ethiopia, 1270–1527.* Oxford: Clarendon Press, 1972.

______ . *The Church in Ethiopia.* Addis Ababa: Ethiopian Orthodox Church, 1970.

______ ."Hagiographies and the Reconstruction of Medieval Ethiopian History." *Rural Africana* 11 (1970): 12–18.

Tesfaye, G., and J. Pirenne. "Inscriptions sur bois de trois églises de Lalibäla." *Journal of Ethiopian Studies* 17 (1984): 107–26.

Trimingham, J. Spencer. *Islam in Ethiopia.* New York: Barnes and Noble, 1965.

Turaev, Boris, ed. *Vitae sanctorum indigenarum: Gadla Aron; Seu Acta Sancti Aaronis; Gadla Filpos; Seu Acta Sancti Philippi.* Rome: De Luigi, 1908.

Uhlig, S., ed. *Encyclopaedia Aethiopica*, vol. 1, *A–C.* Wiesbaden: Harrassowitz, 2003.

______ . *Encyclopaedia Aethiopica*, vol. 2, *D–Ha.* Wiesbaden: Harrassowitz, 2005.

______ . *Encyclopaedia Aethiopica*, vol. 3, *He–N.* Wiesbaden: Harrassowitz, 2007.

Uhlig, S., and A. Bausi, eds. *Encyclopaedia Aethiopica*, vol. 4, *O–X.* Wiesbaden: Harrassowitz, 2010.

______ . *Encyclopaedia Aethiopica*, vol. 5, *Y–Z.* Wiesbaden: Harrassowitz, 2014.

Velat, B. "Le mawāše'et et les livres de chant liturgique éthiopien." In *Mémorial du cinquantenaire: 1914–1964*, 159–70. Paris: Bloud & Gay, 1964.

Von der Nahmer, Dieter. *Die lateinische Heiligenvita: Eine Einführung in die lateinische Hagiographie.* Darmstadt: Wissenschaftliche Buchgesellschaft, 1994.

Wadi, Awad. "The Arabic Lives of Saint Takla Haymanot." *Studia Orientalia Christiana* 45 (2012): 131–36.

______ ."The Western Fathers in the *Confessio Patrum*." *Studia Orientalia Christiana* 45 (2012): 105–29.

Weninger, Stefan. "Sounds of Gə'əz—How to Study the Phonetics and Phonology of an Ancient Language." *Aethiopica* 13 (2010): 75–88.

Wolde Aregay, Merid. "Gondar and Adwa: A Tale of Two Cities." In *Proceedings of the Eighth International Conference of Ethiopian Studies, University of Addis Ababa*, 2: 57–66. Frankfurt: Peter Lang, 1988–89.

Wright, William. *Catalogue of the Ethiopic Manuscripts in the British Museum Acquired Since the Year 1847.* London: British Museum, 1877.

Zare'a Ya'eqob. *Il libro della luce del Negus Zar'a Yā'qob (Maṣḥafa Berhān).* Trans. Carlo Conti Rossini and Lanfranco Ricci. Louvain: Secrétariat du Corpus SCO, 1964–1965.

Zelleke, Kinefe-Rigb. "Bibliography of the Ethiopic Hagiographical Traditions." *Journal of Ethiopian Studies* 13, no. 2 (1975): 57–102.

Index

Note: Illustrations are indicated by page numbers in *italics*.

A

Äbba Anthony, 31

Äbba Daniel, 27, 31

Äbba Ǝsṭifanos, 37, 63, 81–82, *83*, 157n45

Äbba Garima, 9, 70, *71*, 81

Äbba Hor, 27, *29*

Äbba Mätta', 23, 31, 148n5

Äbba Menas, *27, 29*

Äbba Nafer, 31

Äbba Samuel, 27, 31, *55*

Äbba Shenuti, 31

Äbba Täklä Hawareyat, 47–49

'Abiyä Ǝgzi' of Däbrä Mädḥanit, 82

Abraham, 15, 40, *41*, 42, *55*

Abrahamic tradition

    defined, 15

    pilgrimage sites in, 17–19

Abuna Maba'a Ṣəyon, 46

Acts of the Apostles, 70, 79, *102*

Acts of the Martyrs, 78–79, 153n36

Adafa, 148n2

'Adal, 54, 65, 95, 105, 112, 128

Adoration of the Magi, *92, 131*

African Zion (exhibition), 8–10

Agäw, 113

Aḥmad b. Ibrāhīm al-Gāzī, 112

Akalä Krəstos of Däbrä Maḥəw, 86

Aksum, 15, 25, 59, 70, 77–78, 80–82, 99, 105, 115, 118, 133

Aläqa Estazya, *93*

Alaqa Gabra Selasse, 8, *51*

Amdä Ṣəyon (Emperor), 15–16, 100–101

Anba Marina, 31, 148n13, 149n14

Ancient of Days, 43, *45*, 47, *48*, 49, 106

Annunciation, 39, 70, *72, 92, 108, 131*

Apostles, *36*, 37, 43–45, *45, 50*, 51, 54, *62*, 70, 79, 88, 106

Arabic Gospel Book, 119, *120*

Arägawi, 81

Ark of the Covenant, 150n18

Ascension of Christ, 70, *72*

Assumption, 39, 56, *57, 131*

Atronsä Maryam, 103

B

Bä'ədä Maryam, *94*, 102–3, *103*, 105

Baraki, Almaz, 8

Barbara, 27, 31, 148n13

Bäṣälotä Mika'el, 84, 99

Bäträ Maryam of Zäge Giyorgis, 86

Benjamin II (Patriarch), 81

Berry, LaVerle, 13

Betä Ǝsra'el, 15–17, 19

    as Abrahamic, 15

    in *Short Chronicle*, 15

    Susənyos and, 113

    Yeshaq and, 17

Bəstawros, 84